Gandhi's Pilgrimage of Faith

D1571504

Gandhi's Pilgrimage of Faith

From Darkness to Light

Uma Majmudar
with a Foreword by Rajmohan Gandhi

State University of New York Press

Published by
State University of New York Press, Albany

For information, address State University of New York Press,
194 Washington Avenue, Suite 305, Albany, NY 12210-2365

Production by Michael Haggett
Marketing by Michael Campochiaro

Library of Congress Cataloging-in-Publication Data

Majmudar, Uma, 1936-
Gandhi's pilgrimage of faith: from darkness to light/written by
Uma Majmudar; foreword by Rajmohan Gandhi.
p. cm.
Includes bibliographical references and index.
ISBN 0-7914-6405-9 (hardcover : alk. paper)—ISBN 0-7914-6406-7
(pbk. : alk. paper)
1. Gandhi, Mahatma, 1869–1948—Religion.
2. Statesmen—India—Biography. I. Title. DS481. G3M2735 2005
954.03'5'092—dc22
2004014223

10 9 8 7 6 5 4 3 2 1

This book is dedicated to all those who are interested in the spiritual journey from

"untruth to Truth,
darkness to Light,
and death to Immortality."

Contents

Foreword

By Rajmohan Gandhi, Grandson of Mahatma Gandhi

Let me explain why I welcome and commend this study.

First, and here the study is quite distinctive, it theorizes Gandhi. It sets his life against a theory of a life of faith. It is one thing yet again to examine, if possible from a fresh angle, Gandhi's life in all its dilemmas, ironies, and challenges. An instructive portrait could well result. But it is a different thing to suggest a pattern of obstacles and conflicts in any individual's life of faith, and to look at Gandhi in the light of such a pattern.

I am not aware that this has been done before in Gandhi's case. The theory that Majmudar invokes is not her own, but it is clearly one yielded by painstaking and informed research. Tested against Fowler's theory, Majmudar's Gandhi emerges not as a strange great figure on an exotic stage but as a pilgrim on an obstacle course to which other pilgrims too are drawn, and to which we too, no matter who we are or where we come from, might potentially be drawn.

My second and third reasons are connected to the first. In addition to theorizing Gandhi, Majmudar's study universalizes him. As happens to Fowler's theoretical figure, we find that before long Majmudar's Gandhi too is "freed from the confines of tribe, class, religious community or nation."

That Gandhi, who for decades was seen in India as the most authentic Indian of them all, has been universalized is now well-known. All over the world men and women seem touched by him; all over the world a courageous, self-restrained, and compassionate individual in the neighborhood is at times spoken of as "a Gandhi"; in the mind, on a billboard, or on a blackboard, Gandhi is an easily summoned suggestion of the brave, self-denying, and imaginative dissenter.

Majmudar's Gandhi is also a very human Gandhi. Not only is he seen as, and termed, imperfect, he faces pulls and conflicts and doubts that any of us might face. Majmudar wants us to touch and feel Gandhi. He is not on a pedestal, he is not made of granite or bronze, he is warm and vulnerable.

Finally, Majmudar's is, in a helpful sense, a summarized Gandhi. Not only are the numerous rich episodes of his life summarized here; the study makes good use of, even if at times it seeks to differ from, some of the "lives" and studies of Gandhi provided by others.

I am glad to be associated with this study. The author informs us that she has always lived with her childhood memory of the blow of Gandhi's assassination. May this study clarify, and help sustain, the legacy of pilgrimhood and of a pilgrim called Gandhi.

Rajmohan Gandhi

Urbana, Illinois
November 3, 2002

Preface

I have never seen Mahatma Gandhi, nor have I met him in person. I have only heard his voice on All India Radio in the mid-forties, a voice so feeble it was hardly audible. But what a magical effect it had on all its listeners—young and old, men, women, and children! *Bapu*'s (*Bapu*: father) was the voice that stirred souls, that inspired the people and spurred the whole nation to action—to launch the first bloodless revolution in history against the mighty British Empire that had ruled over India for 150 years.

When the Mahatma spoke, the Indians were awakened and the British alarmed. Gandhi's voice had the same charisma and character of the man; it made the weak strong and it made the strong softened by kindness. Gandhi's was the clarion call that awakened the people of India to "do or die" for freedom—to win over the British by suffering for truth, for justice, and for human dignity.

Many a poignant memory of my childhood flashes back on my mental screen. The first to come alive in my mind is the year 1942. The Indian independence movement was in full swing. The slogans—"British quit India," "Mahatma Gandhi ki jay" ("Hail to Mahatma Gandhi"), "Jay Hind" and "Gandhi is our Hero!"—still keep ringing in my ears! Not only the slogans but also the ongoing nonviolent protests and parades, the curfews, and the Indian flag-holding students being shot down by English officers—all come alive from somewhere in the labyrinth of my mind.

My second flashback emerges from my preteen years. Like feeling the dizzying raptures of falling in love for the first time, I still feel the thrill of that momentous moment in history when, at the stroke of midnight on August 15, 1947, India became "free at last." I vividly remember how India, adorned like a young bride, looked stunningly beautiful that night—a night that was impregnated with great expectations of a new dawn awakening for us and for our beloved country! Close to midnight, I joined the teeming millions who milled around the *Bhadra Killa* (fort) in downtown Ahmedabad (in the Gujarat State in West India) to see the most dazzling display of lights on all the government buildings. The people danced wildly in the streets as the sounds of *shahnai* (Indian instrument played at all auspicious occasions) sweetened the air; the temple bells chimed in harmony as the devotees chanted prayers in Sanskrit and offered coconuts, flowers, and sweets to their deities. The decorated elephants and horses, the trucks, buses, cars, and rickshaws all vied with pedestrians to make their way through the needle-narrow streets, but nothing moved. Traffic stood still. The people, shoving and pushing one another, climbed up the telephone poles or into the treetops for a better view. Some managed to go onto the rooftops of buildings or to hang out from windows. Small children, perched up on their parents' shoulders, had the best view of the lights, the parades, and the fireworks. Not an inch of space was unoccupied.

Only the father of the nation, Mahatma Gandhi himself, stayed away from the Independence Day celebrations; for him it was a "Day of Mourning," because much against his will and efforts, what he called "the vivisection of his Motherland" or the "partition" took place. Upon Muhammad Ali Jinnah's insistence, a separate nation of Muslims was carved out of India; it was called Pakistan (*Pak*: pure, *stan*: place).

The third memory that still stabs my heart is that of Mahatma Gandhi's assassination on January 30, 1948, less than six months after India's independence. I cannot forget that cold and dark, dreary winter evening when, arriving home from school, I heard my older brother sobbing. I knew in my heart someone must have died. But who? Even though afraid, I asked him what was wrong, and my heart sank as he continued sobbing like an orphaned baby. I ran inside to my mom. Grieving, yet in control, she told me that an extremist Hindu had shot and killed Gandhi just prior to his evening prayer session in New Delhi. The whole country mourned like a widow that night, which seemed longer and darker than any other night in the history of India.

At eight o'clock that evening, like millions of other families in India, our family huddled together to hear the national radio broadcast by Jawaharlal Nehru, the first prime minister of independent India, speaking from New Delhi. He bid his last farewell to his "Beloved Bapu"; the words, coming straight from his heart, have gone down in history:

> Friends and comrades, the light has gone out of our lives and there is darkness everywhere. … The light has gone out, I said, and yet I was wrong. For the light that shone in this country was no ordinary light. … For that light represented something more than the immediate present, it represented the living truth. … the eternal truths. (Nehru 1948a, 127)

Today I am reviving my childhood and teenage memories of Gandhi not for nostalgia but because they serve a specific purpose in both personal and developmental ways. Personally, these vignettes touch a deeper chord in my heart because it is through them that I am connected to my past—to my "Indianness." Developmentally, it is Gandhi's spirituality and integrity that have continued to influence me indirectly but positively throughout my life.

Fifty years stand between then and now, and yet I am more aware now than ever before of my continuously growing and maturing interest in Gandhi and his profound influence on my thinking, values, and ideals. I also realize today that my earlier interest in Gandhi, although sincere, was emotionally biased and intellectually limited; I had not yet developed a critical or reflective ability to delve deeper into the workings of Gandhi's mind and soul. I needed to step back and look at Gandhi with a renewed perspective.

A golden opportunity came in 1986 when I enrolled as a doctorate student in the Graduate Institute of Liberal Arts of Emory University. I took James W. Fowler's[1] Ethics course, "Wholeness, Evil, and the Ethical," which introduced me to Erik Erikson's major works and to his two psychobiographies: *Young Man Luther* (1962), and *Gandhi's Truth* (1969).[2] The latter touched me deeply, as the major historical drama of Gandhi's *satyagraha* (Truth campaign) for the textile mill workers in 1918 was played in no other city but my own hometown of Ahmedabad. I was motivated all the more to dig deeper into Gandhi's life history.

During the summer of 1988 Professor Fowler taught another short, intensive course, this time on his own Structural Developmental Theory of "Stages of Faith" to which I was partially introduced from our discussions of Erikson and Gandhi in the previous class. This course opened for me a wide vista of learning and exploring in two ways: first, I found a fresh new angle and a comprehensive approach to investigate the stages of Gandhi's spiritual growth; and second, to my surprise, I discovered that in spite of countless biographies of Gandhi, no systematic, structural developmental study had yet been undertaken about the process of Gandhi's spiritual growth. It was a moment of awakening—of knowing from within—that this was *the* subject for me to explore, to research, and to write.

The selection of the book's title—*Gandhi's Pilgrimage of Faith: From Darkness to Light*—reflects, my own scholarly, developmental journey of seeking and finding what I had been looking for, albeit unconsciously, all these years. This book is a culmination of everything I experienced, felt, heard, knew, and studied about Gandhi, including those childhood reminiscences and adolescent fascinations for this extraordinary spiritual genius of our times and perhaps of times to come. Above all, this is the ripened fruit of my years of researching and making meaning of Gandhi as a spiritual seeker after Truth.

Acknowledgments

It takes not one person to write a book but an entire community-at-large. I am deeply indebted to my family, friends, and mentors for their invaluable contributions.

First, I am enormously thankful to my husband and lifelong friend, Dr. Bhagirath Majmudar, for being as committed to my personal goals and growth as to his own. Sangini, my younger daughter, proved to be my long-distance lifeline and cheerleader, believing in me and my project all the way. I also appreciate my one and only (so far) son-in-law, Joe Meyer, for his no-nonsense insistence on my being at my desk, producing a certain number of pages each day.

But it is Nija, my older daughter, who deserves my Extra Special Thanks for being my biggest helper, with her extraordinary talent of editing. She, being a Harvard MBA, made a "win-win" deal with me: that I watch over my two precious grandchildren, Hans and Arya, while she edits my work-in-progress. Nija, where would this book be without you?

I also take this moment to pay homage to the dear departed souls of my dad and my aunt-cum-mom. Dad, this book is actually your dream coming true through me!

In addition to my family, I was fortunate to have the moral support of so many friends—whose names I cannot list here but whose faith in my ability I will never forget.

I also express my deeply felt appreciation to all my teachers, mentors, and fellow writers of the past and present: the late Professor John Fenton, the late Dr. Chester Herman, and the late Professor Paul Kunz; also, Professors James Fowler, Preston Williams, K. L. S. Rao, P. V. Rao, Laurie Patton, Ivy George, Edith Blicksilver, and to Beatrice Bruteau, and John Schlenk. I am grateful to Shri Rajmohan Gandhi for his time and kindness in writing the Foreword to my book on his grandfather.

It is because of these individuals that my dream became possible— God Bless one and all.

Introduction

The Mystique and the Myth of
the Mahatma

"Out of my ashes a thousand Gandhis will rise," forebode Mahatma Gandhi in *Harijan* (January 16, 1937). His words could not have proved more prophetic, although Gandhi never claimed to be a prophet or a saint. Out of one Gandhi who freed India from the foreign British bondage rose an American Gandhi (Martin Luther King Jr.), who fought and died for the civil rights of his fellow African Americans; a South African Gandhi (Nelson Mandela), who suffered in jail for more than two decades for resisting apartheid, and many more Gandhis, who silently carry on Gandhi's message of peace and nonviolence in their own countries. Like an Indian Banyan tree spreading its branches in all directions, Gandhi's message and his methods have spread far and wide, changing lives and changing even the political map of the globe.

Millions around the world revere Mahatma Gandhi, yet only a few know the man Mohandas Gandhi and the internal journey of his soul. What manner of man was he at the core? Which power nourished his soul and held together his complex and paradoxical personality? What was the secret of his universal appeal and influence?

Although the market today is flooded with books on Gandhi, none seems to focus on the soul and substance of the man, namely, his ever-growing, expanding and deepening faith in God as Truth and his own internal self-developmental journey to Truth.

The charismatic Mahatma seems to have overshadowed the man, who remained a mystery to most people—not only to strangers but even to his intimate friends. One of his disciples wondered, who was the "real Gandhi?"

1

Like the Taj Mahal, the multifaceted Mahatma looked different in different lights and at different times.

In addition to being a mystery, the Mahatma was controversial. One who transformed the lives of so many people of dissimilar temperaments, backgrounds, and talents also exasperated the British; he shocked both orthodox Hindus and Muslims by his unorthodox religiosity, and made the Maharajas squirm in their seats by his outspoken truths upon his return to India from South Africa.

Yet controversy only added to Gandhi's charisma. Not even his staunchest enemies could resist the spell of this man who did not fear death and was not attracted to pleasures of the flesh or things material—wealth, power, position, prestige, or honors. They could not but respect this man, who, though adamant on principles, harbored no ill-will or hatred toward anyone, but only love and forgiveness for all. Friends and foes alike admired Mahatma Gandhi's superior spiritual stature; yet, they knew not this ordinary yet extraordinary man of flesh and blood. The Mahatma was worshipped, but the man and what he stood for was forgotten; the real Gandhi lay concealed behind a veil of mystery and the cobwebs of myths began to grow around him.

Regarding the "myth-making" of the Mahatma, Jawaharlal Nehru[1] wrote in his foreword to D. G. Tendulkar's biography of Gandhi (1951, vol. 1): "Even during his life innumerable stories and legends had grown around him," and he saw that "this legend will grow and take many shapes, sometimes with little truth in it." Nehru, with his extraordinary ability to see through the myths surrounding Gandhi, observed:

> Certain rare qualities which raise a man above the common herd and appear to make him as made of different clay. The long story of humanity ... is a story of the advance and growth of man and the spirit of man. (ibid.)

Referring to Gandhi's "rare qualities," even Albert Einstein, Gandhi's great contemporary, wondered: "if generations to come, it may be, will scarce believe that such a one as this ever in flesh and blood walked upon this earth!"

At the same time, one of the rare qualities of Gandhi was that he never claimed greatness or infallibility, but considered himself to be only "a simple individual liable to err like any other human being." Gandhi was humble enough to admit his "Himalayan blunders" as well as courageous enough to retrace his steps. He knew courage was costly; he also knew he was making himself vulnerable to enemies, embarrassing friends, and inviting criticism of "being inconsistent." Yet, unruffled, he rebuffed in *Harijan* (April 23, 1933): "I am not at all concerned with appearing to be consistent, my only commitment is to be consistent to Truth at any given moment." He implied thereby that Truth had never been a static point in his spiritual journey, but rather a dynamic, divine force activated by nonviolence or "the largest love." His faith in and commitment to Truth kept growing, expanding and deepening, as he too grew in wisdom and maturity.

Because Truth was the sine qua non of Gandhi's life, searching for his own true self-identity became a part of his ongoing search for Truth, which is why he called his autobiography, *The Story of My Experiments with Truth* (1948).[2] Although he started out telling the story of his inward journey to Truth, he could not continue or finish it because of his constant mobility and incarceration during the Indian independence movement. Thus, "the story of the advance and growth of the man and the spirit of man," which Nehru mentioned, still remains untold despite countless biographies of Gandhi.

This "unfinished story of Gandhi's spiritual experiments" needs to be told the way Gandhi intended—in the spirit of scientific inquiry and with Truth as its objective. With that intent, I have authored this book based on a systematic, developmental study of Gandhi's life and faith—his internal spiritual journey to Truth. I argue that above all, Gandhi was a spiritual seeker after Truth, a man of prayer and vision, with a deep, ever-growing faith in God as Truth. As Carl Heath put it, "Gandhi is himself an incarnation of soul-force. Above all his political and social activity he remains always the man of the soul" (Radhakrishnan 1944, 99).

This book focuses on the inner developmental journey of Gandhi, "the man of the soul." It proposes that the power that nourished Gandhi's soul and sustained him through the darkest hours of his life—the thread that wove together the multiple dimensions of his complex personality and made him whole—was his ever-growing faith in the ultimate triumph of Truth and in the innate Godliness of the human soul.

To understand and interpret Gandhi's multidimensional personality and faith, we need a critical-analytical method that is both comprehensive and competent enough to achieve the goal. To this end, I have selected James Fowler's structural theory of "Stages of Faith" as a heuristic guide to explore, analyze, and interpret the continuously changing patterns of Gandhi's evolving identity and faith across his life time.

FOWLER'S THEORY OF STAGES OF FAITH DEVELOPMENT

The best way to understand the stages of faith development is to first understand its four cornerstones: faith, structure of faith, stage of faith, and faith stage transition. A brief explanation of each follows.

Fowler describes *faith* (1981, 14) as "the most fundamental category in the human quest for meaning in relation to transcendence." Faith is a generic and universal feature of human living, which is deeper, more personal, and comprehensive than both *religion* and *belief*; it is a "primary motivating power on the journey of the self," says Fowler (1985, 25).

Fowler uses the term *structure of faith* as a formal way of describing *how* faith functions in life, and *how* it organizes our implicit thought patterns, emotions, responses, and relationships in reference to transcendence. By the same token, the structural theory focuses on faith as a *lifelong process* in which structures of faith emerge, evolve, develop, and are transformed in interaction with persons and events that we encounter throughout our life.

Fowler uses the term *stage of faith* to identify and communicate differences in the *styles* or the ways of being that is faith. Each stage denotes its own specific structural features of faith as a way of "construing meaning, interpreting and responding to the factors of contingency, finitude, and ultimacy in our lives," explains Fowler (1984, 52). "Development" in faith involves a process of transformation of the internal thought structures at a given time. This developmental process is invariably in the direction of greater or more sophisticated differentiation, complexity, flexibility, and stability, according to Fowler.

Faith stage transition represents significant and specific alterations in the operational structures of a person's knowing, understanding, responding, and valuing. Transition from one stage to another is not "analogous to climbing stairs or ascending a ladder," as Fowler clarifies (1984, 57). The transitional process is rather prolonged, often imperceptible, and hardly without pain; it begins when the existing coping mechanisms to life's challenges become powerless.

Using these cornerstones as a foundation, I can now describe each of the stages of faith development and their characteristic components.

Infancy and Pre-Stage Primal Faith

According to Fowler, "We all begin the pilgrimage of faith as infants." All humans are born with an innate capacity or potentiality to relate to

Transcendence, or what Fowler calls the "ultimate environment." As we emerge from the comfortable, symbiotic existence in our mother's womb, we are thrust into a strange new environment where we still do not have fully viable capabilities. That is why we need a mother and a loving, supporting, and trustworthy "mothering environment," which is a precursor to the "ultimate environment."

Although largely inaccessible to empirical research, this pre-conceptual and pre-linguistic pre-stage holds the key to our first rudimentary sense of self and our predisposition toward God. Fowler explains how our first "pre-images of God" have their origins in our first environment:

> In the pre-stage called Undifferentiated faith the seeds of trust, courage, hope and love are fused in an undifferentiated way and contend with sensed threats of abandonment, inconsistencies and deprivations in an infant's environment. ... The quality of mutuality and the strength of trust, autonomy, hope and courage (or their opposites) developed in this phase underlie (or threaten to undermine) all that comes later in faith development. (1978, 121)

Adequately performed mothering rituals (holding, feeding, cleansing, interacting) and a dependable, complementary relationship of symbiotic mutuality are most likely to generate our first-felt sense of self and the universe as basically trustworthy or untrustworthy. Transition starts with the convergence of thought and language around the age of two, when a toddler, standing on his or her feet, starts exploring the world, using speech symbols and ritual play.

Early Childhood and Stage 1 Intuitive-Projective Faith

According to Fowler, children between the ages of two and seven undergo a revolutionary convergence of thought and language, together with an explosion of imagination and active imitation, all the hallmarks of Stage 1 Intuitive-Projective Faith. As Fowler describes:

> Stage 1 Intuitive-Projective Faith is the fantasy-filled, imitative phase in which the child can be powerfully and permanently influenced by examples, moods, actions and stories of the visible faith of primarily related adults. ... This is the stage of first self-awareness. The self-aware child is egocentric as regards the perspectives of others. (1981, 133)

Compared to the previous undifferentiated pre-stage of infancy, this stage marks the beginning of a child's first self-awareness, but the self-aware child is egocentric and not yet capable of taking the perspectives of others. In this stage, imagination is fertile and fantasies are wild; the thinking is still fluid and uninhibited by logical linking or reasoning. Because young children's imaginations are extremely powerful, they acquire knowledge through primary mental processes, including nonverbal, visual, and sensual images, as well as moods, rhythms, vibrations, voice inflexions, exaggerated actions, and so on.

Transition to the next stage occurs with an emergence of concrete operational thinking, which makes a child inquisitive about his or her world, what is real and what only seems to be so.

Mid-Childhood and Stage 2 Mythic-Literal Faith

In contrast to the Stage 1 Intuitive-Projective preschooler, a child of age seven to twelve becomes capable of inductive and deductive reasoning. Whereas the Stage 1 child "fuses fantasy, fact and feeling, the Stage 2 boy or girl works hard and effectively at sorting out the real from the make-believe," says Fowler. He describes the main characteristics of Stage 2:

> Mythic-Literal faith in which the person begins to take on for him—or herself the stories, beliefs and observances that symbolize belonging to his or her community. Beliefs are appropriated with literal interpretations, as are moral rules and attitudes. ... In this stage the rise of concrete operations leads to the curbing and ordering of the previous stage's imaginative composing of the world. ... The new capacity or strength in this stage is the rise of narrative and the emergence of story, drama, myth as ways of finding and giving coherence to experience. (1981, 149)

A vital strength of Stage 2 is an emergence of the narrative—story, drama, or myth—as a way of making meaning and giving coherence to experience for a school-age child. Transition takes place, however, when excessive reliance on literalness and reciprocity breaks down, and an implicit clash or contradictions of stories lead the adolescent-in-the-making to reflection on meanings and mutual interpersonal perspective taking.

Early Adolescence and Stage 3 Synthetic-Conventional Faith

"Puberty brings with it a revolution in physical and emotional life," says Fowler (1981, 151). An adolescent needs mirrors of all sorts. Besides a vanity mirror, a young person needs a social mirror to see him or her self as others see him or her. Similarly, one sees the images of others as reflected in one's own eyes. Fowler says, "I see you seeing me: I see the me I think you see," and conversely, "you see you according to me: you see the you you think I see" (ibid., 153).

This complex ability to compose hypothetical images of oneself and others is called "mutual interpersonal perspective-taking" or "social perspective-taking." What others see, say, think, approve, or disapprove dictates every move of an adolescent, who defines the self in terms of its roles and relationships. Sharon Parks calls this "the tyranny of the they" (Fowler 1981, 154). The youth structures even the ultimate environment in interpersonal terms.

Among all relationships, however, the "chum relationship" becomes crucially important to a teenager. Fowler describes the "chum" relationship as "a first experience of adolescent intimacy outside the family. In the chum—of either the same or opposite sex—a youth finds another person with time and with parallel gifts and needs" (ibid. 151).

How does an adolescent's experience relate to the title of Stage 3, called "Synthetic-Conventional Faith?" As Fowler explains:

> The adolescent's experience of the world now extends beyond the family. A number of spheres demand attention: family, school, work, peers, street society and media, and perhaps religion. Faith must provide a coherent orientation in the midst of that more complex and diverse range of involvements. Faith must synthesize values and information; it must provide a basis of identity and outlook." (1981, 172)

If the adolescent world is ridden with interpersonal roles, relationships, conflicts, and tensions, how can his or her faith be "synthetic?" In order to answer this question, we need to mark the use of the verb "must" in that faith "must provide a coherent orientation," which means that faith should serve as a unifying agent that brings meaning, order, and coherence into the chaotic world of a teenager. According to Fowler, faith "forms and conforms" one's self-identity at this stage. This kind of synthesis, however, does not happen automatically or smoothly. It can be a rather painful and prolonged process in which the adolescent can take years—spilling over into young adulthood—to achieve that "unification of a sense of self."

"Conventional," the other term in the title, signifies the conformist quality of the stage, which entails "a *forming with*" others through shared commitments and loyalties. In Stage 3, values, commitments and relationships are
seen as central to identity and worth" (Fowler 1987, 65). Thus, a teenager is
heavily dependent on the affirmation-confirmation of significant others.

Moreover, the youth begins to form his or her personal myth of self-
projecting into future roles and relationships. As Fowler puts it, "the emer-
gent capacity of this faith is the forming of a personal myth—the myth of
one's own becoming in identity and faith, incorporating one's past and
anticipated future in an image of the ultimate environment unified by
characteristics of personality" (ibid., 173).

The transitional process to the next faith stage, according to Fowler,
includes:

> Serious clashes or contradictions between valued authority sources;
> marked changes, by officially sanctioned leaders, or policies and practices
> previously deemed sacred and unbreachable ... Frequently the experience
> of "leaving home"—emotionally or physically, or both—precipitates the
> kind of examination of self, background, and life-guiding values that
> give rise to stage transition at this point. (1981, 173)

Stage 4 Individuative-Reflective Faith

According to Fowler (1981, 179), "the two essential features of the emergence
of Stage 4 are the critical distancing from one's previous assumptive value system and the emergence of an executive ego. When and as these occur a person is forming a new identity." Acquiring a new identity involves "a double
development," says Fowler. Two important movements must occur, together
or in sequence. In the first, a person must learn to relinquish his or her earlier
reliance upon external sources of authorities, and begin to critically question
or reflect over one's tacitly held previous assumptions, beliefs, values, and relationships. This means the Stage 3 "tyranny of the they" must be broken or the
roles and relations must be redefined. Sometimes "they" can also be present as
"the internalized voices" that may keep bothering until one learns to be free
from their control; this is the first part of the "double developmental" process.

In the second movement, along with the dislocation of authority from
outside, there should also be a "relocation of authority in the self." Not
others, but the self is now the ultimate source of authority. Fowler calls this
the "emergence of a strong executive ego"—I take command; I am in command of myself (ibid., 179).

In order for a "strong executive ego" to emerge, a person must develop a critical, analytical faculty to examine or re-examine whatever was given, inherited, or tacitly held before. This kind of critical distancing cannot be possible without what Fowler calls "a third-person perspective-taking" or "social perspective-taking" (ibid.). Critical judgment requires distance from the scene as well the objectivity of an onlooker or a third person. "The third-person perspective provides an angle of vision from which evaluations and expectations of others and from which conflicting claims or expectations can be adjudicated" (ibid.).

If critical distancing is necessary for the emergence of an "executive ego," its maintenance requires the young adult to develop a new outlook or "ideology." As Fowler explains, "To sustain that new identity, Stage 4 composes a meaning frame conscious of its own boundaries and inner connections and aware of itself as a 'world view'" (ibid., 182). Thus, ideology is the oxygen of the young adult faith.

Because of the importance of the critical-analytical faculties, and ideology based on reason and conviction, Stage 4 faith is a "demythologizing stage," says Fowler (1987, 70); he further explains, "creeds, symbols, stories and myths from religious traditions are likely to be subjected to analysis and to translation to conceptual formulations." A young adult perceives an ultimate environment in terms of an "explicit system of meanings." To sum up Stage 4 exposition, its ascendant strengths appear to be: critical distancing or critical reflection (third-person perspective-taking), the emergence of an executive ego, and the birth of explicit ideology with a tendency to "demythologize" symbols and creeds.

What are the factors that signal a person's readiness for transition from Stage 4 Individuative-Reflective to Stage 5 Conjunctive Faith? According to Fowler:

> Restless with the self-images and outlook maintained by Stage 4, the person ready for transition finds him or herself attending to what may feel like anarchic and disturbing inner voices. Elements from a childish past, images and energies from a deeper self, a gnawing sense of the sterility and flatness of the meanings one serves—any or all of these may signal readiness for something new. (1981, 183)

Stage 5 Conjunctive Faith

Stage 5 Conjunctive Faith is more complex, dialectical, and multidimensional in its approach to life and truth. The name "Conjunctive Faith" can be traced to Nicolas of Cusa (1401–1464), according to Fowler. It suggests the "coincidentia oppositorum," which means "the conjunction of opposites and contradictions" in our apprehensions of truth. Moving beyond the dichotomizing strategy of Stage 4 Individuative Faith, one sees all sides of the issue simultaneously. Suspecting that things are organically and intricately interwoven, one begins to accept the multidimensionality of truth. A Stage 5 person also needs to hold together several conscious and unconscious elements and polar tensions within the self, and in the experience of ultimate reality, which does not usually occur before the mid-thirties. According to Fowler:

> Stage 5 Conjunctive Faith involves the integration into self and outlook of much that was suppressed and unrecognized in the interest of Stage 4's self-certainty and conscious cognitive and affective adaptation to reality. This stage develops a "second naivete" (Ricouer) in which symbolic power is reunited with conceptual meanings. Here there must also be a new reclaiming and reworking of one's past. There must be an opening to the voices of one's deeper self. (1981, 197–198)

The dimensions of breadth and depth characterize Stage 5. The breadth of vision entails a widening of one's perspective-taking which requires "an ability to be not only self-critical, but also to be open to identify with perspectives that may be radically different from one's own." It means an acceptance of a plurality of ways of looking at things. As Fowler remarks, "one must also seriously commit to justice, human dignity, and truth that is freed from the confines of tribe, class, religious community or nation."

Fowler affirms that "new depths of experience in spirituality and religious revelation also characterize Stage 5" (1987, 71). It requires a critical recognition of one's social unconscious (myths, ideal images, and prejudices) built deeply into the self-system, which should not be confused with Stage 3's pre-critical subjectivity and pluralism.

Regarding the transition, Fowler states, "the transition involves an overcoming of this paradox through a moral and ascetic actualization of the universalizing apprehensions." He explains it further:

> Heedless of the threats to self, to primary groups, and to the institutional arrangements of the present order, ... Stage 6 becomes a disciplined, activist incarnation—a making real and tangible—of the imperatives of absolute love and justice of which Stage 5 has partial apprehensions. The self at Stage 6 engages in spending and being spent for the transformation of present reality in the direction of a transcendent actuality. (1981, 200)

Fowler adds persons who can make such a transition "are only few and far between"; they are "rare individuals"—"the finest exemplars of faith and the ultimate hope of mankind."

Stage 6 Universalizing Faith

"Stage 6 is exceedingly rare," says Fowler; very few persons, like Gandhi, Martin Luther King Jr., Mother Teresa, Dietrich Bonhoeffer, and exceptional others, have exemplified this stage. "The persons best described by it have generated faith compositions in which," says Fowler, "their felt sense of an ultimate environment is inclusive of all being. They have become incarnators and actualizers of the spirit of inclusive and fulfilled human community" (1981, 200). He explains further:

> Living with a felt participation in a power that unifies and transforms the world, Universalizers are often experienced as subversive of the structures (including the religious structures). ... Many persons in this stage die at the hands of those whom they hope to change. Universalizers are often more honored and revered after death than during their lives. (ibid.)

From this I derive that the Stage 6 persons must fulfill these criteria: inclusiveness of community, a radical commitment to justice and love, and a selfless passion for "a transformed world" that is "in accordance with an intentionality both divine and transcendent."

According to Fowler, "Universalizing faith is marked by the radical completion of two tendencies." The first is an "epistemological decentration from self," which involves "the gradual qualitative extension of the ability and readiness to balance one's perspective with those others included in an expanding radius" (1984, 69). This is "a qualitative expansion in perspective taking" in which at each stage, we keep gradually widening our circle of awareness and concern beginning with our "self" and immediate family to an extended circle of friends and colleagues to eventually include the outer groups, classes, nations, and the world. This "all-encompassing knowing" and "a compassionate perspective-taking," especially of strangers, becomes one of the hallmarks of Stage 6. As Fowler explains, persons in Stage 6 experience "a powerful kind of kenosis or an emptying of self" into God. They are able to "love even the enemies" who are seen "transformingly as God's children who must be loved radically and redemptively" (ibid., 76).

The second "decentration from self" that Fowler describes involves an "axiological expansion"; it is related to one's "valuing and valuation" of the self and others. Fowler explains it as "conferring meaning and worth" to self and others; it is "resting our hearts on God or Transcendence," putting our total trust in this one supreme source of value and power. In this process of "decentration in valuing, the self is drawn beyond itself into a new quality of participation and grounding in God, or the Principle of Being" (1987, 75). It is called the "relinquishing of self as epistemological and axiological center" in which "the self is no longer the prime reference point from which the knowing and valuing of faith are carried out" (ibid.). "God or the Transcendent" remains the highest source of all knowledge, value, and power. The "self" becomes now "the God-grounded Self."

PARALLELS: GANDHI'S APPROACH TO TRUTH AND FOWLER'S DEFINITION OF FAITH

I found three strong parallels between Fowler's concept of faith and Gandhi's approach to Truth, which encouraged me to undertake this comparative, cross-cultural study. First, Fowler conceives of faith not only as "a human phenomenon, an apparently generic consequence of the universal human burden of finding and making meaning," but also claims that "all humans are genetically potentiated for partnership with God, whether or not they are religious in any traditional way" (1987, 54). Gandhi too, in accord with his *Advaita* Vedanta (non-dualistic) philosophy of Hinduism, believed that the *Brahman* (cosmic spirit) pervades the whole universe and flows through every human being. Therefore, every *atman* (human soul) inheres an infinite capacity for unconditional love, compassion, and forgiveness. Gandhi further affirmed that even the most hardened hearts melt under the soft, persistent pressure of love, because love as active nonviolence proves to be the most positive transforming power.

Second, Fowler claims that faith, being a deeper and dynamic dimension of life, is not confined to religion or beliefs; it is free to embrace all humans across religious and cultural boundaries. Gandhi, who was a deeply devoted Hindu, also did not believe in the narrow confines of dogmas, rituals, and sectarianism. Although he said that his motive in undertaking any activity was "purely religious," he was not religious in its commonly understood sense. He described Hinduism as the "Religion of humanity"—of Truth and love in its broadest sense.

Third, Fowler conceives of faith as "a comprehensive and holistic stance of life; it is not a separate dimension of life or a compartmentalized specialty" (1981, 14). To Gandhi too, "the whole gamut of man's activities today constitutes an indivisible whole; you cannot divide social, political and purely religious work into watertight compartments" (Hoyland 1944).

Unfortunately, despite Gandhi's all-encompassing vision of life as an "indivisible whole" and his assertion that he believed only in the "Religion of Truth and nonviolence or love in the broadest sense," he and his actions were often misunderstood. The myths and misconceptions about Gandhi kept perpetuating through hagiographies and hero-worship of Gandhi; some of them were even overtly dramatized by the major motion picture *Gandhi*. Below I have provided an overview of some common myths versus the realities of Gandhi, which I will discuss at length in the upcoming chapters.

Some of the most common myths about Gandhi are:

1. Gandhi was born as a Mahatma or the Mahatma-hood came easily to him.
2. Gandhi underwent a sudden conversion at Maritzburg in South Africa.
3. Gandhi's London experience was wasteful; it gave no hint of the future Mahatma.
4. Child Gandhi had an Oedipal relationship with his mother and father.

In reality:

1. Gandhi was not born as a Mahatma, nor did Mahatma-hood come easily to him. His serenity of mind was hard-earned through a painful and prolonged process of practicing various spiritual disciplines (fasting, abstinence, observance of silence, for example) and conducting rigorous experiments with truth and nonviolence.
2. Gandhi had no sudden conversion, nor a religious revelation. His nonviolent defiance of apartheid at Maritzburg in South Africa was a well-considered response with emotional and psychological connections to his past experiences.
3. Contrary to what most biographers of Gandhi have opined, Gandhi's London years were not wasteful; rather, they were his silently formative years that initiated him into the British culture, democratic system, and the British character, as they also whetted his religious appetite.
4. Erik Erikson's Oedipal interpretations in *Gandhi's Truth* (1969) of child Gandhi's strong attachment to his mother and his ambivalence toward his father are challenged in this book and the social, cultural and psychological differences in the "child-mother-father" relationship in the Indian context are explained.

Indigenous Cultural Perspective

As most Western writers, including Erikson, and readers are not familiar with Gandhi's native language and culture, throughout this book I offer an insider's perspective of culture-specific concepts that played a decisive role in Gandhi's transformational process, such as:

- mother and mother veneration in Indian society and religion;
- the Indian mythological ideal of filial obedience and piety;
- reasons for adolescent Gandhi's "guilt and shame" on the night of his father's death;
- Gandhi's views on marital sex;
- Gandhi's vow of *brahmacharya* (abstinence) after witnessing the Zulu war violence;
- the profound influence of Rajchandra on Gandhi's inner self-transformation; and
- Jain influences: Gandhi's passion for purification, perfection, truth, and nonviolence.

By introducing myself as "an insider/outsider," [3] I want to clarify at the very outset that I do not intend to create any artificial distinction between the natives of India versus non-Indians about their right to speak with authority regarding anything associated with India. Nor do I want to suggest that simply by virtue of being born into a country, culture, or religion that a person automatically becomes "an insider"; by the same token, it would be presumptuous for me or for anyone to disclaim the rights of those outside of India to speak with authority and authenticity about India, about her culture and people.

My point is that I feel doubly blessed for having been born and raised in India in the very cultural milieu, language, and part of the era that I happen to share with Gandhi. As I have indicated earlier, I grew up as a child under the influence of the Gandhian era at the height of the Indian Independence Movement. What I saw, felt, heard, witnessed, and sometimes participated in have all become a part of me that connects me with my "Indian-ness." I have felt all the emotions of tremendous elation as well as the dark dejection and pain, associated with the struggle for freedom. But feelings and emotions tend to be subjective and could be misleading, too, without an added perspective of "critical distancing" from the scene, to use Fowler's language in his description of Stage 4 Individuative-Reflective Faith. I was fortunate to have an educational opportunity to study Gandhi outside of India, in the United States, to be able to develop a different kind of objective, analytical-critical interest in Gandhi. I do cherish my roots, but I also hold in high esteem all scholars who have contributed a great deal before me to unravel the mystery of this infinitely intriguing man and his multidimensional faith.

GENERAL FORMAT AND CHAPTER OVERVIEW

Each chapter in this book is divided into two components. In the first part, I cover the life story of Gandhi. In the second part I review the same in the theoretical light of the corresponding stage in the faith theory. I give my final evaluation of Gandhi's evolving identity and spirituality in view of the stage criteria and discuss if and how they help us understand some of the yet undisclosed or ambiguous aspects of his personality and faith. At this point, I also examine if there were any other indigenous influences that might be playing a culture-specific role in shaping Gandhi's views, responses, and general outlook on life and faith.

Chapter 1 paints with broad strokes the picture of Victorian colonial India under the British *Raj* (Rule) in the latter half of the nineteenth century. Because Gandhi was born into this historical-political background marked by political unrest, a complex British–Indian (sahib–servant) relationship, and a rising spirit of nationalism, he could not escape the influence of the national maladies and psychological preoccupations of his times.

Chapters 2 and 3 cover Gandhi's early childhood environment, which was soaked in devotional faith; they show the supreme significance of the role of his parents, extended family, and the whole social-cultural milieu in which he was raised. Most important, in chapter 3 I refute Erik Erikson's interpretation in *Gandhi's Truth* (1969) that the child Mohandas had an Oedipal relationship with his mother and father; on the contrary, I argue from the Indian cultural perspective that this period proved to be the most positive in shaping Gandhi's personality, values, morals, and his trust in God.

Chapter 4 delineates the mid-childhood period of Mohandas Gandhi's life, his morbid shyness and his extraordinary moral sensitivity. This is the period that marks the beginnings of the "Moral Mahatma" with his intense passion for seeing mythological plays that extolled the virtues of truthfulness and self-sacrificing for parents.

In Chapter 5, adolescent Mohandas Gandhi is seen through a turbulent period of "identity-crisis" brought on by his early arranged marriage, his friendship with a Muslim boy named Mehtab, his religious skepticism, and his divided loyalties. From the faith developmental perspective, Gandhi is struggling with his "guilt and shame" feelings on account of some of his juvenile indiscretions and deceptions. Adolescent Gandhi's honest confession of his wrong-doings to his father, and his father's compassion in return, mends their estranged relationship; Gandhi describes this as "the first visible proof of the power of *ahimsa*," or a nonviolent approach, which awakened the best in both father and son.

In Chapter 6 I argue that contrary to what most biographers have suggested, Gandhi's London years as a law student were not wasteful; rather, the whole experience broadened his intellectual horizons, kindled his religious appetite, and acquainted him with the British culture, people, and political system—which prepared him for his future leadership role in confronting colonial governments in South Africa and India.

Chapter 7 shows that the first phase of Gandhi's South African years contributed not only to his emergence as a leader but also to his intellectual and spiritual growth. This is the country where he fought the apartheid government with the only weapon in his hand—nonviolent resistance—which he later developed into the well-honed technique of *satyagraha* (Truth campaign) based on nonviolence and voluntary suffering. The period is also marked for Gandhi's increasingly serious religious inquiries to his Indian spiritual mentor, Rajchandra, his reading of Tolstoy's *The Kingdom of God is Within You*, and his self-reflections. His meeting with the poor, indentured laborer named Balasundaram proves to be another catalyst to make Gandhi think seriously about his life, and to make it more service-oriented than self-oriented.

Chapter 8 introduces us to *Gandhibhai* or Brother Gandhi, the leader of the Indian community in South Africa. Gandhi goes through intense soul-searching after reading Ruskin's *Unto This Last* and after witnessing the Zulu War violence; as a result of both, he takes his vow of celibacy, founds the Phoenix Ashram, and resides in it with his family. In his determination to abandon his prosperous law career and comfortable lifestyle for a simple, austere life of public service, we see the first glimpse of the future Mahatma.

In Chapter 9, *satyagraha*—Truth campaign based on nonviolent resistance—is born and led by Gandhi for the first time in South Africa. During this period Gandhi writes *Hind Swaraj* (1909), and under the profound influence of Tolstoy's *The Kingdom of God is Within You*, (1899), he founds his second ashram named Tolstoy Ashram. Gandhi's inner life becomes more service-oriented and God-centered.

Chapter 10 shows Gandhi returning to India and being hailed as *Mahatma*—the Great Soul. He impressed his fellow Indians as an unusual leader who used politics only as a means for the spiritual regeneration of himself, others, and the whole nation. We see Mahatma Gandhi emerge on the Indian political scene as a strong leader of rare moral integrity, who organized a nationwide *salt satyagraha* (1930) against the British salt monopoly. Alongside his active involvement in India's freedom struggle, Gandhi is deeply engaged in his "constructive programs," such as the removal of untouchability, promotion of village industries, and Hindu–Muslim unity. In this chapter we also see the complexities and paradoxes in Gandhi's personality, which are all held together by his ever-deepening faith in God or Truth.

Chapter 11 covers the last radical phase of Gandhi's life and faith journey, which encompasses his intense political and spiritual struggles as he approaches the end of his life. Gandhi gives the British the ultimatum to "Quit India" in 1942 and prepares the nation "to do or die" for freedom. We see the Mahatma moving toward martyrdom for peace and for the brotherhood of Hindus and Muslims in the wake of India's partition in 1947. As war and violence rage outside, Gandhi conducts his most rigorous experiments in *brahmacharya* to purify and strengthen his soul power; at the same time, he undertakes his fast unto death as a token of a collective penance for communal sins. The chapter covers the last tragic episode of Gandhi's death by an extremist Hindu assassin's bullets. Gandhi died as he lived—for Truth, for nonviolence, for peace, and for the brotherhood of mankind. This ultimate stage of his life and faith proved to be the most eloquent testament of Fowler's Stage 6 Universalizing Faith.

In Chapter 12, I give final observations and conclusions regarding Gandhi's continuously evolving identity and spirituality in light of Fowler's Theory of Stages of Faith. In addition, I offer my cultural perspectives and interpretations of Gandhi as a pilgrim of Truth.

Mine is not a typical biographical approach; it does not simply narrate what happened and when in Gandhi's life, but rather explains the true significance of what happened from the perspective of his inner self and faith development. The primary focus is not on events, nor is it on the contents of Gandhi's thoughts and philosophy, even though both are integral parts of the whole process of his faith development and self-transformation. The purpose of this book is to show the metamorphosis of an ordinary man, Mohandas Gandhi, into Mahatma Gandhi—an extraordinary spiritual genius who showed mankind the way from darkness to Light, from untruth to Truth, and from death to Immortality.

1

Victorian Colonial India

The British colonial Indian environment preceding Gandhi's birth was disturbing yet promising at the same time. The Indian Mutiny of 1857 against the oppressive British regime was suppressed; as a result, Indian spirit was crushed, their self-esteem wounded, the economy ruined, and the whole country submerged in deep despair. Although the British now had no choice but to relent their policies a little by granting special favors and Western educational opportunities to a few eligible Indian elite, their overall attitude to Indians remained that of a sahib to a servant—arrogant and overbearing or patronizing and scornful by turns. This problematic British attitude generated four major Indian responses to the British, which played a critical role in shaping Gandhi's responses to the British and the British rule.

FOURFOLD INDIAN RESPONSE TO THE BRITISH

In his book *Colonialism, Tradition and Reform* (1989), Bhikhu Parekh suggests four broad categories of "Hindu Responses to British Rule" (between 1820–1920): modernism, traditionalism, critical modernism, and critical traditionalism. These responses provided the basic conceptual framework within which Gandhi formulated his own unique response.

The modernists were convinced that modernity was incompatible with the old Indian civilization and culture; they suggested a clean break with all things traditional—its plural, rural, feudal governing system, orthodox religious beliefs, sectarianism, caste barriers, and narrow parochialism. The younger Gandhi tended to be a modernist who emulated the British lifestyle and manners, as discussed later in this book.

The modernists came under heavy fire, however, from the traditionalists, who called them traitors, copy-cats, sycophants, and even the brown sahibs. Convinced that India was in its present sorry state of affairs because of the English, Muslim, and other foreign invaders, the traditionalists denounced them all. They thought that compared to their glorious, ancient Indian civilization, the European civilization was barbaric, inferior, and morally bankrupt. Consisting largely of upper-caste orthodox Hindus, this group used the scriptures to justify and maintain caste barriers and unsociability. They even forbade anyone to cross the black seas to go to Europe for higher education; violators were ostracized. (Young Gandhi with his entire family was excommunicated for his daring to go to England for higher studies.)

The third group of responders comprised critical modernists or syncretists. They advocated a judicious combination of Indian moral values and European political values, of the Western scientific spirit of rational inquiry and the Eastern mystical inquiry into the human spirit. They were great reformers, such as Raja Ram Mohun Roy, Keshab Chandra Sen, Bankim Chandra Chatterjee, Gopal Krishna Gokhale and others, whom I shall discuss in more detail later.

The fourth category of responses consisted of the critical traditionalists like Bankim Chandra Chatterjee (in later times), B. C. Pal, Shri Aurobindo, and Swami Vivekananda, of whom the latter had a profound influence on Gandhi. Unlike the critical modernists who advised borrowing the good from other cultures and rejecting the bad, the critical traditionalists suggested that each person first rethink and revise his or her own tradition from deep within and then get rid of whatever seemed to be irrational or obsolete. Unlike those New Age proponents who knowingly or unknowingly held the European civilization to be superior, the critical traditionalists upheld their own civilization, valued their culture, and suggested only to eliminate the diseased, dysfunctional, or dead parts.

GANDHI AS A CRITICAL TRADITIONALIST

Although the younger Gandhi tended to be a modernist, we shall witness his gradual metamorphosis into a critical traditionalist later in the book. Gandhi's role as a critical traditionalist needs special attention as most of his leadership style and ideals emanated from his deep, yet not blind devotion to his own Indian tradition. Gandhi loved Hinduism, but he was not an orthodox Hindu, or as Bhikhu Parekh (1989) put it, "though Gandhi valued tradition, he was not a traditionalist." Unlike most other critical tradition- alists, Gandhi diagnosed the disease of the Indian degeneration as a severe moral decline of the Hindu character. Whereas other critical traditionalists pointed the finger of blame at the British, Gandhi turned it toward his own countrymen who had lost their physical, intellectual, and moral courage, and therefore lacked character. Gandhi firmly believed that when the char- acter of the people falls, the nation falls. As a critical traditionalist, he resem- bled his spiritual predecessor, Swami Vivekananda—the monk-disciple of the sage Ramakrishna of Calcutta—who regretted the loss of Indian social and moral conscience.

SWAMI VIVEKANANDA'S INFLUENCE ON GANDHI

Speaking at the Parliament of World Religions in Chicago in 1893, the saffron-robed Swami Vivekananda first introduced Vedanta to the West and mesmerized Westerners by his fiery personality and matchless eloquence. Swami Vivekananda was the first one to awaken his fellow Indians from their deep slumber with his inspiring words: "Arise! Awake! Rest not till the goal is achieved," the goal being to gain freedom from the foreign British yoke. He exhorted his countrymen to straighten their backs so no foreigner could ride on them. A few years later, Gandhi, too, would admonish his people, saying that the reason the British ruled India was because Indians allowed them to do so. Time and again Vivekananda reminded Indians to be "mighty lions" and "not meek lambs." Above all, what the Swami instilled in his fellow Indians was the spirit of nationalistic pride and vigor based on their own unique spiritual heritage of the *Vedas*, *Upanishads*, and *Vedanta*; Swami Vivekananda's spiritualistic nationalism greatly inspired Gandhi. Moreover, like Vivekananda, Gandhi not only identified with the poor millions of India, but he, more than any other leader, continued the Swami's unfinished work of serving the poor and downtrodden as the *Daridra-Narayana* or "God of the Poor." Although Gandhi did not directly mention his indebtedness to Vivekananda, as Bhikhu Parekh observed (1989), he was deeply influenced by the latter's ideas of national unity, religious harmony, service to the poor, and culti- vating "manliness." To become as "manly as a mighty Englishman" was the motto of every young Indian in British India, and young Gandhi was no exception. He would change that later, however, by reinterpreting the meaning of "manliness."

GANDHI AND THE COLONIAL STEREOTYPES

If the younger Gandhi fell prey to the colonial stereotypes of "manly Englishman" and "feminine Indian," the more mature Gandhi fought against it; he rewrote the entire negative colonial script of "Indian effeminacy" with a new one of "positive androgyny." As Ashish Nandy observed (1983, 54), "Gandhi's nationalism ... undermines the imperialist ethos of hyper-masculinity by de-linking courage and activism from aggression and violence and making them compatible with femininity." Gandhi drew upon the ancient Hindu concepts of *Sakti* (positive androgyny), or dynamic womanhood, which is an alternative model of masculinity. He strategically harnessed this spiritual feminine power of "suffering love" and "nonviolent courage" into his *satyagrahas* and thus redefined the very concept of "manliness." Women represented the power of *tapasya* (spiritual forbearance), which is more potent and healing than brutal power. To Gandhi, "the power of the sword was as zero before the power of the soul." Both in himself, and in his political campaigns, Gandhi made creative use of feminine spiritual strengths, thereby helping to change not only the male stereotypes (of colonial India) but also restoring the positive images of femininity of the *Vedic* and *Upanishadic* Hinduism.

PREDECESSORS PAVE THE WAY

In rewriting the negative colonial script, however, Gandhi was not alone, nor was he the first Indian leader-reformer to undertake the task of national regeneration. Many a brilliant reformer before him had brooded over the current moral degeneration of India under British colonial rule and had paved the way for him. In imperceptible ways Gandhi was inspired by those reformers' fervent nationalism, their social and religious reformist zeal, and their examples of selfless work and devotion to India. Because of their shining light, which pierced through the darkness and turmoil of the post-Mutiny period, the skies looked brighter in the second half of the nineteenth century. It was the British Orientalism movement that first sparked off the Hindu cultural and religious renaissance, giving birth to many reformist movements all across India.

British Orientalism Spreading to
Europe and America

The years from 1772 to 1830 under British colonial rule in India can be described as the golden era of Orientalism, which fired up the imagination of a group of "acculturated civil, military and judicial officials," according to David Kopf (1969). Through their painstaking study of Sanskrit, this earliest batch of English scholars—William Jones, Charles Wilkins, Thomas Colebrooke, and William Carey—discovered the spiritual wisdom of the *Vedas*, the *Upanishads*, and the *Bhagavad Gita*; they also translated into English the two Hindu epics of *Ramayana* and *Mahabharata*, the *Puranas* and other sacred Sanskrit texts. The wind of British Orientalism spread from England to Germany (Muller, Schopenhauer). It also swept over America, giving rise to the transcendental movement spearheaded by Ralph Waldo Emerson and Henry David Thoreau. The Oriental movement received additional reinforcement from the Theosophical movement in England (Madame Blavatsky, Annie Besant), which would later kindle the young law student Gandhi's interest in his own religions, especially Hinduism and Buddhism.

Hindu Cultural-Religious Renaissance
and Reformist Movements

Nationally, India was awakening in herself; psychologically and culturally, she was awakening in her people. New winds of change were blowing and reform was in the air. The two-way process of acculturation or intercultural borrowing, initiated by British Orientalists, was now being reciprocated by British-influenced Indian intellectuals who set the whole nation afire with their reformist zeal. As a part of the Hindu cultural and religious renaissance, various reformist movements flourished all across India, but Bengal became the very hub of a sociocultural and religious revolution. Bengali reformers like Rammohun Roy, Ishwar Chandra, Keshab Chandra Sen, Radhakant Deb, Bankim Chandra Chatterjee, and others were particularly drawn to the newfound ideas of freedom, justice, and equality. "Rammohun Roy, one of the most fascinating and complex Indians to have emerged during the Orientalist period," (Kopf 1969, 196) was the founder-editor of the *Sambad Kaumudi*—a Brahmmanical magazine. He wrote fiery editorials on "the Folly of caste," the "abolition of the Hindu custom of *suttee*," and the "rights of women." He also founded the *Brahmo Samaj*, the "cornerstone of Hindu reformation movement." Similarly, in Saurashtra (now a part of Gujarat), Dayanand Saraswati founded the *Arya Samaj*; like Roy, he opposed idol-worship. Another radical reformer of Gujarat, Veer Narmad practiced what he preached and married a widow himself. Besides these, a host of other Indian reformer-nationalists who preceeded Gandhi and influenced him included Dadabhai Naoroji, called the "Grandshire of Indian Nationalism," Bal Gangadhar Tilak, Aurobindo Ghose, and Gopal Krishna Gokhale.

GANDHI'S DISTINCT IMPRINT ON HIS TIMES

Although some of the nineteenth-century Hindu reformers profoundly influenced Gandhi, he set his own style and put his own distinct mark on his *yuga* (epoch) to regenerate himself and his people, and to free his beloved India from British bondage. He created his own concoction of spiritual nationalism based on social reforms, religious openness, and an all-encompassing humanity in order to seek first his own true identity, and in that process, the identity of his people. We may also note here that though Gandhi worked all his life to purge Hinduism of excrescences such as unsociability, caste barriers, religious sectarianism, and racial prejudices, he was never an iconoclast like Dayanand Saraswati, nor a demythologizer like Raja Rammohan Roy. More like Swami Vivekananda, Gandhi firmly believed in retaining his own Hindu tradition and in revitalizing and reinterpreting it in the context of his time.

Deriving inspiration from the precepts and examples of his predecessors, Gandhi would later lead a bloodless moral and spiritual revolution from the grass roots level and not just the elite level. Gandhi envisioned life, to use his own metaphor, "not as a pyramid with the apex sustained by the bottom," but rather, as an "oceanic circle whose center was the individual." Thus, Gandhi's reformist approach was not only more comprehensive than that of any of his predecessors but also more pragmatic and democratic to involve people at the grass roots; he was convinced that what India needed at the time was moral and spiritual regeneration.

2

Gandhi's Roots

Gandhi's favorite saint-poet from his own native Gujarat, Narsimha Mehta,[1] summed up one of the profound truths of the Hindu *Advaita* philosophy in these lines:

> O Lord, as You are the seed from the tree,
> So are you the tree from the seed.[2]

The idea is not only that the seed and the tree are contained in each other, but that both symbolize one of the greatest principles of the universe, namely, that the phenomenon of the rooting of the seed and its gradual growth, blossoming, expansion (and eventually extinction) is all part of an organic process—a visible proof of God's miracle at work.

The roots of Gandhi's faith were firmly and deeply planted in his native Indian culture of Kathiawar-Gujarat,[3] from where they continued to grow and spread like an Indian Banyan tree. Mohandas Karamchand Gandhi was born in 1869 in Porbandar or Sudamapuri,[4] a seacoast city in the British-ruled princely Kathiawar peninsula in west India. Gandhi was every inch the son of his soil, influenced by the Kathiawar culture and the Porbandar community that nurtured child Gandhi, helped shape his early personality, and formed the first images of his surrounding world. What was the nature and significance of his first environment from which the infant Gandhi absorbed, albeit unconsciously, his morals and cultural characteristics that would lay the foundation of his own identity and faith? Do we find in his infancy a confirmation of the basic premise of Primal faith in the theory of Stages of Faith?

25

KATHIAWAR

The Kathiawar peninsula, surrounded by the Arabian Sea on India's west coast, formed a conglomerate of miniature, princely kingdoms in the post-Mutiny Victorian era. At one time or another, Gandhi's ancestors had been employed as *Diwans* or Prime Ministers of such small states as Porbandar, Rajkot, and Vankaner, ruled by the local *Ranas* or princes with their privileges of "eleven-gun salutes" but no real power in British India.

Regarding Kathiawari politics, the region was notorious for its petty power struggles, courtly intrigues, gossiping, and backstabbing. One of the main reasons Gandhi left home for South Africa was because of his utter disapproval of such a polluted political environment. Although Gandhi abhorred dirty politics, he adopted some of his native political traditions of demanding justice by nonviolent retaliation, such as *dharana* (sitting at the door of the debtor and fasting), *risamanu* (refusing to speak), and *traga* (courting self-punishment for justice). It was customary for a creditor to sit at the door of his debtor and not eat or drink until the latter came out and paid off his debt. Non-communication was like non-cooperation, and the inviting of self-punishment was equivalent to self-suffering for the sake of truth and justice. Gandhi's forefathers were known to have used some of these techniques, which were meant to bring moral pressure on an adversary by rousing his conscience rather than threatening or physically attacking him. Child Gandhi may have absorbed these tactics through the stories and examples of his own family sires and grandsires who internalized them from what Sudhir Kakar calls the "community unconscious," which is "so much in a Hindu's bones he may not even be aware of it" (1981, 15).

We may note here two pertinent pieces of information. First, since the population of Kathiawar was an intermixture of Gujaratis and the Muslims, Gandhi was exposed early on to Muslims as his neighbors, and one of his closest childhood friends was a Muslim boy. Second, when he later became a barrister, his very first employment in South Africa was with the firm of Dada Abdulla, a Muslim merchant from his hometown, Porbandar, in Kathiawar.

PORBANDAR

Gandhi's birthplace, Porbandar, was a once-booming business port of the Gujarati *banias* (businessmen) and Muslim *kharvas* (sailors). The inner city where Gandhi's ancestors lived was a maze of narrow streets and crowded bazaars, interspersed with hundred temples of various Hindu deities. The limestone houses of Porbandar, long exposed to the sun and rain, shone like marble, which earned the city its nickname of the "White City." Gandhi was not only proud of his humble roots in this provincial town, but being a shrewd Kathiawari as well as a *Bania*, he made the most of it: he used his provincial experience as a training ground for working in the national and international fields as a moral-political and spiritual leader, both in South Africa and India.

Gandhi's ancestral house in Porbandar was purchased by his great-grandfather Harjivandas Gandhi in 1777; it is now remodeled and preserved as a national memorial known as "Mahatma Gandhi Kirti Mandir."[5] According to Pyarelal (1965, 190), this home was "a massively built three-storeyed structure, erected on three sides of a courtyard. The rooms were small, low-roofed, airless and dark." The only well-lit place was the top floor (where grandfather Ota Bapa lived), which kept cool due to the balmy, Arabian sea breeze. The house was flanked on one side by a Vaishnava *Haveli* or *Shrinathji* (temple) and on the other side by a Shiva temple. Mohandas Gandhi was born on the ground floor in a dark, small room adjacent to a kitchenette, where his mother Putliba spent most of her life.

GANDHI'S ANCESTORS

The stories and legends of his illustrious forefathers, passed on from generation to generation, became child Mohandas' first family legacy and privilege. According to the earliest available records, Gandhi's roots can be traced back six generations to Lalji Gandhi, who hailed from the Kutiyana province in the Junagadh state of Kathiawar.

Lalji Gandhi began the political involvement of the family in the local princely service and state administration. He served the local Muslim prince of the Khokar family, first as his *karbhari* or *daftari* (estate manager), then rose to the position of *Naib Diwan* (Assistant to the Prime Minister) in Porbandar. Lalji's son Ramji followed in his father's footsteps, as did his son Rahidas and Rahidas' two sons, Harjivandas Gandhi and Daman Gandhi. Harjivandas Gandhi's only son, Uttamchand Gandhi (Ota Bapa), the father of Karamchand Gandhi and grandfather of Mohandas Gandhi, was the first to become the *Diwan* or Prime Minister of Porbandar, a highly prestigious position in the British-ruled princely India.

The members of the large Gandhi clan never tired of narrating with pride the larger-than-life career of their grandfather Uttamchand Gandhi, the illustrious prime minister of the state of Porbandar and Junagadh successively. Usually addressed by all as Ota Bapa (*Bapa*: same as *Bapu*, the Kathiawari term for father), Mohandas Gandhi's grandfather earned high reputation and respect for his outstanding skills of negotiation, political diplomacy, moral courage, fiercely independent personality, and fearless loyalty. From grandmother Lakshmima (Ota Bapa's wife) and other women in the family, child Mohandas heard stories of Ota Bapa's exceptional courage and principled rebellion against the tyrannical Queen Rupaliba, the widow of *Rana* (king) Khimoji of Porbandar. Assuming heavy administrative responsibilities of a *karbhari* at age seventeen, the young Uttamchand helped raise the status of Porbandar from a third-class state to an officially classified first-class state in Kathiawar. With his uncanny foresight, Ota Bapa increased the Porbandar state revenues by cultivating some of its sandy wastelands. Besides being a skilled negotiator and financier, Gandhi's grandfather was a large-hearted man who always sided with the underdog and put his own life on the line to defend the rights of a minor official. As it so happened, the new treasurer of the mother-queen fell out of her grace, incurred her wrath, and was given a death sentence by her. The helpless man, running for his life, sought Ota Bapa's protection and took refuge in his home. The enraged queen ordered her prime minister to give up the man or have his house gunned down. More loyal to his principles than to royalty, Ota Bapa suffered the punishment; the subsequent cannon shots destroyed the walls, but the house stood its ground and so did the prime minister.

In yet another incident, Ota Bapa had refused to salute the new king of Junagadh with his right hand. When asked for an explanation, he said that the right-hand salute was reserved only for his original employer, the king of Porbandar. This time he was not punished but rewarded for his loyalty and honesty. These were only a few examples of his grandfather's moral courage, which the infant Gandhi ingested with his mother's milk.

Being the youngest son of his father, Karamchand ("Kaba") Gandhi, the Diwan of Porbandar, and Putliba (ba: mother), the child Mohandas always felt that he was somebody special, that he was the center of their large family universe. His father called him "Manu," and his mother called him "Mo(h)niya" (pronounced Moniya as "h" is silent); both had high hopes in this son, who was livelier, brighter, and more sensitive than their other children. Like his namesake Mohan,[6] Moniya was as playful and full of pranks as *Bala-Krishna* (*Bala*: child); he loved to tease others, to befriend animals by twisting their ears, to eat mangoes, and to bandage the wounded or rotten ones that had fallen on the ground. His older sister described him as "restless as mercury and full of curiosity." The youngster's boundless energy, which Erikson describes as his "locomotor restlessness and energy," remained undiminished through his old age, as the sixty-one-year-old Mahatma out-walked even his younger compatriots during the 1930 Salt March.

Moniya had many a hand to cradle him and many a lap to comfort him. His two grandmothers, Lakshmima and Tulsima; his mother, Putliba; his older sister, Raliatben; his two older brothers, Lakshmidas and Karsandas; countless cousins; widowed aunts; uncles; and Rambha, his special care-taker, all lived together under one roof. They adored him; they told him stories, kindled his imagination, calmed his fears, and taught him right from wrong.

Unlike the Western nuclear family consisting of a mother, father, and their children, a traditional Indian family is a multigenerational, coopera-tive housing community that includes the oldest of the old, the youngest of the young, and all the ages in between. Children are exposed early on to a wide variety of relatives, so they develop not only a special bond with each person but also learn to address each by his or her specific title as well.[7] Although each relative has a specific, honorific title that informs a child about the level of intimacy involved in the relationship, "the aim," writes Ashish Nandy in *Vishnu on Freud's Desk* (Vaidyanathan and Kripal, 11), "is to discourage the growing child to distinguish between 'near' and 'distant' relations."[8]

Although the criteria of jointness may vary from region to region, a joint family operates on the principles of hierarchy, seniority, gender, and age. Obedience rather than independence is expected of all—especially from the younger sons and daughters, who must also be ready to sacrifice their own personal interests in the larger interests of others and elders. An overwhelming importance on filial obedience and duty over pleasure is built into the Indian religion and culture, and it is highlighted in Indian epics, myths, and folklore. In an extended family, the oldest family patri-arch is entitled to all the formal power and authority, but the oldest matri-arch, usually a mother-in-law, pulls the strings and rules over her large family.

It was no surprise, then, that having been raised in such a large joint family, the child Gandhi later became a meticulous and efficient manager of his large ashrams. Not only that, but according to Manubehn Gandhi,[9] he also proved to be a kind and caring *"motherly Bapu"* to all his ashram resi-dents. Baby Moniya learned early in life how to care, share, and serve the needs of all in a joint family—to not only live in harmony with all his ashram residents of different tastes and temperaments but also to bring out the best in them. Thus, children were the beneficiaries of such an extended family system, where not just the two parents but many people loved and valued the child.

Gandhi's Infancy and Pre-Stage Primal Faith: An Evaluation

So, young Gandhi, or Moniya, was doubly blessed to have not only two loving, nurturing, and mutually supportive parents but also many more members in his extended family and in the community at large. Gandhi's first interviewer and biographer in South Africa, the Reverend Joseph Doke, described the effect of listening to Gandhi talk about his parents: "When Mr. Gandhi (yet not a Mahatma) speaks of his parents, those who listen realize that they are on holy ground … and there, in there, are the springs of Divine power and life" (1909, 22). Rev. Doke also recorded how Gandhi invoked the "infant–mother symbiosis" as an example to inspire his countrymen in South Africa during the Indian struggle; Gandhi exhorted them "to leave the world and cling to God as a child clings to its mother's breast."

Gandhi's own experience of "symbiotic mutuality" with his mother was particularly powerful and prolonged, the reasons for which will be discussed at length in the next chapter on Gandhi's early childhood. Here I would comment only that when Gandhi used the metaphor of "a child clinging to his mother's breast" in the Indian context, he was urging his people to fully commit to the national cause and put their full trust into it in just the way an infant trusts in his mother. In his book *The Inner World: Psychoanalytic Study of Childhood and Society In India* (1981, 55), Sudhir Kakar has analyzed the psychology of what "breast" means to an infant: "the infant needs his mother as a whole human being, not merely as a satisfier of hunger and thirst; or to state it plainly, what the infant requires is not a breast but a mother." Another important discussion to be seen in its cultural context—why the child–mother symbiosis is intense and prolonged in India—also belongs to the next chapter when we discuss the alleged Oedipal triangle implications in child Gandhi's relationship with his mother and father. At present it will suffice to say that although Gandhi revered both parents, by his own acknowledgment, he loved his mother more. He felt closer to his mother in terms of physical proximity and emotional intimacy, but more important, both shared a mutual affinity of spirit; they were two halves of the same moral-spiritual entity.

ADDITIONAL INDIAN CULTURAL PERSPECTIVES

What Fowler proposes in the faith developmental theory, that "human beings are genetically potentiated for partnership with God" (1987, 54), finds strong confirmation in the Hindu doctrine of karma and its belief in the *purva-samskaras* or the "innate pre-dispositions" with which a child is born. According to Sudhir Kakar (1979, 47), "the newborn infant is not a *tabula rasa* but comes equipped, as it were, with a highly personal and individual unconscious characterized by a particular mixture of three fundamental qualities or *gunas*." [10] New birth marks new beginnings, which means there is a renewed hope to change the quality of one's karma and the gunas through a continuity of the cycle of births and deaths. Both primal faith and the Indian doctrine of karma take into account the conscious and unconscious thought processes, which have powerful spiritual implications.

Yet another confirmation of the basic premise of primal faith comes from the Indian Ayurvedic medicinal and health system, which acknowledges the existence of the mother–child dyad even before the latter is born. According to this theory, birth begins at conception; a human embryo depends on its mother for its biological needs and growth, as well as for its deeper emotional, aesthetic, and spiritual development as well.

In Gandhi's infancy there is strong evidence of the basic premise of primal faith—that a loving, trusting, and mutually fulfilling mothering environment becomes a precursor of a child's first-felt images of self, others, and God. The infant visualizes the universe through his mother's eyes and sees God in his mother's face. Moreover, what Kakar calls the role of "the community unconscious" is equally important in an Indian context in which the community is part of one's extended family. An infant unconsciously, through his or her parents and from the community-at-large, absorbs most of the social, cultural, and religious influences. I conclude this chapter with Kakar's observation (1981, 82) that an Indian generally emerges from infancy into childhood "believing that the world is benign and that others can be counted on to act in his behalf. The young child has come to experience his core self as lovable: I am lovable, for I am loved." Baby Moniya certainly felt loved and valued by all in his family and community, but most of all by his mother and father, of whom a detailed analysis of character and religious faith will follow in the next chapter.

3

The Seed and the Soil

When the Reverend Joseph Doke remarked that those who listened to Gandhi speak about his parents felt like they were on "holy ground" (1909, 22), he was neither exaggerating nor using a figure of speech. Like most Indian children brought up in the Hindu tradition, child Gandhi learned early in life to revere his parents as human personifications of the Divine; like other children, child Gandhi must also have recited the following prayer in Sanskrit:

> O Lord, You are my mother and my father, You are my brother and my friend as well; You are the Knowledge, You are the wealth, You, my Lord, are all in all and everything to me.[1]

Little Moniya's reverence for his mother and father, however, was not dictated by tradition alone. Those biographers of Gandhi who knew him closely (e.g., Prabhudas Gandhi, Pyarelal, and others) witnessed that even as an adult, Gandhi could hardly speak about his parents without tears welling up in his eyes; those tears spoke even louder than words of his devotional love and gratitude to both parents. He was indebted to his mother and father for being living examples of selfless and dedicated public service. Even after they were gone, they continued to inspire him on his personal, moral, and spiritual journey through life, as well as in his public service mission to India, which included service to humanity at large.

Although he was devoted to both parents, there were times when he began to resent and criticize his father. Never once, however, did he speak or write harshly about his mother, whom he absolutely adored. What were the reasons—revealed and unrevealed—for some of Gandhi's unfavorable remarks about his father in his autobiography? What role did his father play in shaping Gandhi's early ambitions and honing his political and public relational skills? Why was child Gandhi closer to his mother than to his father? Did Gandhi's relationship with his father and mother form an Oedipal triangle as Erikson implied in *Gandhi's Truth* (1969)? Or were there other indigenous social and cultural factors involved? In what religious environment did Gandhi grow up? Following is an examination of these questions for their impact on Gandhi's character formation and faith development in view of Fowler's Theory of Stages of Faith.

FATHER KABA GANDHI

Among all six sons of Ota Bapa, his fifth son, Karamchand ("Kaba") Gandhi, showed the most promise of occupying the family *gadi* or premiership of Porbandar, which had become a family legacy for the last six generations of the Gandhis. According to Prabhudas Gandhi,[2] Gandhi's grandnephew, Kaba Gandhi was an able, morally upright, and well-respected prime minister of Porbandar and subsequently of Rajkot and Vankaner. The adult Gandhi himself acknowledged in his autobiography many outstanding traits of his father, although they were mixed with some personal resentment and negative criticism as well.

In a rather matter-of-fact manner, the middle-aged Mahatma described his father in *Autobiography* (1948, 12) as "a lover of his clan, truthful, brave, generous, but short-tempered... he was incorruptible and had earned a name for strict impartiality in his family as well as outside." As an example of his father's integrity, Gandhi mentions an incident in which Kaba, the prime minister, defended the Rajkot Thakore Saheb (king) when the British political agent spoke insultingly of him. Kaba was ready to suffer the punishment for defying the agent, and suffer he did, willingly as well as bravely. Another quality that Gandhi admired about his father was his total indifference to money and his lack of greed. As Gandhi puts it, "my father never had any ambition to accumulate riches and left us very little property" (ibid.). Gandhi's accounts, supported by others in the family, suggest that Kaba Gandhi had inherited his father Ota Bapa's political acumen—his skills of management and negotiation, combined with integrity and an independence of mind. Having no political degree, Kaba was schooled in the practical management of state affairs. He was skilled in resolving the most intricate political questions, yet he managed to remain above all the political intrigues. Prime Minister Kaba Gandhi was well liked, and respected by all in the family and the community.

Mohandas Gandhi was not only aware of his father's admirable qualities and political achievements but also he later integrated some of Kaba's managerial skills and political techniques into dealing with his own adversaries and supporters. There were, however, some other qualities of his father that son Mohandas perceived as "negative," and for which he later blamed his father. Ironically, history would eventually repeat itself, when Mohandas' oldest son would similarly blame his father in the future.

One of the main reasons for Gandhi's harsh criticism of his father was that Kaba Gandhi married four times, after the death of each wife. Gandhi wrote in his autobiography, "to a certain extent he (father) might have been even given to carnal pleasures. For he married for the fourth time when he was over forty" (1948, 12). Bear in mind, though, this judgmental remark about his father's perceived carnality was made in retrospect by the middle-aged Mahatma, who had given up sexual relations in his early thirties. Several other psychological reasons played a subtle role in the way Gandhi reacted to his father's multiple marriages. The fact that father Kaba married for the fourth time at age forty-seven to a young woman of age eighteen not only irked Mohandas Gandhi but also disturbed him that this young woman was his own beloved mother, Putliba. Gandhi interpreted such "old man-young woman marriages" of his time as an abominable social custom that formally sanctioned male violence over females. Gandhi saw his young mother as "a helpless victim" of his father's carnal passion. He viewed his father in stark contrast to his pious mother, considering his father to be "self-indulgent," but his mother to be "self-restrained."

There was still another reason why Gandhi criticized his father. As he wrote in his autobiography, "little did I dream then that one day I should severely criticize my father for having married me as a child" (ibid.). Gandhi could not forgive his father Kaba for thrusting him prematurely into the fire of sexuality; to Gandhi, "sexuality" was his father's mortal weakness of the flesh, which he passed on to son Mohandas as well.

Whether Gandhi was justified in criticizing his father for marrying four times is questionable considering that during Gandhi's time and place in India it was common for a widowed male to remarry for three reasons: one, if his wife died during childbirth; two, if she was an invalid and hence incapable of conceiving or bearing children; or three, if she failed to give her husband a son. According to biographical evidence, Kaba Gandhi had only two daughters from his first and second marriages, and his third wife had proved incapable of conceiving a child due to some incurable disease. Without any hope now of having a male issue, Kaba yielded to his elders' pressure to remarry for the fourth time. This time, however, the woman he married was not only far younger but also from another sub-caste.[3] According to Pyarelal (1965), what also disturbed Gandhi about his father's fourth marriage was that it took place while his third wife was still living. Even though it is believed that Kaba had asked for and received his third wife's consent to marry again, it must still have been the talk of the town in a community as close and conservative as Kathiawar. Altogether, the impact of his father's marriages and the subsequent rumors must have weighed heavily on Gandhi's mind, and could have affected his views on sexuality and marriage.

MOTHER PUTLIBA

That Gandhi was emotionally and spiritually closer to his mother than to his father is evident from his frequent reverential references to her in his autobiography, letters, interviews, and other writings and speeches. "Saintliness" was the word Gandhi used in his autobiography to describe "the outstanding impression" that Putliba had left on his memory; the word epitomized his deep love, devotion, and reverence for his pious mother. As Pyarelal observed (1965, 202), Gandhi "revered his father, but his mother he adored. … of his father he was sometimes critical in later life, but of his mother never. His father was to him the embodiment of upright-ness, his mother of piety."

Like her husband, Kaba, Gandhi's mother was unlettered but not unintelligent; she was deeply religious but not dogmatic. Though she frequently observed all kinds of *vratas* (religious vows), prolonged fasts, diet restrictions, and many other forms of spiritual disciplines, she never complained or quit. During the *chaturmas* (four months of rainy season) Putliba vowed not to have food without seeing the sun. Gandhi vividly described in his original Gujarati *Atma-katha*, or autobiography, how as young children he and his brothers would stand outside staring at the sky, waiting for the sun to come out so they could run to their mother and give her the good news. Only rarely did it happen, though, that the sun appeared during those dark, cloudy monsoon months of June through September. When the sun finally did appear, the children excitedly ran to tell their mother to come out quickly to see for herself, but by the time she came out, the sun had disappeared again. Gandhi never forgot what his mother said then: "That is God's will, Beta (child or children), He did not want me to eat today," and so saying, with a smile on her face, she would return to her daily chores. Putliba's example of a self-sacrificing yet cheerful piety made a deep impression on Moniya, the Mahatma-to-be.

Putliba was the primary builder of her son's character and conscience. She was the first role model and spiritual guru to inspire and guide him on a lifelong search for Truth through voluntary self-suffering, nonviolence, and selfless service. Gandhi fondly recalled that she would always cook extra meals to feed both the Brahmin and Jain *sadhus* (holy men), and that no *atithi* (unannounced guest) would ever go hungry from her door. Mahatma Gandhi's house also would always be open to welcome unannounced guests not only for dining but also for staying in as long as they wished.

Putliba was a woman of great practical intelligence and was well-informed about affairs of the state; her husband, her neighbors, and the royal queen mother herself often sought her counsel. Gandhi's supreme passion for nursing the sick and giving motherly care to all, including the enemy, was a direct inheritance from his self-disciplined and compassionate mother.

The qualities of his mother that Gandhi admired most were her simplicity, her undogmatic and cheerful piety, her purity, and above all, her self-effacing self-control. Gandhi's drive for self-purification, his faith in human perfectibility and goodness, and his ability to take and sustain the hardest of the hard vows—celibacy, nonviolence, truthfulness, for example—were lessons learned at the feet of his "saintly" mother. As a child, Moniya's personal ambition was to be morally "as flawless as his mother." Mother Putliba and her youngest son Moniya were made in the image of each other; one was the spiritual half of the other.

Was Putliba's influence on Gandhi always positive? For the most part she exerted an influence that was positive for Gandhi's moral and spiritual growth, making him into a kind and caring maternal father to all—friends and foes, colleagues and followers all around the world. It was the mother in him that softened his masculine side, that made him love, serve, nurse, trust, and forgive others. It was also the mother in him who kept him firmly rooted in his own tradition yet open to other religions, peoples, and cultures. However, because of his total identification with his mother, Gandhi was blinded to her faults, such as her extreme, neurotic insistence on cleanliness, self-purification, moral perfection, rigorous fasting, and asceticism.

Gandhi probably knew his mother's faults, but like most Indian children he experienced his mother almost totally as a "good mother." According to

Sudhir Kakar (1981, 83), "The proportion of Indian men who express or experience an active dislike, fear or contempt for their mothers at a conscious level is infinitesimally small." Gandhi was no exception. Later, however, the mature Mahatma was able to convert some of his mother's negative traits that he had inherited into positive ones by using them for his own spiritual emancipation as well as that of others.

MONIYA, MOTHER, AND FATHER: AN OEDIPAL TRIANGLE?

Some western biographers of Gandhi—Sebastian De Grazia, Wolfenstein, Ernest Jones and even Erikson—have read too much into child Gandhi's "mother-attachment" and "father-resentment," implying an Oedipal triangle type of relationship. It would be helpful to examine the reasons for the intensity of the child–mother attachment in the Indian context.

First, in a country and civilization as ancient as India, culture and religion are inextricably interwoven. As a result, the Hindu mythological and religious worship of Mother Goddess has infiltrated into the Indian society and culture through the elevation of the motherhood of a woman. Most Indians, male or female, modern or old-fashioned, urban or rural, would venerate the motherhood of a woman more than her womanhood. The mother occupies a central place, both in the Indian culture and in a child's universe, especially if the latter happens to be a son. "The intensity of the mother-son relationship is a prominent theme in Hindu myths," as Christiane Hartnack observes in *Vishnu on Freud's Desk* (Vaidyanathan and Kripal 1999, 95). "May you bear many a son" is a customary blessing given to a bride by elders in the family; this boon can be found in most Hindu sacred texts, mythology, epics, and lullabies.[4]

Second, the childhood period is far more extended in a traditional Indian family than in its Western counterpart. As a result, an Indian child stays closer to and for a longer time with his mother, not only past his school age but also, in some cases, even after he is married. The father remains only on the periphery, loving the child but not playing with him or her, nor emotionally sharing or involving himself in the day-to-day activities of his son or daughter. Because of social and family restrictions, to an Indian child the father is like a distant star, to be held in awe and wonder but never to come close to like a mother. Moreover, in an extended Indian family system, a child has not just one father, but many older males and uncles who serve as father substitutes. Similarly, "in connection with the development of the Oedipus situation surrogate substitutes ... aunts, elder sisters, maid servants, nurses or any other elderly women are likely to be involved in the sexual situation as mother substitutes," says M. N. Bannerjee (Vaidyanathan and Kripal, 96).

As Sudhir Kakar puts it (1981, 134), "Because it is diluted and diverted to include other elder males, oedipal aggression against the father, in its 'classical' intensity, on the whole, is not common in India." An Indian child is more likely to experience a narcissistic-submissive yearning for his father, rather than a fierce competition with him for the mother's love, the latter being known as the Oedipal complex in the Western hemisphere.

Disregarding the differences in Indian family relationships and gender constellations in comparison with Western models, Erik Erikson, in *Gandhi's Truth* (1969), has superimposed the Freudian theory of Oedipal complex on the interpretation of child Gandhi's play activities and relationship with his father and mother. Sometimes through innuendos and sometimes quite openly, he has implied that child Gandhi unconsciously harbored Oedipal feelings of rivalry, jealousy, and aggression toward his father by wishing to replace him.

For example, Erikson has grossly misunderstood the word *Thakorji*, which means "the image of the Vaishnava deity," but which can also be used in reference to a king; in the latter usage, a king will be honorably addressed as "Thakore-Saheb." Pyarelal used the word *Thakorji* in reference to child Gandhi playing with the images of the deities in his home shrine.

Pyarelal's original version:

If he (child Gandhi) found his way into his father's *puja ghar* (shrine room), he would scatter all the utensils used in the worship, remove the image of *Thakorji* from the stool and seat himself in its place. (1965, 195)

Erikson's version:

He (child Gandhi) would remove the image of the ruling Prince from its customary stool and put himself in its place, a habit of pretending to be his father's master of which we shall make all we can. (1969, 108)

Obviously, Erikson's reference to the image of the ruling prince explains how he has either misunderstood the word *Thakorji* or misunderstood the context to imply the child Gandhi's Oedipal aggression toward his father. Erikson twists both the meaning and the context to imply that Moniya removed the image of his father's master from the stool, put himself in the position of his father's master, and thus surpassed him.

ERIKSON'S INTERPRETATIONS OF GANDHI: A CRITIQUE

It is difficult to determine whether Erikson made an honest semantic mistake of not knowing the word *Thakoreji* (a changed meaning in two different contexts) or whether he twisted the word to suit his own preconceived notion of child Gandhi's Oedipal aggression toward his father. Even if we overlook this as an example of Erikson's unfamiliarity with the nuances of a foreign language (Gujarati), how can we ignore other instances of his heavy use of the Oedipal artillery? Mark, for example, his frequent use of these clinical terms: *infantile curse, cover memory, curse, re-enactment, moral precocity, ambivalence,* and *moratorium*. This is unmistakably Freudian language.

If it is Erikson's purpose in *Gandhi's Truth* to prove that Gandhi, his mother, and father were involved in an Oedipal triangle, he does not argue his case logically, consistently, or convincingly; instead, he confuses his readers by speaking from two contradictory perspectives.

In one breath, he clearly superimposes his Freudian interpretations onto Gandhi, as the following two examples demonstrate. First, "if nursing was another passion of his life, then it all started when in his own unique Oedipal arrangement, he became a mother to his father—a mother who always had time for him" (ibid., 11). Erikson implies thereby that while Gandhi was still a child, he found a redeeming solution to atone for his Oedipal guilt by "nursing his stricken father, and thus becoming his mother." In the second instance, also presuming an Oedipal triangle, Erikson grafts onto child Gandhi his Judeo-Christian, Freudian terminology: "To better the parent thus means to replace him; to survive him means to kill him; to usurp his domain means to appropriate the mother, the house, the throne" (ibid., 129).

In the very next breath, Erikson does an about-face, and contradicts himself regarding these same two instances. First, "There is a passionate transfer of a filial incestuous and jealous affects onto close relatives who provide parental affection and circumspection but escape Oedipal rivalry" (ibid., 42–43). Second, "not even Freud considered it desirable or possible that the Oedipus be conscious" (ibid., 119). Such tongue-in-cheek remarks reveal the ambivalence of the psychoanalyst himself; they also create confusion about the possibility of Oedipal aggression in Indian context.

In the book *Vishnu on Freud's Desk*, several scholars have presented their psychoanalytical perspectives, including the possibility of the Freudian type of Oedipal aggression in the Indian context. Brilliant though their insights are, all of them cannot be covered here. Therefore, I am presenting only the gist of major psychoanalytical perspectives regarding whether the "Oedipal complex of the Freudian variety" applies universally, and if so, how it manifests in the Indian context.

In contrast to Freud's claims for "the universality of his concepts," Indian psychoanalysts affirm their "cultural particularity." The first major difference they notice, of course, is between "the nuclear father-dominated" European family (upon which Freud modeled his Victorian theory), and the colonial Indian joint family system with several mother and father figures. Because of these starkly different family and gender constellations between the two models, and in view of the Hindu cultural and mythological ideals, the "Oedipal aggression against the father, in its classical intensity, on the whole, is not common in India" (Kakar 1981, 134).

Earlier we discussed the reasons for the intensity of the mother–son relationship in Hindu myths, folklore, and in most Indian joint families. Another important point to keep in mind is one of the Hindu mythological ideals of "filial reverence and obedience"—extolled in the characters of *Bhishma* (in the *Mahabharata*), *Rama* (in the *Ramayana*), and the legendary boy *Shravana* (child Gandhi's role model); this ideal acts as a deterrent to a male child's possible fierce aggression toward the father. An Indian son misses his father and yearns for his love, attention, and company; he therefore assumes a rather "submissive-obedient stance" unlike his Western counterpart who turns aggressive to the father. Analyzing the "difference in the flow of aggression in Indian and Western myths, A. K. Ramanujan writes, "Instead of sons desiring mothers and overcoming fathers (e.g., Oedipus) ... we have fathers suppressing sons ... and mothers desiring sons" (Vaidyanathan and Kripal, 95). Thus, by his very submission to the father, the son becomes a hero and attains power.

To sum up our critique of Erikson on the Oedipal Complex in relation to Gandhi, I must say that in the light of all these discussions, I find his interpretations in this regard to be biased, far-fetched, culturally misplaced, semantically misinformed, and therefore ill fitting. Erikson's otherwise excellent psychoanalytical insights into Gandhi are marred by his Freudian superimpositions, or shall I say "superstitions?"

CHILD GANDHI'S RELIGIOUS HOME ENVIRONMENT

Later in life, the adult Gandhi fondly remembered what he saw, heard, felt, and absorbed from his childhood home environment and was grateful to his parents for providing him the best examples of their deeply devotional yet broad-minded religiosity. Not learned or articulate in theology or religion, Kaba and Putliba were two simple, devout people who daily practiced their *Vaishnava* Hindu rituals of *puja* (worship), katha-*varta* (reading and listening to religious discourse), bhajan-*kirtan* (hymn-singing), Ramnam *japa* (repetition of the holy name of Rama), and of visiting temples in their vicinity. As Gandhi recalled in his autobiography, "of religious training he [father] had very little, but he had that kind of religious culture which frequent visits to temples and listening to religious discourses make available to many Hindus" (1948, 12). One of his fondest childhood memories was of holding his beloved mother's hand and visiting different kinds of temples with her in their neighborhood. Interestingly, however, as a grown man, Gandhi himself never liked to go to temples, nor did he believe in worshipping the images of deities (*murti-puja*). What Gandhi truly enjoyed as a child and later as an adult as well, was the deeply devotional nature and the pluralistic religious environment of his childhood home. Gandhi remembered his father having religious discussions at their home with friends of Jain, Parsee, Muslim, and other backgrounds. His family reflected the pluralistic religious constellation of the Gujarat-Kathiawar region, where many sects of Hinduism—including Vaishnavism, Shaivism, the Pranami, the Swaminarayana, and the Kabirpanthis—flourished side by side with other religions, such as *Jainism*, Zoroastrianism, Sikhism, *Islam*, and *Christianity*.

Vaishnavism: The Gandhis' Ancestral Religion

The ancestral faith of the Gandhis was Vaishnavism—a school of *bhakti* (devotion) that believes in Lord Vishnu. Among the many avatars of Vishnu, the two most popular ones are Lord Rama and Lord Krishna. Until Grandfather Ota Bapa's time, six generations of the Gandhis followed a specific sect of Vaishnavism called the "Pushtimarg of Vallabhacharya," which believes in the *Krishna-bhakti* or the path of devotion to Lord Krishna. According to Pyarelal (1965, 178), "it teaches that, with intense love and complete self-surrender, God is accessible to all, irrespective of rank and even culture." Ota Bapa, however, being a follower of the Ramanuja school of Vaishnavism, introduced the family to the *Rama-bhakti* tradition. This particular branch breaks away from the narrow caste, class, and gender divisions, and preaches the gospel of devotion to Lord Rama. Thus, as a child, Gandhi grew up in a Vaishnava family that followed both the Rama and Krishna worship traditions. Just as Gandhi remembered visiting different temples with his mother, he also had a distinct memory of reciting with his father the *Rama-Raksha Stotra*, Sanskrit prayer verses praising Lord Rama.

Among all the saint-poets and devotees of Lord Rama, Tulsidas was the most well-known, whose poem the *Ramacharit Manas*, and whose Hindu epic *Tulasi-Ramayana*, were read and listened to with great devotion in the Gandhi household. One of Gandhi's most cherished memories was listening to the melodious rendering of *Tulasi-Ramayana* by their family priest, Ladha Maharaj, who was said to have been cured of his leprosy just by his faithful reading of the *Ramayana*. Recalling how he felt as a child, Gandhi said he was "enraptured" by Ladha Maharaj's deeply devotional reading, which laid the foundation of his lifetime devotion to Rama and the *Ramayana*.

Hymn singing was another family tradition that Gandhi cherished forever. Later, he even made it a regular feature of all his ashram evening prayer sessions, which included hymns, prayers, and scriptural readings from major faiths of the world.

Mother's Pranami Faith and Jainism

Putliba brought her own maidenhood heritage of the Pranami faith (a sect of Hinduism) to enrich the Vaishnava heritage of her in-laws' family. Prannath (1618–1694), the scholarly founder of this sect, established close scriptural-theological links between the *Bhagavata Purana* of Vaishnavism and the *Qu'ran* of the Islamic faith (Iyer 1970). According to Stephen Hay (1970, 29), "the Pranami sect was noted for its latitudinarianism toward Islamic ideas and social contact with Muslims. One of the distinctive features of the Pranami sect was that it worshipped no images of deities." As Gandhi recalled, there were no deities in the *Pranami mandir* (temple); what he saw instead on the walls were big, lively pictures and beautifully inscribed passages from both the *Bhagavata* and the *Qu'ran*, which made a lasting impression on his child mind.

Jainism[5] is another major religion in India with a large following in the Gujarat and Rajasthan (Marwar) states. Besides following her in-laws' Vaishnava tradition and her own Pranami faith, Putliba had incorporated many Jain practices into her daily routine. One of them was undertaking hard vows, such as going without food and/or water for many days. Another was palate control, which required giving up certain foods or limiting the number of food items one can eat. As Gandhi described in his autobiography, "Putliba would take the hardest vows and keep them without flinching.

Illness was no excuse for relaxing them. ... to keep two or three consecutive fasts was nothing to her (1948, 13)." Should it be a surprise, then, that Putliba's pet son later followed in his mother's footsteps?

Ahimsa (nonviolence) was the most fundamental principle of Jainism, which meant non-injury toward the entire population of God's creation, including animate and inanimate creatures. Gandhi wrote in *Harijan* (December 8, 1946), "*Ahimsa* was also the 'chief glory of Hinduism' as highlighted in the Hindu epic of *Mahabharata*."[6] However, as he further observed, "*Ahimsa* was explained away ... as being meant for *sannyasins* (renunciates) alone." Only in Jainism and Buddhism was nonviolence to be equally and strictly observed by all. Gandhi would later instill a new life and a new meaning into this age-old precept of Hinduism, Jainism, and Buddhism by making *ahimsa* a means to an end of Truth.

Besides *ahimsa*, Putliba practiced other Jain disciplines and austerities for the purposes of self-purification and self-perfection. These included *asteya* (non-stealing), *sunrita* (non-greed), *brahmacharya* (abstinence), and *aparigraha* (non-possession). Although Gandhi's unschooled mother could not have known the logic or the philosophy of another major Jain principle of *anekantvada* (the many-sidedness of reality), she practiced it nevertheless in her day-to-day dealings with people of other faiths. According to George Burch, "*anekantvada* is the fundamental concept of non-absolutism, known also as *syadavada* or somehow-ism" (1964). Just as a truly nonviolent person respects all forms of life and would refrain from hurting anyone physically, mentally, or verbally, so also a truly thinking person who practices *anekantvada* would remain open to the validity claim of all judgments. *Anekantvada* argues that since no one opinion or version of truth is complete, none can claim exclusive rights over truth.

Through his mother, child Gandhi was exposed to the actual practice of these major Jain principles of nonviolence, non-possession, and *anekantvada* or *syadavada*, which postulates that truth is one but multidimensional. These early childhood impressions and felt experiences contributed to Gandhi's character formation and his further moral and spiritual development.

GANDHI'S EARLY CHILDHOOD AND STAGE I INTUITIVE-PROJECTIVE FAITH: AN EVALUATION

In the light of Fowler's Theory of Stages of Faith, confirmation of Stage 1 is found in Gandhi's early childhood phase during which he was most "powerfully and permanently influenced" by his parents' examples of their simple yet sincere faith and practicing rather than preaching. Poor in knowledge, his parents were rich in matters of the heart. Noble action mattered more to them than words, which was the first important lesson their son learned and followed throughout his life. Mahatma Gandhi's penchant for action, and his drive for changing himself before changing others or the world, had their roots in this stage. As Fowler put it (1980, 43), "the drive to world-transformation often has its prime rootage in this stage." In Gandhi's case, however, self-transformation was a prerequisite to the outer world transformation, and that is why he would later interpret *swaraj* not only as political independence but also as "self-rule or self-mastery."

Gandhi was particularly "powerfully and permanently influenced" by his parents' deeply devotional yet diverse faith. As discussed earlier, Gandhi was especially influenced by his saintly mother, whose religiosity was deep but not narrow, traditional but not orthodox, and serene but not morose. Putliba's ascetic self-control, rigorous fasting, selflessness, nursing, and nurturing, and her ability to take and keep the hardest of hard vows instilled in Moniya a desire to be like his mother. With continuous striving, he did eventually fulfill his wish. The future Mahatma, like his mother, was not only an inveterate keeper of the hardest vows but even went further to undertake fasting sometimes to near death.

Along with the positive influence of his mother, Gandhi could not escape from the negative or the shadow side of his mother's influence. To use Sudhir Kakar's analogy, both "the good mother" and "the bad mother" lived side by side in Gandhi. That "bad mother" Putliba, who was rather too hard, too driven for self-perfection, and fastidiously concerned about cleanliness and self-purification, remained in the son's unconscious as his "shadow self." However, Gandhi also had a unique ability to transform his shadows—his unconscious, darker tendencies and traits—into more benign and constructive forms, thus redeeming both himself and others in that process. In this respect the son did surpass his mother.

Similarly, evaluating the impact of his father's faith and character on child Gandhi by the Stage 1 faith criteria, we find that although Gandhi harshly criticized his father, he still emulated his positive qualities, such as living for principles rather than money, and having the moral courage to defy authority despite the consequences. From father Kaba, Gandhi learned his first "ABCs" in clean or unpolluted politics, in putting loyalty before sycophancy, and in valuing character more than power, position, or promotion. The carnal nature that Gandhi perceived to be his father's greatest weakness, however, would later create the guilt and shame feelings in Gandhi during his adolescent phase. Throughout life, sexual issues would continue to haunt him like the ghost of his father, and the "bad father" would revisit him just like "the bad mother." Yet Gandhi would gradually learn to exorcise the "ghost" with rigorous vows, spiritual disciplines, and self-experiments.

Moreover, in view of Stage 1 Intuitive-Projective Faith, one of the most powerful impacts of the visual faith on child Gandhi was what he saw on the walls of the Pranami temple to which he went with his mother. That was the first living example of a peaceful coexistence of faiths as different as Vaishnavism and Islam, which child Gandhi unconsciously absorbed. Similarly, his mother's ascetic Jain practices became a regular feature of Gandhi's faith in later years. Because Gandhi was introduced early in life to the Vaishnava *bhakti*, to the eclectic Pranami faith, and to the rigorous Jain practices in his childhood home, he later began to inquire, explore, compare, reflect, and form his own conclusions about the ultimate nature of reality.

Thus the seeds of Gandhi's faith were sown firmly and deeply in the fertile soil of his childhood through the living examples of his parents' faith, faith that was deeply devotional yet expansive in its outreach to other faiths and to people of other faiths. Being an imaginative and imitative child, Gandhi would continue to learn through imitation and experimentation throughout his life. The same imagination and imitation that are the strengths of this faith stage, however, could turn into the worst nightmares as well. Fowler writes (1981, 134), "the dangers in this stage arise from the possible possession of the child's imagination by unrestrained images of terror and destructiveness." In the next chapter, I will discuss what kinds of fears and terrors possessed child Gandhi, how he handled them, who taught him to overcome his fears, and how he could sustain his faith at such trying times.

4

The Sprouting of Mohan's Faith

Little Moniya's childhood utopia in Porbandar ended abruptly at age seven, when Kaba accepted his new position as the prime minister of Rajkot and moved the family there in 1876. In addition to being prime minister of Rajkot, Kaba Gandhi was on the *Rajasthanik* Court of Appeals, set up by the British to settle revenue disputes between landlords and the ruling prince. Although both positions brought Kaba political honor and social prestige, they also increased his workload and stress, proving detrimental to his health. According to Gandhi's autobiography, his father was neither happy with the new *Thakore Saheb* (king) of Rajkot, nor comfortable in adapting to the new formal British etiquette and attire required of members of the Rajasthanic court. Kaba was also aging noticeably; his political prime now a matter of the past.

If father Kaba suffered, his sensitive son Manu suffered even more as he internalized his father's pain. The father lost his health, the son his carefree childhood utopia. As Erikson put it, "both the father and the son lost their milieu" (1969, 114). Father Kaba's transfer to Rajkot and his resulting illness affected his youngest son's personality and self-perception. However, the change of venue was only the tip of the iceberg, as there were other fears that threatened Mohan's peace of mind and altered his once-buoyant personality into a dark, dejected one. Internal uncertainties plagued this little boy.

Mohandas Gandhi as Schoolboy

Prior to moving to Rajkot, Moniya had started attending his first elementary school in Porbandar, known as the *Dhooli shala*, a dirt-road school

47

where the pupils learned to write their alphabet on the dust, copying the letters written by their village schoolmaster on the blackboard. The only thing Gandhi recalled about his first school was that he had great difficulty learning his multiplication tables by heart, and that like the other boys, he, too, enjoyed calling his teacher all kinds of names rather than learning anything from him. From this Gandhi inferred that his "intellect must have been sluggish, and ... memory raw." His self-perception as a student changed for the worse after moving to Rajkot. He described himself as only "a mediocre student" throughout his primary, middle school, and high school, and said that he had no aptitude for arithmetic, English, and Sanskrit; he liked geography and gymnastics the least.

Gandhi's earliest school records show, however, that unlike how he presented himself, he was not a mediocre student. On the contrary, as Robert Payne observed, Gandhi was "a wildly erratic one, sometimes very good and sometimes inexplicably bad" (1969, 31). This self-label of mediocrity seems to be a post-value judgment of the adult Mahatma, who perhaps expected too much of a young schoolboy. Gandhi's school reports testify that he had received two scholarships and several prizes for his above-average performance in English, Sanskrit, and even Arithmetic. Whether an outstanding student or not, Mohan did have to miss school often, at one point for one year.

Mohan—A Little Boy with a Big Conscience

Come Rajkot, the once outgoing and mischievous Moniya became an excruciatingly shy and timid little boy who avoided all company. He was afraid that bullies in his school might belittle him for his puny physique and timorous personality. He had no friends at this time, nor did he have any interest in making friends with anyone. Gandhi wrote in his autobiography, "My books and my lessons were my sole companions. ... I literally ran back from school because I could not bear to talk to anybody. I was even afraid lest anyone should poke fun at me" (1948, 15).

Not only was Mohan afraid of the school bullies but also of snakes, scorpions, tigers, and ghosts, whom he imagined were lurking in the dark. Given his timidity and vivid imagination, Mohan was afraid of the darkness itself. Imagination, which is the most exciting and powerful faculty of young children, can also prove to be a paralyzing source of fear when nightmares and apparitions of ghosts and goblins disturb their peace of mind.

Rambha and the Ramanama

At such trying times in his mid-childhood, Gandhi found solace in two resources that not only assuaged his fears but also built up his moral and spiritual foundation of faith to last his whole lifetime. The first human source of solace came from a simple, uneducated woman named Rambha, his childhood companion and caretaker, who gave him the guru-mantra of *Ramanama*—the "name of God Rama." She suggested that Mohan repeat the holy name of Rama as a remedy for all kinds of fears. Rambha's remedy proved to be as non-failing as *Ramabaan*—the "arrows of God Rama." The child Mohan followed her advice, which worked like a miracle then and ever after. As Margaret Chatterjee observed (1983, 16), "Gandhi adopted during this early stage of life a devotional practice which was to remain with him all throughout his life, the repetition of *Ramanama*, the '*Japa*' or repetition of a holy word … is a familiar practice in India." Later Gandhi would admit that "thinking of God as 'God' did not fire him as much as the name of Rama did." But how did the repetition of Ramanama help remove child Gandhi's fears? Did he have a real faith in the power and efficacy of the holy name? He explained in his autobiography why it helped him: "I had more faith in her (Rambha) than in her remedy, and so at a tender age I began repeating Ramanama to cure my fear of ghosts and spirits" (1948, 47). He further explained how it worked, "the good seed sown in childhood was not sown in vain. I think it is due to the seed sown by that good woman Rambha that today Ramanama is an infallible remedy for me" (ibid.). This shows how a child learns his or her first lessons of faith—by simple trust and by repetition of a holy name or symbol. A child believes in the person who believes in God; the reasoning develops later.

MOHAN'S PASSION FOR MYTHICAL STORIES AND PLAYS

While Mohan detested reading his schoolbooks, he never tired of reading his favorite mythological stories, and seeing plays based on those stories, which the itinerant showmen brought to his town. With the all-absorbing attention of a ten-year-old, Mohan saw the play performances more than once and recalled enacting the scenes again and again on the stage of his mind. Two plays that Gandhi specifically mentioned in his autobiography as having a profound influence on him were the *Shravana Pitribhakta Nataka* and the *Truthful King Harishchandra*. Mohan was absorbed in reading and

seeing these mythological stories performed that set his imagination afire—
imagination which turned myth into reality and fiction into action.

Devoted Son Shravana

Shravana Pitribhakta Nataka was based on the legendary story of a boy
named Shravana, whose life mission was to love, obey, serve, and protect
his blind, old parents. Their wish was his command; their happiness, his
supreme duty. As the story goes, the little boy Shravana knew that both his
parents had always wanted to go on a pilgrimage, but they could not do so
because they were poor, old, and blind. The son loved his parents so much
that he wanted to fulfill their last wish. He was only a little boy with no
money or means to send them on a pilgrimage, yet, in spite of that, he
made for them two hanging baskets that attached by slings to his shoulders
and upon which he carried them to different pilgrimage places. Sometimes
Shravana had to pass through jungles, cross rivers, climb mountains, and
confront wild beasts, snakes, and other creatures, but he remained
undaunted as he continued his journey. At intervals and at night, they
would rest under a shady tree or near to a river. As if the Gods were testing
his devotion, just as Shravana was filling his pitcher with water from
a river, King Dasharatha (Lord Rama's father), who had gone hunting,
mistook the sound for that of an animal drinking water from the river.
Guessing it was his *shikar* (prey), he shot an arrow that killed Shravana.
The resulting tragedy, the heartrending lament of the helpless parents (and
set to tune), were all so vividly portrayed by the vaudeville performers that
the scenes and the tunes pierced child Gandhi's heart and stayed alive forever. More than that, the story drove home an important moral: No risk
was to be considered too high for serving one's parents, and no sacrifice
was great enough to fulfill their wish. As Gandhi wrote in his autobiography, "The book and the picture (show) left an indelible impression on my
mind. Here is an example for you to copy" (1948, 16).

Truthful King Harishchandra

If the Shravana story extolled the Indian cultural ideal of parental devotion, the story of King Harishchandra highlighted truth as the summum
bonum of life. The king exemplified that truth must be lived and that
promises must be kept at any cost. Hearing about King Harishchandra's
great reputation for truthfulness, the sage Vishwamitra decided to test

him. Disguised as a poor Brahmin, the sage went to the king and challenged whether he would give him anything that he desired. The king
promised the sage that he would do so at any cost. The sage first asked for
the king's wealth and kingdom; the king complied. Next, the sage
demanded that the king give up his wife, family, and palace, and that he go
live in a forest, taking nothing, not even his royal clothes. The sage also
made another condition that during his forest stay, the king must not stay
with his wife and child, and should work incognito like any ordinary citizen. Per the sage's wish and command, the king parted ways with his wife,
Taramati, and their only son to live in the forest. From time to time sage
Vishwamitra would reappear just to trick the king into breaking his vow of
truthfulness. But the king remained adamant. The enraged sage now put
the king through his worst ordeal.

King Harishchandra's only son died of a snakebite in the jungle and
was brought by his distraught mother to a *Chandala* (the king incognito),
who was in charge of cremation. The bereaved queen had no money to pay
for her son's cremation, so she begged the *Chandala* to work gratis. The
Chandala refused because if he granted any favors he would violate his
dharma (sacred duty). Harishchandra's steadfast adherence to truth and his
power of endurance finally convinced sage Vishwamitra of the king's
truthfulness. In all humility, Vishwamitra accepted his defeat and restored
to the king his kingdom, his wife, and their son. Mohandas Gandhi
derived from the story one of his first moral principles: Truth always ultimately triumphs.

Gandhi wrote in his autobiography that King Harishchandra's story
"captured" his heart, the impact of which lasted all his life. He said that
ever since he saw the play, he wondered, "Why should not all be truthful
like Harishchandra? To follow truth and to go through all the ordeals
Harishchandra went through was the one ideal it inspired in me. I literally
believed in the story. ... The thought of it all often made me weep" (ibid.).

Three points regarding child Mohan's extraordinary liking for the story
of Harishchandra, who was not even a historical king, bear emphasis. To
Gandhi, historical truth did not matter as much as the moral truth. He was
drawn to the story because the king demonstrated that truthfulness is not
a virtue of expediency; truth must be practiced at all times, under any circumstances and at any cost. In order to reach the highest ideal of the
Absolute Truth, one must first adhere to the relative or the existential truth.
Taking hard vows and keeping them—as the king kept his vow or promise
to the sage—were ways to enter the gateway to truth. As Margaret
Chatterjee explained (1983, 68), "Gandhi began to attach special importance

to the vow not as a formalistic framework to keep one on the rails to say, but as a way of entering more deeply into the truth, of being in the truth, of belonging to it, or being rooted in it." The Harishchandra story reinforced the ideal of adherence to truth through keeping the vow.

Second point to bear in mind is what Gandhi says—that he "literally believed" in the story in spite of knowing that Harishchandra was a mythical character. From childhood onward, myths to him were as real, if not more, as reality itself. Why? Because myths conveyed an ideal, a goal, a vision to which everyone must aspire. That is why Gandhi questioned, "Why should not all be truthful like Harishchandra?" He believed that mythical as well as spiritual ideals, such as truth and nonviolence, must be lowered from their high pedestal to become a part of everyday reality, as he later demonstrated in and through his *satyagrahas*. If myth does not translate into reality, then reality must rise to the level of myth. To Gandhi, the means and the end not only should match, but both must also be interchangeable.

Third, child Mohan's understanding of truth at this stage is limited to truthfulness only. This is still the Mythic-Literal stage of his mid-childhood faith. Hence, his intellectual and reflective abilities have not yet developed for him to hold a metaphysical inquiry into the nature and meanings of Truth. Gradually, through further experience and through developmental stages, his definition and understanding of truth will grow, expand, and deepen.

So, Mohan's primary source of inner joy came through reading his favorite mythological stories and their play versions, which laid the foundation of his morals, self ideals, and his basic spiritual stance of life. Though Gandhi's poor self-perception, fears, and terrors were real, he found ways to cope with his childhood anxieties by turning to mythical stories of irreproachable moral characters who epitomized the Indian cultural-religious ideals. Developmental significance can be found in the faith perspective of Fowler's Theory of Stages of Faith.

GANDHI'S MID-CHILDHOOD AND STAGE 2 MYTHIC-LITERAL FAITH: AN EVALUATION

As examined previously, child Moniya absorbed the meanings of his experiences through powerful images, symbols, and stories. Beginning school, however, around age seven, Mohan began to be acutely aware of the reality of his new world.

Mohan's newly emerging ability of self-awareness and awareness of others, according to Fowler, is typical of children between the ages of six and eight, who undergo "a revolution in knowing and valuing," which relates to what Piaget calls "concrete operational thinking." The concept of "self" at this stage is primarily rooted in "self-competence and self-esteem depends on how well one is able to do things."

In the light of Stage 2, why Mohan's poor self-perception during his school years was directly related to his school performance can be understood. Another trait of Gandhi, even as a little boy: He tended to be a perfectionist. Hence, he expected to have a perfect score in each subject, even those in which he had more difficulties, such as Arithmetic, Geography, and others. When he failed to meet his own standards, his self-esteem suffered, causing him to dub himself a mediocre student.

The other characteristic typical of children of this stage—taking a one-dimensional view and not taking a full perspective of things—also applies to the way Mohan interpreted his school performance, which fell short in his eyes but not in the eyes of his teachers. Though capable of logical reasoning, Mohan was not yet able to think of the long-term advisability of selecting certain courses, such as Geometry or Arithmetic. Only after one of his teachers explained to Mohan the future benefits of taking Geometry, which required "a pure and simple use of the reasoning powers," did he agree. This shows how his choice of subjects was based not on reflective thinking but purely on what he could do with ease, which also determined whether he judged himself to be a smart student or one with sluggish intelligence.

In Stage 2, children's perception of others is based on "concrete imagery," that is, the obvious size, shape, appearance, demeanor, actions, and their consequences. For example, the reason Mohan "literally ran back from school and avoided all company" was because he saw himself as a "weakling" in comparison with other stronger boys in his school. Most of his fears and anxieties at this period were rooted in the way he saw himself.

The most telling testimony we find in Mohan's boyhood faith is that of what Fowler calls "the new capacity or strength—the rise of narrative and emergence of story, drama and myth as ways of finding and giving coherence to experience." Unlike the Stage 1 child who enjoys listening to a story with rapt attention, and who can also describe it but only episodically or haphazardly, the Stage 2 child can do better. Because of his or her newly developed organizing and logical reasoning ability, the older child in Stage 2 can "narratize" events and experiences—whether in life or in a story. Although a child can narrate and connect events as well as cause and effect, he or she still cannot reflect on the underlying meaning, nor can he or she link the meanings to form the "master story" or "the core" story.

Like other children in Stage 2, the boy Mohan thrived on retelling his favorite mythical stories—of *Shravana* and *Harishchandra*. Also like the other children, he could "narratize" or reproduce some of the scenes and replay on his concertina the piercing tunes of the grieving parents lamenting over their son Shravana's accidental death. That Mohan loved not only to see the play performances over and over but also reenacted the same scenes and tunes in his mind, confirms the Stage 2 characteristic of "conserving, communicating and comparing meanings and experiences" through repetition and reproduction of stories, plays, and other forms of narratives.

It is natural for children in this stage to ask the logical question, "Why should not all be truthful like Harishchandra?" Child Mohan not only asked the question but also took it a step further—something that, though not profound, is distinctively Gandhian in character. Mohan was not aware of the ontological meaning of Truth or that "Truth is many-faceted yet One"; he still saw the connection, however, between morality and Truth in the story of Harishchandra. Given his moral proclivity, the boy Mohan was inclined to think that all must practice the quality of truthfulness, which Harishchandra exemplified. This is the early indication of the moral Mahatma-to-be, who believed in making the ideal real and the real to imitate the ideal. To the boy Mohan as well as to the adult Mahatma, mythical characters like those of Harishchandra, Shravana, and Rama (the God-hero of *Ramayana*) were more real than the real because they lived up to their ideals. Mohan's early moral passion for truthfulness will develop into a lifelong yearning and search for Truth; it will be the ground motif of his life tapestry and the ultimate end of his journey of faith.

INDIGENOUS ASPECTS OF MOHAN'S BOYHOOD FAITH

In a tradition-bound culture like India, community and the community ideals play a seminal role in shaping a child's morals, values, self-ideals, and his or her conceptions of God or "the ultimate environment." Kakar writes (1981, 11), "cultural traditions are internalized during childhood in the individual's superego, the categorical conscience which represents the rights and the wrongs, the prohibitions and mores, of a given social milieu." What Kakar adds to this is even more important, that "the superego of the child is not really built up on the model of the parents, but on that of the parents' superego." Parents' superego is derived from the age-old values, religious and community ideals, and ideologies that are passed on to them by their parents and their parents' parents, to become what Kakar calls, "the vehicle of tradition." Thus, the ideologies of the superego perpetuate the past. This is a slow and hardly perceptible process by which the community ideals become a permanent feature of the parents' superego, which becomes a part of the child's inner psyche.

Let us illustrate this point in reference to child Mohan. Gandhi's parents were deeply tradition-bound people, with their ego-ideals based on the virtuous and pious characters of Rama and Sita in the great Hindu epic of *Ramayana*. It is important to note that Mohan's father worshipped Rama not only as his chosen family *ishtadevta* (deity) but also emulated him as an ideal king, as well as an exemplary son to whom filial duty took precedence over personal pleasure. Similarly, Mohan's mother emulated the character of Sita—the chaste, pious, virtuous, and an ever-enduring wife of Rama—the supreme Hindu ideal of womanhood. This is not to say that Gandhi's parents self-consciously imitated these ideals, but as Kakar observed, these Hindu world images and cultural beliefs "silently pervade the community unconscious." Similarly, Gandhi's later views of women— as loving, enduring, and self-suffering role models of virtue—were also based on the example of his own mother (and later, that of his wife) who personified the Hindu ideal of a wife in her chastity and fidelity. These, then, were some of the cultural ideals and Hindu world images that the child Mohan learned early in life, and which contributed to the "Indianness" of the future Mahatma Gandhi. As Kakar explained, "such images are absorbed early in life as a kind of space-time which gives coherent reassurance against the abysmal estrangements emerging in each successive stage and plaguing man throughout life" (1981, 15).

Mohandas Gandhi's mid-childhood period substantiates the biggest strength of Stage 2—that children's first self-awareness, their self-image, their ego-ideals, and their images of the world and God are absorbed through the stories, beliefs, and observances that symbolize those of their community. In this period lay the beginnings of the future "Moral Mahatma" and of "Mahatma the truth-seeker" as well. Gandhi's idealistic bent of mind turned naturally to such mythological stories that extolled and exemplified the Hindu cultural ideals of parental devotion (Shravana), filial duty before personal pleasure, and of observing truthfulness (Harishchandra) to reach the ultimate goal of realizing Absolute Truth. This was the stage when the theme of truth made its first strong impact on Mohan's inner psyche. What Gandhi meant by truth continued to change, grow, expand, and deepen as he, too, developed in his self-understanding, life experience, and in his ongoing experimentation with truth. This idea of continuous growth is vitally important to understanding Gandhi's self and faith development which, in Fowler's Theory of Stages of Faith, is an ongoing, dynamic process of seeking and finding meaning of self in relation to others and God or Truth.

5

A Crisis of Identity and Faith

Come adolescence, Mohandas Gandhi began to show certain changes, not only in his physical appearance but also in the patterns of his thinking and relating to others. A new spirit of inquiry, a defiance of authority, and a desire for self-autonomy began to surface. The appearance of these traits suggests "significant alterations in the structures of knowing and valuing," said Fowler, which called for a transition to Stage 3 Synthetic-Conventional Faith.

In his autobiography, Gandhi has described two incidents that happened around age twelve, which indicated his freshly emerging capacities of moral reasoning and valuing, of taking a bold step even if it meant going against the tide, and of making a choice between two clashing principles. The first incident is that of a spelling test during his first year at Alfred High School in Rajkot. The visiting British educational inspector, Mr. Giles, had given Gandhi's class a spelling test. Whereas all the other students had spelled every word correctly, Mohandas had misspelled the word kettle. The teacher tried to prompt Mohandas to copy the correct spelling from his neighbor's slate, but he would not. Later, "the teacher tried to bring this stupidity home to me, but without effect," wrote Gandhi in his autobiography, "but I never could learn the art of copying" (1948, 15). What the teacher called Mohandas' "stupidity" was actually a sign of his rising ability of moral reasoning, which put him in a quandary—should he be prompted by his teacher or by his conscience? The voice of his conscience said, "obedience must not override truth." Should it be surprising, then, that the boy Mohandas who was a fan of Harishchandra voted for truth rather than for blind obedience to his teacher?

The other incident involved Mohandas teasing his mother by touching Uka—the untouchable scavenger who came daily to clean their latrines. This time he wanted his mother to explain to him as to "why he should not touch Uka." [1] Gandhi noticed that his mother, who was otherwise open-minded, could not give him any reason. According to Pyarelal (1965, 217), "simply out of reverence for his mother he often did what he was told. But his heart rebelled; it planted in his soul the seed of rebellion against the institution of untouchability."

In terms of Gandhi's developing faith and self-identity, the above two incidents and others indicate adolescent Mohandas' rising new ability to notice contradictions and what Fowler calls "the limitations of literalness" in accepting anything at its face value. Not only could Mohandas notice discrepancies but also he could reflect and raise moral questions, demand answers, and if not satisfied, follow what he thought to be right. Fowler explains how this transition occurs:

> A factor which initiates transition to Stage 3 is the implicit clash or contradiction in stories that leads to reflection on meanings. . . . previous literalism breaks down; it leads to disillusionment with previous teachers and teachings. (1981, 150)

At the threshold of adolescence, Mohandas Gandhi encountered five cataclysmic events that not only embroiled him in a conflict of roles and relationships but also catapulted him into an acute crisis of identity and faith. The first involved his pre-arranged marriage coinciding with his father's serious illness. The second entailed his juvenile experiments in self-autonomy and search for identity, which led to the third—his fateful friendship with a Muslim boy named Mehtab. The fourth was his letter of confession to his dying father, and the fifth related to his feelings of guilt and shame around his father's death.

Early Marriage

As we saw earlier, Gandhi severely criticized his father for marrying four times and interpreted that his father was a man given to carnal pleasures. Similarly, Gandhi could neither forgive nor forget that his father thrust him into what he called his "preposterously early marriage." In Gandhi's eyes, Kaba was to be blamed for passing on to his youngest son his own mortal weakness of the flesh, a weakness that Gandhi would spend his whole lifetime trying to control, master, and finally, sublimate for his spiritual enlightenment.

At first the adolescent Gandhi seemed to thoroughly enjoy his early marriage. He was actually excited by the months of long wedding preparations, which he mentioned in his autobiography, as "the prospect of good clothes to wear, drums beating, marriage processions, rich dinners and a strange girl to play with" (1948, 19). Above all, Mohandas enjoyed being the center of attention in the large Gandhi family. For strictly economic reasons, however, his father decided that Mohandas, along with his older brother Karsandas and a cousin, should be married in one big, joint Hindu wedding ceremony. Gandhi remembered how on the evening before their weddings, the ladies smeared the bridegrooms with *peethee* (a specially prepared, fragrant turmeric paste), which was supposed to enhance their complexion and their sexual appetite. Mohandas, the young husband-to-be, was instructed on how to behave on his wedding night. More than anything, he looked forward to having a new playmate in his thirteen-year-old bride, Kasturbai Makanji, the daughter of a rich *Modh Bania* family in Rajkot.

"Two innocent children all unwittingly hurled themselves into the ocean of life," is how the adult autobiographer Gandhi recalled his wedding night. Both he and his bride were too nervous to even look at each other, much less to talk. No previous coaching came to their rescue, because, as Gandhi said, "no coaching is really necessary in such matters. The impressions of the former birth are potent enough to make all coaching superfluous" (ibid., 21). Gradually, however, both began to relax and to speak freely with each other. Gandhi added, he "took no time in assuming the authority of a husband."

The new marriage enthusiast, Mohandas Gandhi, aspired to be an ideal husband. He also wanted his beautiful but strong-willed wife to be an ideal wife—someone as sweet, submissive, faithful, and virtuous as Sita, the ideal of a Hindu wife. Unconsciously, he may have wanted her to be like his own mother, who emulated the ideal of Sita. So, Mohandas began to read whatever inexpensive "little pamphlets" he could get that would give him the formula for a perfect marriage and the duties of a husband. From cover to cover, he read booklets that inculcated the ideal of "lifelong faithfulness to wife," which "remained permanently imprinted in my heart," wrote Gandhi. "Furthermore," he added, "the passion of truth was innate in me, and to be false to her was therefore out of the question" (ibid., 22). The idealistic young husband thought it was not enough or right that only he take the pledge of faithfulness to his wife, insisting that she must do the same. Looking back, Gandhi took total responsibility for being a jealous husband and described the damage his distrust and jealousy caused to their early marriage:

> Her duty was easily converted into my right to exact faithfulness from her, and if it had to be exacted, I should be watchfully tenacious of the right. I had absolutely no reason to suspect my wife's fidelity, but jealousy does not wait for reasons. I must needs be for ever on the look-out regarding her movements, and therefore, she should not go anywhere without my permission. This sowed the seeds of bitter quarrel between us. The restraint was virtually a sort of imprisonment and Kasturbai was not the girl to brook any such thing. (Ibid., 22)

Gandhi's jealousy, distrust, and spying on his wife continued even after he left India for England and until midway through his stay in South Africa, for which he called himself a "cruelly kind husband." Deep beneath, however, other unconsciously ingrained Hindu concepts of an ideal husband and ideal wife must also have been working, which we recognized earlier as a part of "the community unconscious." In a predominantly paternalistic Indian society, men and women usually played their stereotypical roles of husband and wife. It is hardly surprising, considering that Gandhi was brought up in a close-knit, conservative community like Kathiawar, that he, too, wanted to follow the same. In addition to his conscious and unconscious role-playing, it was his idealistic bent of mind that set the highest moral standards not only for himself, but also for others, especially if they were as close to him as his wife and family.

Yet another reason for the young husband to want to control his wife was that she was a free spirit, brave and confident, whereas he was inhibited, timid, and diffident at this point in his life. Even though he was in high school and married, his earlier fear of ghosts, snakes, spirits, and darkness had not yet left him. Kasturbai fully used this to her advantage when they quarreled. If her husband tried to bully her or restrict her comings and goings, the willful wife ran away, turning off all the lights and leaving him alone in the darkness. Their marital battles continued except for small breaks when Kasturbai would either go to her parents' home or when she would be driven away by her irate husband. With time, however, little Kasturbai mellowed and grew in wisdom along with her husband, who later fully acknowledged her self-suffering love, her patience, and her superior power of endurance.

Mohandas Gandhi was not only an authoritative and jealous husband, he was also "passionately fond of" his young and beautiful wife, as he admitted in his autobiography. It seems from Gandhi's description that it was a one-sided passion for which he did not blame her but rather he blamed himself. He was so fond of her, he said, that the thought of nightfall and their subsequent meetings used to titillate him during daytime, during school hours, and even while he was nursing his bedridden father. Kasturbai's illiteracy and her resistance to learn anything from him also aggravated this problem. The more he tried to teach, the more she resisted. He did not dare approach her during the daytime because of the presence of elders,[2] so the teaching had to be done in private and at night. Gandhi wrote that although he was very anxious to teach her, his "lustful love" left him no time. He took the entire blame upon himself, saying, "had my love for her been absolutely untainted with lust, she would have been a learned lady today" (ibid., 24). In Gandhi's eyes, it was his so-called lust that came in the way of his teaching his resisting pupil-wife.

As mentioned earlier, Kaba Gandhi's health was fast declining after his move to Rajkot. He was suffering from a persistent health problem of fistula,[3] and surgery was not advisable because of his advanced age. On top of it, in the rush of getting from Rajkot to Porbandar in time for his sons' weddings, the coach he was riding in toppled over, causing Kaba severe injuries from which he could not completely recover.

Being the most sensitive and conscientious son, Mohandas could not bear his father's pain and agony. With Shravana as his self-ideal, he wanted to serve and nurse his father day and night. Father Kaba preferred Mohandas to anyone else for mixing his medicines, for massaging his aching feet, and for just being around him. The obliging son was also a young and passionate husband, however, who admitted later in his autobiography, "Every night whilst my hands were busy massaging my father's legs, my mind was hovering about the bedroom" (ibid., 29). Attending to both his father and his young wife meant neglecting his studies, and Mohandas could not afford to miss any more days as he had already lost one whole year of school on account of his wedding. Erikson (1969, 116) has described the pitiable predicament of Mohandas: "His account of life suggests a certain frantic rush from one to the other, from wife to father and father to wife and to and from both, to and from school."

Gandhi's Juvenile Experiments in Self-Autonomy

Mohandas Gandhi felt overwhelmed by too many responsibilities too early in life. Besieged from all sides, he craved freedom—freedom to be, to do, and to go anywhere without adult supervision, religious restrictions, or

social constrictions. As discussed earlier, Gandhi was born into a highly traditional and conservative Vaishya-Vaishnava family. His parents practiced
the Vaishnava, Pranami, and Jain traditions, which all had in common several religious prohibitions. They were all forbidden to eat flesh or meat, to
smoke, to drink alcoholic beverages or use any other intoxicants including
drugs and tobacco, or to dine with any member outside of their own caste
or religion. Mohandas and other boys of his age revolted against these restrictions, but above all, against their elders' encroachment on their freedom.

As Gandhi reported in his autobiography, like many other boys of his
town, he too was "enamored of the smell of cigarette, and imagined a sort
of pleasure in emitting clouds of smoke from their mouths" (1948, 39).
Gandhi remembered his uncle smoking stealthily, and perhaps he had also
seen some of the servants doing the same. So, off these boys went, out of
everyone's sight, and took a few puffs of stolen or discarded stubs of cigarettes. But contrary to what they had imagined, smoking was no fun at all;
it resulted in uncontrollable bouts of coughing. Besides, who had money to
buy cigarettes, anyway? Thus the smoking experiment went up in smoke.

Frustrated, the boys made a suicide pact and chewed some poisonous
dhatura plant seeds. The half-comic and half-tragic scene of the boys' cer-
emonious preparations for their joint suicide comes out more hilarious in
the original Gujarati version of Gandhi's autobiography. The boys go into
the wilderness to a Shiva temple, light a lamp, and pray to God before sacrificing themselves. After eating only one or two seeds, however, they begin
to vomit; they pause, they think, they panic. What would happen if they
did not die but lingered on? That would be worse than death. Then why
not live and face the adults? The way they argue themselves out of their
mock-serious suicide pact elicits both laughter and sympathy for the boys.

Mohan and Mehtab: Positive versus Negative Identity

Mohandas Gandhi's juvenile experiments in smoking had fizzled out, his
suicide attempt with the other boys had gone awry, and his self-esteem had
hit rock bottom. He was now desperately in search of someone who was
vastly different from him, but someone that he would like to be. When
he entered high school, Mohandas came under the spell of Sheikh Mehtab,
a Muslim (Meman) boy who was originally a friend of his older brother
Karsandas. Little by little, the charismatic Mehtab spread his net and lured
Mohandas into it. Mohandas felt honored to be called a friend of someone
as big, strong, and brave as Mehtab.

Mohandas and Mehtab were poles apart in all aspects. Excruciatingly shy, Mohandas was small and timid; rakishly handsome, Mehtab was a big, brave boy with an intimidating demeanor. Mohandas was the son of a Vaishnava Hindu prime minister, whereas Mehtab was the son of a Muslim police chief. Mohandas was a *Bania*—proverbially known for its meekness, physical weakness, and aversion to all forms of valor and violence. He was no match for the stout and sinewy Mehtab, who exuded strength, dare-devilry and above all, fearlessness. Mohandas was married, careworn, and scrupulous. Mehtab, by contrast, was single, carefree, and as conniving as Iago in Shakespeare's *Othello*. By his own admission, as a young boy, Gandhi was "a coward—afraid of the thieves, ghosts, serpents and the darkness." Mehtab, by contrast, could hold live serpents in his hand, defy thieves, and chase ghosts.

Mehtab did almost everything that Mohandas could not—smoke with style, gamble with ease, eat meat often, drink heavily, and even frequent brothels. Mohandas desired, albeit unconsciously, to be like Mehtab and do what he did, but without guilt or fear. Mehtab sensed that deep down, Mohandas envied him; he was ready to be converted by this Muslim guru.

Mehtab masterminded a superb plan to make Mohandas eat meat. He knew, however, that it would be impossible for someone who had never seen meat to eat it. So Mehtab first tried to excite and inspire Mohandas to want to eat meat. Mehtab pushed the right buttons; he touched Mohan's most vulnerable spot—his desire to be as strong, as invincible, and as impressive looking as the tall and mighty Englishman. He quoted the famous lines of a Gujarati reformer poet, Narmad:

> Behold the mighty Englishman
> He rules the Indian small
> Because being a meat-eater
> He is five cubits tall.

The trick worked. Mohandas tasted goat's meat but found it so chewy and tough that he felt nauseated and could not eat or sleep that night. Here is how Gandhi described the scene in his autobiography: "A horrible nightmare haunted me. Every time I dropped off to sleep it would seem as though a live goat were bleating inside me, and I would jump up full of remorse" (ibid., 35). The whole scene comes off better in the Gujarati version in which he even mimics the sound of a goat bleating and his springing out of his bed with acute stomach pains!

Mehtab initially succeeded in his efforts to convert Mohandas because he appealed to him in the name of reform, which was a national preoccupation of the day. Most reformers enthused the nation's youth "to be manly and strong" so they could stand up to the Englishmen, defy them, and even defeat them. The great Hindu monk Swami Vivekananda exhorted the young people of his time, "You must first be strong. Religion will come afterwards. . . . you will be nearer to Heaven through football than through the study of the *Gita*" (*Complete Works of Swami Vivekananda*, 3, 242). Adolescent Gandhi was doubly attracted to this national theme of strength, first because he himself was physically weak and suffered from poor self-esteem, and second because he was an idealist who wished to "re-form" what is into what should be. As Susanne Rudolph and Lloyd Rudolph observed (1983, 15), "The dilemmas of the young Gandhi did in many ways approximate those of the surrounding generations."

Erikson (1969, 134) has called Mehtab "an evil genius" who "tried to ruin the son of the Vaishnavite prime minister morally." Nevertheless, Mohandas was also a willing pupil, too eager to learn all his master's secrets and the tricks of his trade. Mohandas' fatal attraction to Mehtab was not only because of his devilish charm but also for what he projected—everything that Mohandas desired to be, but must not be. As Erikson put it, "Mehtab played perfectly the personage on whom to project one's personal devil and thus became the personification of Mohandas' negative identity, that is, of everything in himself which he tried to isolate and subdue and which yet was part of him" (ibid., 135).

It is true that Mehtab perfectly played the role of "a devil," who brain-washed a Vaishnava boy into meat-eating and stealing money to pay for it. At first, Mohandas began to pilfer coins from his servant's pockets but that was not enough. So he even had to steal a bit of gold from his brother's armlet to pay off his mounting debts. Not only that, but Mehtab tried to instigate Mohandas against his wife, luring him to a brothel in the name of virility and reform. One must not forget, however, that Mehtab was only an exaggerated version of most adolescent boys then and even now. Mehtab appears to be a devil, probably because at the other extreme was Mohandas. As Sudhir Kakar argues in *Intimate Relationships* (1989, 88), "Reading about their youthful transgressions a hundred years later, to us Mehtab does not appear especially evil. He is neither more or less a representative of the world of male adolescence with its phallic displays and the ethic of a devil-may-care bravery." Kakar has a point in that Mehtab was not an atypical youth considering the bravado-braggadocio world of young males. However, he crossed a boundary by taking Mohandas to a brothel with the intention of making him cheat on his wife. Although Mohandas froze with fear and nothing happened, the act involved a betrayal of marital trust for which Mohandas felt intense remorse.

Another point worth discussing regarding Mohan's and Mehtab's friendship is Erikson's remark that "any intense friendship among men which excludes or demeans women cannot be without a homosexual element"[4] (1969, 137). Without proper proof or justification, Erikson has insinuated an "element of homosexuality" in Gandhi's friendship with Mehtab. Once again I find Erikson to be guilty of making wild inferences and interpreting the Mohan-Mehtab friendship in Freudian terms. I challenge his observations and also object to his far-fetched superimpositions for three reasons.

One, it is not at all uncommon in the Indian context for two males or females to have intense and tender emotional or physical attachment without sexual implications. For example, the characters of Krishna and Arjuna in the *Bhagavad Gita*, and of Rama and Sugriva in the *Ramayana*, illustrate the cultural and religious emphasis on such lifelong loyalty, devotion, and emotional commitment between two same-sex friends. Not only that, but the Indian society, religion, and mythology all value such friendship above all other relationships, even husband and wife, parent and child, or siblings. Two, I want to clarify here that my objection is not meant as an affront to gaymen or homosexuality. Moreover, it is not Erikson's claim of homosexuality itself that bothers me, but it is the unsubstantiated nature and cultural ignorance of his claim. Three, just as when Erikson superimposed the Oedipal triangle onto the Mohan-Mother-Father relationship, so also here he has tried to force-fit his Freudian theory by making ill-founded inferences. I was surprised that a Pulitzer prizewinning psycho biographer like Erikson would engage in a gossipy tone and instigate insinuations that cannot be proved one way or another.

Confession Letter to Father: The First Lesson in Nonviolence

Mohandas was deep in debt, both morally and monetarily, on account of his youthful escapades, which Erikson (1969) calls his "experiments with delinquency." I would rather call them Mohandas' "experiments in search of his true identity." Although these were acts of indiscretion, Mohandas did not intend to violate the rules or cheat his family, but rather wanted to exert his self-autonomy. He followed Mehtab because he wanted to exercise his right to experiment in order to test his beliefs [find out where he stood]. Having tasted the fruit, however, he began to feel intense remorse and guilt for violating the trust, love, and values of his family.

An acute anxiety attack paralyzed Mohandas. How was he going to face his parents and his wife? How would they feel knowing that he was not only a cheat but also a thief? The only way out was to go and tell it all. But to whom? To his mother, of course. Gandhi's mother listened with sympathy, as was her nature, and forgave her son. But now how would he face his gravely ill and bedridden father, and how would his father take it? Putliba suggested that Mohandas write a letter of confession and take it to his father. So Mohandas wrote a letter, and trembling like a goat before a lion, he handed it over to his father and waited in silence.

In his letter, Mohandas confessed his guilt and asked for adequate punishment. He closed the letter with a request to his father not to blame himself for his son's offense. Because of his long illness and the unbearable pain of his unhealed fistula, the aged Prime Minister Kaba was now too weak to sit up, but he propped himself up on the wooden plank on which he slept and began to read the note. Head down, Mohandas waited for the guillotine to fall. When it did not, he looked up and saw:

> Kaba read it through, and pearl-drops trickled down his cheeks, wetting the paper. For a moment he closed his eyes in thought and tore up the note. . . . I also cried. I could see my father's agony. If I were a painter I could draw a picture of the whole scene today. It is still so vivid in my mind. (1948, 41)

The quality of the confession—coming straight from the son's heart, transparent in its honesty and sensitivity—began to penetrate and purify the father's heart. Mohandas was surprised. Kaba was short-tempered, and when angry, he was prone to strike his own forehead and to shout. But this time he did neither; instead, he looked "so wonderfully peaceful!" What Kaba felt was something akin to a conversion of heart. He melted. He cried. His tears spoke louder than words—of his love for his son, his understanding and compassion, his acceptance and forgiveness. Young Gandhi was deeply touched.

Reflecting later on the miraculous effect of the letter, Gandhi wrote in his autobiography, "I believe this was due to my clean confession. A clean confession, combined with a promise never to commit the sin again, . . . it is the purest type of repentance" (ibid., 42). The letter proved to be mutually uplifting and redeeming for both the father and the son. Kaba was touched not only by his son's disarming honesty but also by this proof in hand that his beloved son Manu was primarily worried about the pain and the shock he had caused to his parents. It was the son's truth that inspired the father to be nonviolent, and it was the father's loving forgiveness that revealed the calming and healing power of *ahimsa* or nonviolence. Reflecting later, Gandhi wrote in his autobiography:

> This was for me an object-lesson in Ahimsa. Then I could read in it nothing more than my father's love, but today I know that it was pure Ahimsa. When such Ahimsa becomes all-embracing, it transforms every-thing it touches. There is no limit to its power. (41)

Father Kaba's Death and the Son's Double Shame

Kaba's health deteriorated quickly, and Mohandas served his father around the clock—compounding his drug mixtures, feeding him like a baby, fanning him, and massaging his feet. Occasionally, Mohandas would let his mother or servant relieve him of his pious duties. The father and the son spent more time together now than ever before, until almost that last fateful moment, when the father died without the son at his side.

When Kaba's illnesses progressed further, his older brother came to be with him and to help nurse him. Around 11 p.m. one night, when Mohandas was still busy massaging his father, his uncle offered to relieve him for the night. Gandhi described how "glad" he was to go straight to his bedroom and be intimate with his wife, although she was fast asleep and in an advanced state of pregnancy. In less than ten minutes or so, the servant knocked on the door, saying, "Get up, Father is very ill." Gandhi knew what "very ill" meant at that moment. Springing out of bed, rushing to the servant, he pressed him to tell him the truth. The servant said, "Father is no more." For Mohandas, no more was left except for guilt and shame.

Mohandas was overcome not only by grief but also by the guilt of his absence at the time of Kaba's death. Even worse than feeling guilty, Mohandas felt ashamed for the reason for which he had left his father. He thought it was his lust that separated him from his father, and that his lust was his shame. Mohandas fell in his own eyes. He thought he failed his father when Kaba needed him the most. Intense pain, guilt, remorse, and shame, like ghosts, haunted his thoughts. Day and night Mohandas kept thinking, "If animal passion had not blinded me, I should have been spared the torture of separation from my father during his last moments. I should have been massaging him, and he would have died in my arms" (ibid., 45).

Gandhi's autobiography (43–46) overflows with the "shame" vocabulary. His frequent use of words and phrases like "in the grip of lust," "my animal passion," "sinking into the ground for shame," "the shame of my carnal desire," "my lustful cruelty," "shackles of lust," and others, indicate that in Gandhi's mind then and forever, sexuality and shame were not only connected, but sexuality itself constituted shame.

The cataclysmic configuration of circumstances at the time of his father's demise did not cause but only confirmed his earlier feelings of inadequacy and self as a failure. This unfortunate incident aggravated his inner turbulence, setting into motion the whole cycle of self-blame, guilt, and shame. Gandhi had blamed his father for what he perceived to be his carnal weakness. He also criticized father severely for passing this on to his son by throwing him so early in life into the all-consuming flames of adolescent sexuality. This time, however, it was not the father who failed the son but the son who failed the father.

Why does Gandhi use the word "double shame" (in the title of chapter IX of his autobiography)? And what was his "double shame"? According to Gandhi, his first shame was that he failed to restrain himself while yet he was only a *vidyarthi* (student) who must totally dedicate himself to the acquisition of learning.[5] The second was an even greater shame in his eyes—that he failed in his filial duty and responsibilities to his parents, especially his father. And actually there was also a third shame, which Gandhi mentioned but only in passing, and that was he indulged in sexual union with his wife who was in an advanced state of pregnancy. Here, too, he blamed himself because the baby died within the first few days after its birth. Here is how Gandhi sums up the chapter of his "Father's Death and My Double Shame":

> The shame to which I have referred . . . was this shame of my carnal desire even at the critical hour of my father's death. . . . It is a blot I have never been able to efface or forget, and I have always thought that, although my devotion to my parents knew no bounds, . . . yet it was weighed and found unpardonably wanting because my mind was at the same time in the grip of lust. (Ibid., 46)

What Gandhi wrote toward the very end of this chapter of his double shame reveals that, in his eyes, he also failed as a husband to his wife: "I have therefore always regarded myself as a lustful, though a faithful, husband. It took me long to free myself from the shackles of lust, and I had to pass through many ordeals before I could overcome it" (ibid.).

Arjun Appadurai: "Understanding Gandhi"

Regarding Gandhi's overwhelming feelings of guilt and shame, we need to understand that Gandhi was reflecting, albeit unconsciously at this point, his culture's perspectives on human sexuality, which are markedly different from Western views.

As Arjun Appadurai observes in, "Understanding Gandhi," in *Childhood and Selfhood* (1978), there are two fundamental differences between Indian and Western understanding of human sexuality. First, in the Indian cultural and religious context, sexuality is seen as wasteful versus the Western Judeo-Christian interpretation of it as sinful. In Appadurai's words, "sexuality in Hindu culture is not so much sinful as wasteful, and . . . the core psycho-religious problem, in the Hindu view, is ignorance (*avidya*), not guilt: most religious ideologies and technologies are directed to the removal of ignorance and not the expiation of guilt" (132). Sexual indulgence is "construed as a waste of potent bodily substances" (semen in males) and therefore, as depleting one's energy. Gandhi bought into this widely spread Indian belief that sexuality even in marriage should be regulated and gradually sublimated for the purpose of God-realization. Excessive sexual indulgence is associated with animality, impurity, and sheer wastefulness of vital human energy. As Gandhi put it later in *Hind Swaraj*, "A man who is unchaste loses stamina, becomes emasculated and cowardly." Gandhi's later strivings for sexual abstinence were aimed at first controlling his sex drive, and then converting this vital energy into a spiritual power directed to God for self-liberation.

Appadurai also recognizes the link in adolescent Gandhi's mind between the traditional Hindu ideal of *brahmacharya* (abstinence) and that of filial duty. As Appadurai explains:

> The most powerful connection that the circumstances of his father's death seems to have made in Gandhi's mind is between the carnal indulgence and filial duty. . . . The Hindu view provides a specific and widely accepted theory of the link between carnal indulgence, construed as a waste of potent bodily substances, and the failure to perform one's duty. (1978, 132)

We also need to bear in mind that since childhood, Gandhi's self-ideals were based on the mythological and religious characters of Shravana, Rama, and Grandsire Bhishma (in the Hindu epic of *Mahabharata*), who gladly sacrificed their personal pleasures (including sexual) when they were found clashing with their service and duty to parents. It was in the light of this traditional, cultural-religious ideology that adolescent Gandhi judged himself as "an unworthy son" who failed at a critical time in his filial duty and loyalty.

During Gandhi's early adolescence—the years between ages thirteen and sixteen—he went through many traumatic experiences. These unfortunate incidents created a severe identity crisis, which also affected Gandhi's faith, as examined from the faith developmental perspective.

GANDHI'S EARLY ADOLESCENCE AND STAGE 3 SYNTHETIC-CONVENTIONAL FAITH: AN EVALUATION

Examining Mohandas Gandhi's early adolescent years in the light of Stage 3 criteria, we find him overwhelmed by too many conflicting roles and responsibilities too early in life. We also witnessed how this congenitally shy and introspective young boy of thirteen felt inadequate, guilty, and shame ridden—partly because of his own acute self-consciousness and partly because of the pressures and demands of his family and society. There cannot be a more powerful example of the "tyranny of the they" in the life of adolescent Mohandas Gandhi, who fell prey to both the imagined and real expectations of his family, his teachers, his "chum," and significant others in his community. Gandhi's internalization of the expectations and evaluations of others provides a compelling proof of one of "the dangers or deficiencies in this stage," according to Fowler.

We are therefore unable to see, at least in the early years of Gandhi's adolescence, any evidence of the "synthetic" quality of Stage 3 faith. For Mohandas, the unification process seems to be a rather long, painful, and difficult journey interrupted by doubts, dilemmas, and disappointments; he will continue to struggle, search, and experiment in order to find his true self-identity and faith. We may note here that for Gandhi, his "personal myth of becoming in identity and faith" would have to wait for a prolonged process of "transition," which is yet to take place.

Although adolescent Gandhi's life did not show at this point any positive proof of the "synthetic" side of Stage 3, it certainly provided solid evidence of its "conventional" side. As discussed earlier in the chapter, young Gandhi had to conform—whether he liked it or not—to the rules and expectations of his parents, his teachers, his wife, and his friend Mehtab. We saw young Gandhi trying to please both his adolescent bride, Kasturbai, and Mehtab, who represented what Erikson called Gandhi's "alter-ego" or "negative identity." Gandhi felt that he failed to win either one of them, and as a result, sank further into the morass of guilt and shame.

Just as Mohandas had to first experiment with his negative identity in order to find his positive or true identity, he also had to struggle to seek answers to his questions about religion at this stage. No book or scripture at this time, nor any person—parent, teacher, or other elder—could resolve his doubts or satisfy his intellectual queries. Although he was brought up in a deeply religious environment and was taught early in his life the lessons of religious openness and acceptance, he felt that what was important then was not sufficient for now. As Gandhi put it in his autobiography, "I had learnt to be tolerant to other religions did not mean that I had any living faith in God" (1948, 50). About this time, he happened to read *Manusmruti* or "Laws of Manu"—a Hindu text of laws of ethics written by Manu—which Mohandas found among his father's small collection of books at home. This book, however, failed to pacify Gandhi's doubts, nor could it satisfactorily answer his questions regarding whether "to eat meat or not eat meat!" Similarly, Gandhi wrote, "The story of the creation and similar things in it did not impress me very much, but the contrary made me incline somewhat towards atheism" (ibid.).

We recognize adolescent Gandhi's disappointment in not getting satisfactory answers to his religious queries, and that he came close to being an atheist at this stage. Yet we need not confuse his "disappointment" with "despair," for Gandhi had not given up his intellectual search for adequate or more informed answers. We may say that his faith at this moment was partially eclipsed, but not annihilated. Given his drive for self-perfection and inwardness, Mohandas continued to look for answers by conducting self-experiments with Truth and by his contact with other more knowledgeable people. For example, although Gandhi experimented with his negative identity and even indulged in juvenile indiscretions in the company of Mehtab, he found a way out by writing a clean confession letter to his father. This letter, written by fifteen-year-old Gandhi, is an early yet eloquent testimony of the "transforming power of love, acceptance, and forgiveness," called *ahimsa* or nonviolence. It shows that even as a teenager, Gandhi possessed this ethical capability to turn inward for strength and for seeking answers.

6

A Law Student in London

While not yet eighteen years of age, Mohandas Gandhi came face-to-face with the harsh realities of life. In addition to his intense grief, trauma, guilt, and shame related to his father's death, he had to carry on his young shoulders the extraordinary financial burden of his family. In the Indian cultural context, the eldest son usually performs not only his father's *shrāddh* (death rites) but must also bear the financial burden of the family. Even though Mohandas was the youngest son, he still took upon himself the cross of filial expectations for two reasons. One, because he had known all along that his father held high hopes only in him. Even while dying, Kaba Gandhi's last wish was, "Manu will be the pride of our family; he will bring luster to my name" (Pyarelal 1965, 1, 202). The deceased father's expectations now became his favorite son's moral obligation. Two, ever since Mohandas was a little boy, he had admired the story of the devoted son Shravana; this was his chance to be Shravana.

Among all Kaba's sons, only Mohandas had shown some academic promise. Kaba knew the times had changed, and that none of his sons could ever hope to become a prime minister like him or his ancestors without a respectable college degree that offered education in English. Proficiency in English brought not only prestige but also high position in British colonial India. Determined to fulfill his father's dream and to keep the prime ministry in the family, Mohandas studied hard and passed his matriculation examination in 1887 with fairly good marks. He was now eligible for admission in any well-established college with high-quality English educational standards. Although the best choices for Mohandas would have been the well-reputed

Elphinston College in Bombay or Gujarat College in Ahmedabad, both cities were too far away from Rajkot; the railway journey then was too cumbersome and expensive. However, there was the newly opened Shamaldas College in Bhavnagar, which not only had the best English faculty (of Anglo-Indian and Parsee professors) but also was no farther than ninety miles from Rajkot. Thus, because of the formidable distance of Bombay and Ahmedabad, and because of dwindling family finances, Mohandas had to settle for joining Shamaldas College in Bhavnagar.

For the first time, this provincial Kathiawari boy left his home, home-town, family, and friends. Gandhi has described in his autobiography how lonely and ignorant he felt in his new environment: "I went, but found myself entirely at sea. Everything was difficult. I could not follow, let alone taking interest in, the professors' lectures" (1948, 52). One reason Mohandas found his courses so difficult was that until then, he had not been exposed to instruction in the English language, much less the stiff and formal Macaulayan style of English college lectures of his time. Mohandas again blamed himself for being "so raw" as not to understand his erudite, Western-educated professors. At this time he began to suffer from headaches and nosebleeds. Maladjusted, homesick, and psychosomatically sick, Mohandas quit college after only one term and returned home to face a yet bigger question—what to do now.

For the dejected prodigal son Mohandas, who came home empty-handed without earning a degree from college, his father's trusted friend and family adviser, Mavji Dave, seemed to be a messenger of God, or at least a spokesman of his father's voice. Mavji Dave advised Putliba to send Mohandas to London, England, to become a barrister-at-law. Mavji argued that to be a "London-returned barrister" would not only make the whole Gandhi family and community proud of Mohandas, but would also enhance his chances of becoming the next prime minister of Rajkot. After all, was that not the last, supreme wish of his late father, Kaba Gandhi? Mavji's advice could not have been more timely, for every aspiring young Indian male in those days dreamed of going to London and coming home as a barrister. Mavji also pointed out the futility of earning a lackluster B.A. degree that would make Mohandas no more than a clerk, whereas a bar-at-law degree from London would put him at par with the high society of both the Western and Indian elite; it would also improve the family's economic and social status. Mavji's own son, Kevalram, had earned his law degree from London in less than three years.

No sooner than Mavji had left, Mohandas began to "build castles in the air." London was the only way to keep his father's heritage and the only way out of all his current problems. Besides, was London not the land of the English poets and philosophers about whom his college professors had spoken in such adulatory tones? Like most young men of Victorian India, Mohandas, too, entertained dreams of visiting London and becoming a "brown sahib"—one whom Lord Macaulay had described as "Indian in blood and color, but English in taste, in opinion, in moral and in intellect." (in Pyarelal, 1965 Vol. 1, 47) We may note here the paradox that despite having immense difficulties in following English, Mohandas was enamored of the English language, literature, and metropolis of London. Before leaving, however, for what he called, "the Mecca of my dreams," Mohandas, like Harishchandra, would have to pass through many an ordeal.

Family Opposition

The first opposition to his plan came from inside his own family. His dearest mother, Putliba, was not only afraid of letting her pet son go so far away but also of his getting corrupted in an alien land and culture. Putliba had heard stories of many *desi* (native) boys shamelessly indulging in the vices of drinking, womanizing, and meat-eating, all of which her dual religious heritage of Vaishnavism and Jainism prohibited. She passed the decision, however, to Mohandas' uncle, who, being the patriarch in the family, had to be consulted first. Gandhi described how he undertook the five-day journey from Rajkot to Porbandar, halfway by a bullock cart and halfway by a camel ride, just to get his uncle's approval and blessings. Like Gandhi's mother, his uncle was afraid that Mohandas, being so young, might go astray in a big city. Yet, he diplomatically passed the decision back to Putliba, saying that if she consented, he would.

Back to his mother again, Mohandas wanted to pacify her doubts about going astray in London. Just then, as if God-sent, came the trusted family priest Becharji Swami—a Brahmin turned Jain monk—who administered three vows to Mohandas: not to touch wine, women, or meat in Europe. Mohandas solemnly took the vows, which, at this stage meant nothing more to him than honoring his mother's wish and allaying her fears. Because his mother was sacred, so were the vows given to her. Besides, to this fan of the Truthful King Harishchandra, a pledge or a vow was always irrevocable.

Caste Ostracism

For Mohandas, the hardest hurdle to cross before going overseas was the opposition by his *Modh Bania* caste. To the caste elders, "crossing of the black seas" was an act of sacrilege punishable by excommunication. Holding a huge meeting of all the caste members, the elders put Mohandas in a witness box. They questioned him, intimidated him, ridiculed him, and even shamed him for violating the caste prohibitions by going to a foreign country of *mlecchas* (the "polluted ones"). Polite yet unyielding, Mohandas stayed adamant and gave his eternal negative answer: "I am helpless in this matter. I cannot alter my resolve to go to England" (Autobiography 1948, 58). The enraged caste leaders now passed their "guilty" verdict on Mohandas and ostracized not only him and his entire family but also anyone who would keep relations with them. The violators were forbidden to marry within the caste or even to mix with members of the same caste. Until the very last moment of Mohandas' departure from Bombay, he was harassed by some of the more vengeful caste elders. Mohandas, however, was determined to sail against the tide—a character trait that was to become the Gandhian trademark.

Financial Woes

Finances posed another thorny problem. How to raise funds for Mohandas' sea voyage and for his minimum three-year stay in London was a matter of great anxiety for the Gandhi family. Father Kaba had left little money behind as he was indifferent to all things material. Some relatives, who initially had promised large sums of money, turned their backs at the last moment for fear of ostracism and physical harm from malicious caste authorities. As a last resort, his oldest brother, Lakshmidas, sent Mohandas to the British political agent, Mr. Watson, to seek his favor for financial help. Curtly refusing to provide any help whatsoever, Watson insulted Mohandas by calling his older brother a political intriguer, and a troublemaker. Mohandas had previously had humiliating experience when he went to see another British officer, Mr. Lely, for his educational advice; Mr. Lely had abruptly brushed him off, asking Mohandas not to bother him until he first got his B.A. degree from India. Although he "pocketed the insults," as Gandhi put it, he could not forget the arrogance of the British sahibs and his humiliation at their hands.

TRANSITION TO STAGE 4
INDIVIDUATIVE-REFLECTIVE FAITH

The unusual courage and determination of eighteen-year-old Mohandas— to stand alone, to defy his caste elders, and to stick to his decision of going to London to become a barrister—mark a new shift toward transition from Stage 3 to Stage 4 Individuative-Reflective Faith. However, these are only the preliminary signals of this transition, which will be a long and painful process for Mohandas before he becomes fully capable of the Stage 4 well-reasoned and well-reflected decisions. Mohandas has slowly begun to move toward what Fowler calls, "the forming of a personal myth—the myth of one's own becoming in identity and faith," which requires "incorporating one's past and anticipated future in an image of the ultimate environment" (1981, 173). Thus far, adolescent Gandhi's "personal myth of becoming" had remained unfulfilled because of his early marriage, conflicting roles, identity crisis, and his guilt and shame concerning his father's death. He has now arrived at a crucial juncture between adolescence and young adulthood. Mohandas shows all the telltale signs of shedding his earlier identity of a provincial home-boy and adopting a new identity that will allow him to learn, grow, and explore the wider intellectual, social, and religious horizons in London.

En Route to London

With dreams of London dancing in his head, Mohandas was free at last to set sail from Bombay to England on September 4, 1888, via the S. S. *Clyde* steamship. This was his very first voyage abroad to explore the uncharted seas. Gandhi said that he did not feel seasick, but terribly homesick. No sooner than the ship had left Bombay, his whole world turned upside down. Earlier he had used the expression "entirely at sea" metaphorically, when he had difficulty following the lectures in English in his college classes. This time, however, he literally found himself "at sea" for several reasons.

The first reason was his crippling shyness, which kept him cooped up in his cabin day and night. His congenital shyness and timidity assumed titanic proportions during the voyage, partly because of his language handicap. Even at home he had difficulty with English, but on board it grew even worse. He could barely understand, much less converse in English without first forming the thoughts and sentences in his mind. So he would mutter or stutter so badly that nobody understood what he was saying. As a result, he decided to avoid company altogether, except for talking to his senior fellow passenger, Tryambakrai Mazmudar, also a native of Kathiawar. Mohandas noticed that Mazmudar not only spoke English fluently but had no qualms about drinking or eating meat. Mohandas had never liked or approved of drinking, but food was the mother of all his problems.

Mohandas' food ordeal had just begun. None of his other three vows proved as problematic as abstaining from meat. A vegetarian diet was a rarity in those days, and one with spices was almost nonexistent. Even if he could eat meat, he had never learned to eat with a fork and knife. To make matters worse, the other passengers seemed to have adjusted quite well. Even Mazmudar relished meat and coaxed Mohandas to do the same. Mohandas declined, however, not only because he was bound by his vow but also because he did not like what was offered. Gandhi recalled in his autobiography, "even the dishes I could eat were tasteless and insipid" (1948, 63). He survived on home-packed sweets and snacks for as long as they lasted, but considering his voracious appetite, it was only a tease. Mohandas literally starved.

On top of these handicaps of language and food, Mohandas had nil knowledge of European customs—dining, dancing, socializing, formal dressing, and others. Lonely, starving, and miserable, Mohandas missed both his mother and his motherland. As he wrote later in his autobiography, "my mother's love always haunted me. At night tears would stream down my cheeks, and home memories of all sorts made sleep out of the question" (ibid.).

Despite all these hardships, Mohandas derived great satisfaction that like his hero Harishchandra, he, too, had remained true to his vows throughout his eight-week-long journey. After having come this far, he was determined to keep his vows in London come what may.

IN LONDON AT LAST

Upon landing on the fog-shrouded London shores in late September 1888, Mohandas realized he was the only person dressed in a white flannel suit. He felt frozen not by the wintry weather but by the icy cold stares of the prim and proper Victorian British. There was nothing he could do. His baggage had not yet arrived. Mohandas felt like sinking into the ground. He was greeted there by one of the elderly friends of his family, Dr. Pranjivan Mehta, who, looking at his white flannel suit, gave a certain smile. Mohandas knew the meaning of that part-critical, part-amused smile and smiled back nervously. Mehta took him to the Victoria Hotel, one of the early luxurious hotels, now called Northumberland House, close to Trafalgar Square. Upon entering, Mohandas felt like Alice in Wonderland, which is evident from his descriptions in his diary, "A Guide to London" ([1893–1894]; 1959, 1: 66–120). The hotel's glitter and glamour, the lights, the marble floors

and fountains, the servants in fine livery and the waiters in frock coats daz-
zled him. At first he mistook the spacious "lift" (elevator) to be a hotel
room. Later, after seeing his real room for the first time, he exclaimed, "I
thought I could pass a lifetime in this room" (ibid.).

Gandhi mentioned in his autobiography that when he first met
Dr. Mehta, he casually picked up Mehta's fur top hat and passed his hand
over it the wrong way, which ruffled both the hat and the wearer of the hat.
Angry yet understanding, Dr. Mehta taught Gandhi his first lessons of
British etiquette: "Do not touch other people's things; do not ask questions as we usually do in India on first acquaintance, and do not talk
loudly. Never address people as 'sir' as we do in India" (1948, 62). Mehta
also advised him to live with a private family to save money and to become
acquainted with the English ways of living.

From a Customary to a Voluntary Vegetarian

As per Dr. Mehta's advice, Mohandas moved in with Dalpatram Shukla,
a Kathiawari friend, living in Richmond. Now that he had found accom-
modation, finding a good vegetarian restaurant became a matter of life and
death for this starving young law student. He soon realized his friend
Shukla did not approve of his die-hard vegetarianism. Shukla tried to talk
to Mohandas about the health advantages and convenience of adopting
a meat diet but to no avail. He then gave Bentham's book, *Theory of Utility*,
to Gandhi hoping it would help change his mind. Mohandas, however,
turned it down, saying politely yet firmly that he found the author's language and arguments too abstruse to follow. As Gandhi reported later in
his autobiography, Shukla now lost all his patience with him, and con-
fronted Mohandas with a question: "What is the value of a vow made
before an illiterate mother, and in ignorance of conditions here? It is no
vow at all" (ibid., 65). Not knowing how to convince Shukla about the
virtues of vegetarianism, Gandhi answered in his "eternal negative," just
as he had before in dealing with his caste elders. He said, "I am helpless.
A vow is a vow; it cannot be broken" (ibid.).

Gandhi's desperate food hunt sent him walking ten to twelve miles a day
in search of a vegetarian restaurant where he could eat to his heart's content.
One day, looking for the Porridge Bowl Restaurant, he found instead the
Central Restaurant on Farringdon Street. Gandhi described in his autobiography, "The sight of it filled me with the same joy that a child feels on
getting a thing after its own heart. ... this was my first hearty meal since

my arrival in England. God had come to my aid." (ibid., 67). Gandhi felt
doubly blessed, because he found there food for the body and food for
thought as well. To his pleasant surprise, he saw in the restaurant window
Henry Salt's pamphlet, *A Plea for Vegetarianism*. There and then he bought
it for a shilling and devoured it from page to page along with his meal. The
psycho-spiritual impact of the same was long lasting. Salt's book gave
Gandhi a scientific rationale as well as a moral basis for making vegetarianism a meaningful life choice rather than a custom or a habit. Ironically,
food, which was Gandhi's great weakness, would now become his formidable spiritual strength. Food also served as a catalyst to introduce Gandhi
to England's New Age radical thinkers, vegetarians, theosophists, puritans,
naturopaths, vivisectionists, and devout Christians.

The Vegetarians

Reading Henry Salt's pamphlet led Gandhi to meeting the author himself
and a whole group of leading vegetarians who were also radical reformers
of the day. Salt, who played a prominent role, invited Gandhi to a tea party
at his home. In *Salt and His Circle* (1951, 118), Stephen Winsten
described Gandhi as "the shy Indian, in silk hat and black coat, who ...
meant to be more English than the English, especially now that he had met
so many who were open-minded, unreserved and helpful. Salt was kindness and understanding itself."

Gandhi said that with a "neophyte's zeal," he joined this "new cult of vegetarianism in England." Next to the Central Restaurant were the offices of the
London Vegetarian Society, or the famous LVS. LVS members spread the vegetarian gospel of wholesome food (fruits, vegetables, and grains), of humanity, simplicity, purity, and spirituality in all walks of life. In January 1888 it
launched the weekly *Vegetarian*, "A Paper for the Promotion of Humanity,
Purity, Temperance, Health, Wealth, and Happiness" (Hunt 1978, 20–30).

"With a convert's enthusiasm for his new religion," said Gandhi, he
became a member of the LVS Executive Committee in 1890. He worked
shoulder to shoulder with prominent vegetarian reformers such as Henry
Salt, Howard Williams, Anna Kingsford, Dr. Allinson, Joshua Oldfield,
A. F. Hills, and Edward Maitland. He organized meetings, arranged lectures, took minutes, wrote articles in the *Vegetarian*,[1] participated in discussions, and nervously gave some speeches on behalf of the LVS.

If Gandhi liked an idea, he breathed it, lived it, and experimented
with it in day-to-day life. Only if it passed his rigorous testing, would he

develop the idea further and implement it in every possible manner. Ever since he read Salt's book, it whetted his appetite for extensive dietetic studies. He began to read as many books as available on the subject, including Howard Williams' *The Ethics of Diet*, Anna Kingsford's *The Perfect Way in Diet*, and Dr. Allinson's writings on health, hygiene, and the benefits of a strictly vegetarian diet. Gandhi said that in the early stage of his dietetic experiments, his principal motive was only health. "But later on," he said, "religion became the supreme motive" (1948, 68).

Shukla was now alarmed about his new Indian friend's consuming interest in vegetarianism. To save him from what he considered to be Gandhi's foolishness and folly, Shukla tried one last time to convert his friend to a nonvegetarian diet, but in vain. Although Gandhi knew he had disappointed his friend, he confessed that he was helpless in the food matter; he decided to make it up to Shukla by becoming a stylish and sophisticated Englishman.

Playing the English Gentleman

Gandhi gave two reasons in his autobiography for undertaking "the all too impossible task of becoming an English gentleman." The first reason was to make up for his clumsiness and inflexibility regarding food to his friend Shukla. Another reason was to learn the proper English manners and accomplishments worthy of the sophisticated, high English society. Perfectionist as he was, Gandhi passionately pursued the task of total Anglicization starting with his dress. To look the part of a London dandy, Gandhi bought from the respectable Army and Navy stores the most stylistic clothes and accessories—a Dickensian high silk hat, stiff collar shirt and tie, leather gaiter and leather boots, and even a silver-mounted cane. Gandhi had his evening suit custom-tailored on Bond Street, the ultimate fashion center of the day. He asked his oldest brother to send to him from India a double watch gold chain which, dangling from the waistcoat pocket, made a fashion statement of the Victorian gentleman. This provincial Indian boy, who never had the luxury of even a mirror at home, was now spending enormous amounts of time before the mirror to part his hair perfectly and to tie his necktie correctly. Just one look at the picture of an earnest eighteen-year-old Gandhi—dressed immaculately from head to toe, with each unruly strand of his jet black hair neatly parted slightly off center—makes us laugh at his youthful frivolity, yet love him at the same time for his desire to fit into the English mainstream.

Gandhi took private lessons in dancing, violin, French, and elocution. However, having neither an ear for music, nor a sense of rhythm or a flair for speaking, Gandhi soon realized it to be a huge waste of money, which he simply could not afford.

Crushed by an acute sense of financial and moral responsibility toward his family, Gandhi thought of his obligation as a student or his *vidyarthi-dharma*. He was now not only a son, a brother, and a husband but also a father of an infant son. His family had given an enormous sacrifice in sending him so far away to the other end of the globe so that he could fulfill his dream. Struck by conscience, the fashion-bug Mohandas Gandhi now turned to the other extreme, economic austerity.

Notice this developing pattern in Gandhi's character. Just as in his early adolescence he experimented with his negative identity (Mehtab) in order to find his true self-identity, here, too, he stretched the limits of his English experiment to find out where he belonged. Although Gandhi called this his "infatuation" lasting about three months, in terms of his faith and self-development it was his twin desire to join the English mainstream and to "belong to" and "to be okayed" by significant others. Still hovering between Faith Stages 3 and 4, Mohandas is not yet completely free from the "tyranny of the they" (Stage 3), nor yet capable of independent judgment (Stage 4). He is undergoing a rather protracted stage transition.

FIRST EXPERIMENTS IN ECONOMIC LIVING

Mohandas' English experiments served as eye-openers to see his true identity as an Indian and his primary responsibility as a student. From his heedless pursuit of becoming an English gentleman, Gandhi now took a U-turn to live like an austere Indian student—simplifying life, reducing expenses, saving money, keeping and tallying accounts, and feeling gratified about it. Instead of living with a friend or a family member, he now took rooms of his own (first two, then one) and learned to cook, to clean, to wash, starch and iron clothes, and to even cut his own hair. He began walking everywhere, whether far or near. His experiments in economical living sometimes made him the butt of ridicule, but he did not mind. For example, his over-starched shirt would shed white material in public, or sometimes people would make fun of his unevenly cut hair. Gandhi would join them in laughing at himself; he enjoyed poking fun at himself as much as he enjoyed poking fun at others.

Experiments in Dietetics

Gandhi's dietetic experiments were part of his larger experiments in economic living as a student. Having learned to cook his own food, he realized that the simpler the meals and the fewer the food items, the more time and money it saved him. The only criterion of good food, he learned from his vegetarian friends, was its nutritive value; it was neither the taste, nor an elaborate menu. Besides health considerations, Dr. Allinson, Anna Kingsford, and other LVS members introduced him to the humanitarian, scientific, and ethical perspectives of a purely vegetarian diet. They argued that if mankind were superior to animal kind, then man should not make animals their prey but should instead protect and nurture all subhuman species. Scientifically, the human physical structure suggested man should not be "a cooking but a frugivorous animal" who, as a baby should only subsist on his or her mother's milk, and after cutting teeth, should only eat foods such as organic fruits, vegetables, and grains. Ethically, man should eat to live rather than live to eat. "These changes," said Gandhi, "harmonized my inward and outward life. It was also more in keeping with the means of my family. My life was certainly more truthful and my soul knew no bounds of joy" (1948, 75).

TWO FACES OF SHYNESS

As mentioned earlier, by nature Gandhi was shy and timid. His shyness had two faces. One face of Gandhi's shyness was embarrassing, humiliating, and even shameful. He felt ashamed of himself about the shyness that caused him acute embarrassment whenever he got up to speak in front of people; it made him a laughing stock in the public eye. As an executive member of the LVS he had to make many presentations in London and beyond to promote the vegetarian cause. He distinctly remembered how, while giving a farewell speech at the Holborn Restaurant, his vision blurred, and his tongue was tied, his mouth felt parched, and he trembled like Arjuna,[2] the warrior-hero, in the *Bhagavad Gita*. Sometimes he could not even read his own written speech beyond a few lines; becoming flustered, he had to sit down and give it to somebody to read it for him. Gandhi retained this shyness throughout his London stay, and though he made great improvement later in South Africa, he could not completely overcome it.

Gandhi's shyness proved to be embarrassing not only while speech making but also in his dealing with young women in the earlier days of his arrival in London. But the same shyness had another face, which was benign, discreet, and protective like a mother. Gandhi counted the many advantages of his God-given shy nature. His hesitancy in speech that once caused him embarrassment, ridicule, and shame proved to be a blessing in disguise in that it taught him the economy of words. It also taught him to speak and act discreetly, to restrain his anger, and not to exceed his limits. "My shyness," said Gandhi (1948, 84), "has been in reality my shield and buckler. It has allowed me to grow. It has helped me in my discernment of truth."

His congenital shyness also saved him from moral fall, as when he had visited a brothel with Mehtab in the earlier years. Like most other Indians arriving in London, he, too, had posed himself as a bachelor, but in the words of Gandhi, "Only my reserve and my reticence saved me from going into deeper waters" (ibid.).

In the last days of his stay in London when Gandhi had gone to Portsmouth for his LVS conference with other members, his shyness pulled him out once again from the "den of vice," as he put it. While playing cards with a woman of questionable virtue, he joined the others in making indecent jokes with her. Before he crossed his limits, however, friends who knew he was married and committed to his vow of chastity brought him to his senses. Although deeply ashamed, Gandhi was grateful to his friends and to God, as he said:

> I did not then know the essence of religion or of God, and how He works in us. Only vaguely I understand that God has saved me on that occasion and on all occasions of trial. (ibid., 95–96)

ACQUAINTANCE WITH RELIGIONS THROUGH THE THEOSOPHISTS

Through his association with the members of the London Vegetarian Society, Gandhi came to know prominent theosophists of the day, like Helena Petrovna Blavatsky, the Olcott brothers, Annie Besant, Edward Maitland, and others. Just as Salt initiated young Gandhi into vegetarianism, these theosophists introduced him to his own great Hindu heritage, philosophy, and the Sanskrit scriptures. Gandhi's thirst for formal religious knowledge had remained unquenched and his queries unanswered. He was at that time hovering between theism and atheism.

Theosophy was the New Age religion, according to Martin Green (1993). It was officially founded in New York in 1875 by Madame Blavatsky and Colonel Olcott, who were inspired by Hinduism and Tibetan Buddhism. They espoused esoteric doctrines, the Law of Karma, reincarnation, and beliefs in the occult, such as magic, witchcraft, clairvoyance, and hypnosis, as well as communication with the spirits of the dead. Also interested in Orientalism, Unitarianism, and Transcendentalism, theosophists comprised a motley group of vegetarians, antivivisectionists, radical reformers, writers, and activists.[3] Three major objectives of the Theosophical Society were: the universal brotherhood of humanity; the study of comparative religion, philosophy, and science; and investigation of the unexplained laws of nature and powers latent in man. Gandhi was attracted to the philosophical side of Theosophy but not by its occultism. He admired its brilliant women leaders, such as Madame Blavatsky and Annie Besant; later, he would also work with the latter for the cause of Indian independence.

Gandhi was approached by two theosophist friends who needed his assistance in reading the original Sanskrit text of the *Shrimad Bhagavad Gita* alongside its English translation by Edwin Arnold, titled *The Song Celestial.* To Gandhi this first formal study of the *Bhagavad Gita* was a humbling as well as humiliating experience because he only had a nodding acquaintance with Sanskrit. Gandhi admitted in his autobiography, "I felt ashamed, as I had read the divine poem neither in Sanskrit nor in Gujarati" (1948, 90).

The shame of his own religious illiteracy, however, became a strong incentive for Gandhi to study the *Gita* (short for *Bhagavad Gita*) as well as other scriptures of the world. Deeply impressed by the *Gita* in particular, Gandhi used it as his "spiritual dictionary" and referred to it in all moments of doubt and despair. Later he wrote a book titled *Gita—My Mother,* in which he said, "Today the *Gita* is not only my Bible or Koran, it is more than that—it is my mother" (1945, 4–5). He regarded the *Gita* as the book par excellence for the knowledge of Truth, and he especially liked its second chapter, verses 62 and 63:

> Man, musing on the objects of sense, conceiveth attachment to these; from attachment ariseth desire; from desire anger cometh forth. From anger proceedeth delusion; from delusion confused memory; from confused memory the destruction of Reason; from destruction of Reason he perishes.

Once kindled, Gandhi's religious appetite began to grow by leaps and bounds. Soon after finishing the *Gita,* Gandhi read another of Edwin Arnold's masterpieces, *The Light of Asia* about the life of Buddha, which he liked even more than Arnold's translation of the *Gita*. As Judith Brown observed (1989, 26), "Many of the Buddha's teachings echoed his Jain inheritance and his own movement through vegetarianism towards non-violence and compassion for all life." Next Gandhi began to read the Bible, both the Old Testament and the New Testament. Although he was disenchanted by the Book of Genesis, the New Testament made a deep impact on him, especially the Sermon on the Mount.

THE BHAGAVAD GITA AND THE SERMON ON THE MOUNT

That Gandhi was profoundly moved by Christ's words is evident here:

> The Sermon on the Mount went straight to my heart. The verses, "But I say unto you, that you resist not evil: but whosoever shall smite thee on your right cheek, turn to him the other also. And if any man take away thy coat let him have thy cloak too" delighted me beyond measure. (*Autobiography*, 92)

Although Gandhi had never read the Bible or the Sermon on the Mount before, he was deeply touched by Christ's words, which reminded him of something he had heard as a child. Christ's message of human compassion, renunciation, and forgiveness revived Gandhi's memories of his own Gujarati saint-poet Shamaldas Bhatt's verse: "For a bowl of water, give a goodly meal." His moral mind began to make the connections: Return evil with good; give more than asked, or give until it hurts. He recalled another didactic Gujarati *chhappa* (verse), which raised a moral question: "Who is more virtuous? One who does good in return of good, or one who does good to all—even to those who hurt, speak ill or take away?" We may note that just as what he had heard in childhood came back to him with double force and extraordinary clarity at this stage, what he is reading now will go a long way in shaping the moral and spiritual philosophy of the future Mahatma. The lessons will be lasting.

Gandhi now began "to unify the teaching of the *Gita, The Light of Asia* and the *Sermon on the Mount*. That renunciation was the highest form of religion appealed to me greatly." His religious appetite being whetted, he read many more books, especially on the lives of the saints and religious teachers of the world. One was Carlyle's book *Heroes and Hero Worship*, in which the Muslim prophet Mohammad's life of piety, bravery, and austerity made a deep impact on Gandhi.

Until now Gandhi was standing on the brink of atheism not because of lack of faith, but because his faith was not nourished by convincing moral reasoning. It was at this crucial juncture that Gandhi came in contact with Annie Besant and read her famous book, *How I Became a Theosophist,* which told the story of her own transformation to theism from atheism. This was the book that helped Gandhi "cross the Sahara of atheism," as he put it. If Salt's book convinced him about why he should remain a vegetarian, Besant's book explained why he should not be a religious skeptic anymore.

In London, Gandhi met esoteric Christians, puritans, ethicists, Quakers, Theosophists, and vegetarians who impressed him with their deep piety, faith, humanity, and integrity. They helped him to remove his earlier prejudice and negative boyhood memories of the zealot Christian missionaries who forced conversion on people of other religions; they also helped him to learn and grow intellectually, morally, and religiously.

THE BARRISTER

Interestingly, Gandhi did not seriously apply himself to his legal studies until the fall of 1890. Most of his books on Roman law and Common law were in Latin, but Gandhi had never had any Latin courses in his high school or college. So, in order to learn Latin and to gain proficiency in English as well, Gandhi decided to take the London Matriculation examination, which he passed in his second attempt in June 1890. He could not have made a wiser decision, because his knowledge of Latin stood him in good stead later in South Africa, where the Dutch law was founded on the base of Roman law. Similarly, the rigorous English standard of the London matriculation helped him gain mastery over both spoken and written English. In *Gandhi in London* (1978), James D. Hunt says that barristers received their training in one of the four Inns of Court, which were: the Inner Temple, the Middle Temple, the Lincoln's Inn, and Gray's Inn. Gandhi was enrolled in the Inner Temple, which was then the most expensive and most prestigious, as well as the largest law school of all. To qualify for admittance to the bar a student must attend seventy-two dinners, pass two examinations (both written and oral), and be at least twenty-one years of age. A student should keep a minimum twelve terms, and upon the completion of those terms, must pass his exams.

A diligent student, Gandhi read through the Common Law of England and other law books such as Snell's *Equity,* White's and Tudor's *Leading Cases,* William's and Edward's *Real Property,* Goodeve's *Personal Property,* and last but not least important, Mayne's *Hindu Law*. Gandhi passed his examinations, was called to the bar on June 10, 1891, and enrolled in the High Court on the 11th. The very next day, on June 12, the twenty-one-year old Indian barrister set sail for home. Passing the bar exam was easy, but would practicing be as easy?

Protracted but Productive Transition

Discussed earlier were the first signs of the breakdown of Gandhi's Synthetic-Conventional Stage 3 when he defied his caste authorities to go to London to seek his personal identity and fulfill the "personal myth of his becoming." The second sign of stage transition manifested when Gandhi was ready to leave home both physically and emotionally to begin a new life for himself in London. While in London he continued to experience the transitional process from Stage 3 to Stage 4.

London challenged Gandhi in every way—emotionally (homesickness), psychologically (adjustment to food, language, environment), socially (interacting with new people, customs, conduct), intellectually (exposure to new ideas, books, causes, movements), and religiously (reading books and comparing).

The Stage 3 unification process was continuously at work in Gandhi's responses to his multiple challenges in an alien environment. On the one hand, he must remain true to his "Indian-ness," while on the other hand, he must be open to learn and assimilate what is best in the Western culture. For example, his Indian allegiance was first tested by Shukla who was determined to break his vegetarian vow. Though Gandhi could not then defend himself logically, he still adhered to his vow saying that "a vow is a vow and it cannot be broken"; the vow signified both his sacred allegiance to his mother and the culture of his motherland.

In the second instance he was required to study the *Bhagavad Gita* in its original Sanskrit script to help his theosophist friends understand the translation better. Although he was an "insider" who was supposed to have a thorough knowledge and a deeper understanding of his own religious scripture than that of the outsiders, he found himself lacking and disappointed both himself and them. Ironically, this time he needed a Western stimulus to awaken his dormant religious consciousness and to make him aware of his Indian religious heritage.

The most powerful evidence of the continuation of Stage 3 assimilative process can be seen in the third instance of Gandhi's English experiments.

We witnessed Gandhi's earnest yet awkward efforts to become more English than even an Englishman. Yet we should note that his English experiments, unlike his previous juvenile experiments, were more deliberate than defiant. The young Indian novice was determined to find out exactly where he stood in terms of his personal and cultural identity—to know what was right for him and what was not. Having gone through that experience, Gandhi discovered who he was not, no matter how earnestly or foolishly he may have tried to ape an Englishman. Only by experimenting with his alien identity did he arrive at his true Indian identity. To use Erikson's phrase, Gandhi became "an augmented Indian" after his experiments at Anglicization. In terms of Gandhi's ongoing faith and self development, his experiments at Anglicization, in economic living, and in dietetics altogether "precipitate," what Fowler calls "the kind of examination of self, background and life guiding values that give rise to a stage transition at this point." Only by going through this long and painful process of transition will Gandhi eventually arrive at the new Stage 4.

A Critique of the Critics

Many biographers of Gandhi, such as Louis Fischer (1950), Erik Erikson (1969), and B. R. Nanda (1965) have dismissed his London experience as a waste of time, giving no clue at all of the "Mahatma-to-be." Fischer admits, "it is unfair to expect too much of the frail provincial Indian transplanted to metropolitan London at the green age of eighteen." In the next breath, however, he contradicts himself, saying, "the contrast between the mediocre, unimpressive, handicapped, floundering M. K. Gandhi, attorney-at-law, who left England in 1891, and the Mahatma leader of millions is so great, … that the real Gandhi, the Gandhi of history, did not emerge, did not even hint of his existence in the years of schooling and study" (1950, 28).

I find Fischer's appraisal of Gandhi in London to be unfair and unkind. First, Fischer not only makes two contradictory value judgments but also compartmentalizes Gandhi's "pre-Mahatma" period and the "post-Mahatma" period just to highlight the contrast. He pitches the green youth against the mature, middle-aged Mahatma, that is, an unfinished product against a finished and polished human product. Second, by dwelling upon the "Gandhi of history," meaning the moral-political leader, he ignores the clear signs and signals of Gandhi the truth-seeker, an apprentice of faith in the making. Fischer passes the verdict, "only when it was touched by the magic wand of action in South Africa did the personality of Gandhi burgeon" (ibid.). Gandhi, however, was no Cinderella to be turned into a princess by the touch of the magic wand in South Africa. The magician was practicing his art behind the curtains. Or to put it plainly, the apprentice Gandhi was honing his spiritual skills in London.

Erik Erikson (1969, 145–147) interprets Gandhi's London experience as his "adolescent moratorium" in two ways. First, he calls "moratorium" a period of "important delay" when Gandhi is "away from home and not yet constrained to become self-sufficient." Second, "it is a period for meeting one's neurosis" consisting of "the inhibitions and anxieties or what is unresolved in one's personality." I agree with his first observation that London was a period of his important delay not only in terms of his psychological development, but in faith development as well. The point to emphasize, however, is that this delay was not unproductive, but pregnant with the promise of productive new changes. These are the changes that will make him not only "an augmented Indian" as Erikson put it but also an enriched and enlightened Indian because of his Western exposure in London. I do not agree with Erikson that this was a period of Gandhi's "neurosis." Quite to the contrary, this was his first opportunity to face his fears, anxieties, and inhibitions and to work them out in his own way.

B. R. Nanda criticizes (1965, 5) that "not even the most partial observer could have detected in this young barrister-to-be any promise of distinction." Does he not expect too much, and too soon, from a young novice out in the world for the first time? Should a caterpillar be rushed to transform itself into a butterfly?

Without the leasst exaggeration, Gandhi's London years proved to be the most fruitful years, which opened wide his intellectual, cultural, and religious horizons. Let me sum up with Judith Brown's observations (1989, 23), which substantiates my points:

> Gandhi's three years in London were a time of social, moral and intellectual ferment for him. … It was the first time he had the opportunity and the necessity of taking charge of his life, of sorting out priorities and values.

7

A Barrister in South Africa, Phase I

At the age of eighteen, in the spring of his youth and in the spring of 1888, Gandhi had gone to London to fulfill his father's dream as well as his own of becoming a barrister. When he returned home at the age of twenty-two in the summer of 1891, he had already become what the Indians proudly called a "London-returned Barrister." The bar-at-law degree from England not only raised Mohandas Gandhi's status among the educated elite circles but also brought pride and prestige to the Gandhi family. Kaba Gandhi's favorite son, "Manu," had fulfilled his father's last wish; like the devoted son Shravana, he had paid off his final filial debt or to put it in Indian terms, he had offered his true *pitru-shrāddh*.

The London experience greatly contributed to Gandhi's social, intellectual, and religious growth, the latter of which had a particularly lasting impact. Because of his Western cultural exposure, Gandhi's vision had widened, his confidence improved, and his English perfected. Yet somehow, the young barrister seemed to be more anxious than excited about going home. Several fears, anxieties, and uncertainties dampened Gandhi's enthusiasm and marred the joy of reuniting with his family and friends after three years. His apprehensions may have foretold some of the grim prospects ahead.

The first news he received upon landing ashore was that of his beloved mother's death, which his family had purposely kept from him until he returned home. Gandhi admitted in his autobiography that although the news was "a severe shock" to him, and though his grief was even greater than over his father's death, he did not give himself up to "any wild expression of grief" (1948, 112). The reason for this was that Gandhi never felt his mother had died; she was living in him as his "internalized strength," as Erikson (1969) put it. Ever since he was Putliba's little Moniya, Gandhi had adored his mother for her cheerful piety and her ascetic self-control; he endeavored to be "as flawless as his mother." Now that Putliba was gone, Gandhi identified with her so deeply that although he was called a *Bapu* (father), he became softer, kinder, more loving and nurturing like a *Ba* (mother). "This maternal side of *Bapu* attracted particular types of followers and inspired particular trends in the masses," said Erikson; "almost as though he had provided in his own person a new matrix, had become India herself" (1969, 157).

The second initial impediment to his happy resettlement in India was his persistent persecution by the *Modh Bania* caste elders. With a revengeful hostility, they compelled him to go through certain expiating rituals for having committed the sin of going overseas. Although he acquiesced to their demand for his family's sake, he was not the least penitent.

The third factor to dampen his spirits was the persistent problem of his marital disharmony. As Gandhi confessed in his autobiography, "My relations with my wife were still not as I desired. Even my stay in England had not cured me of jealousy" (1948, 116). Gandhi blamed not Kasturbai, but himself for his "squeamishness and suspiciousness" which still continued. But the worst, according to him, was his lust, which came in the way of his efforts to educate her. Toward the latter half of his stay in India and before his departure to South Africa, however, their relationship showed some improvement. They became closer while working together on some of the "home reforms" that also involved their two sons.[1]

The London-returned barrister had imported from the West what he called "reforms," which affected the lifestyle of the whole Gandhi family. The first changes pertained to food and the style of eating. Tea and coffee were now replaced by oatmeal porridge and cocoa, and brass plates by China crockery. Instead of sitting on the floor Indian-style, everyone ate at the dining table, and they ate with forks and knives instead of their fingers. Gandhi also insisted that everyone in his family dress formally in European-style clothes with socks, shoes, boots, and all. Most of all, Gandhi enjoyed teaching his little ones various physical exercises that he had learned in England; he also loved playing and joking with them—a habit that stayed with him until the very end. Children enjoyed Bapu as much as Bapu enjoyed their company.

BRIEFLESS BARRISTER IN INDIA

In addition to all these impediments, Gandhi's biggest frustration was his professional maladjustment. As a young adult beginning his law career in India, he stood once again at the crucial crossroads of his life. In Bombay, where he first opened his law offices, he could not even procure small cases without having to pay commission to the "touts" or the middle men, a custom he considered to be both unethical and humiliating to lawyers. He felt inadequate for not having enough knowledge of Indian law and Civil Procedure Code, nor enough courage to conduct even a small case. His debut in the Small Causes Court where he defended the case of Mamibai turned into a fiasco. In his autobiography Gandhi described his pitiable plight as he stood up to cross-examine his plaintiff's witnesses: "My heart sank into my boots. My head was reeling and I felt as though the whole court was doing likewise" (120). His feelings of inadequacy were partly due to his own initial incompetence, and partly due to the intimidating presence on the scene of such veteran lawyers as Badruddin Tyebji and Sir Pherozeshah Mehta—called "Sir Ferocious" or "the Lion of Bombay." Because he was frustrated in his efforts to make a living as an attorney in Bombay, Gandhi tried his luck at being an English teacher in a Bombay school, but it turned him down by saying he was overqualified for the job.

As a last resort, Gandhi yielded to his family's pressure to start a practice in his own hometown of Rajkot. He could make a moderate living there by writing drafts and memorials for his clients, or he could join his brother Lakshmidas, who himself was a petty pleader and an ex-royal adviser. To his dismay, Gandhi found that here, too, he was required to pay commission to the *vakils* who briefed him. Gandhi would not have agreed to do so but for his brother, who was his legal partner. Gandhi had to compromise his principles, or as he "put it bluntly" in his autobiography, "I deceived myself" (124). He felt suffocated by the corrupt Kathiawari environment reeking with *khutput* (court intrigues) and *kawadawa* (petty power politics) in the small princely towns of Porbandar and Rajkot.

THE FIRST SHOCK

What Gandhi described in his autobiography as "the first shock" was in reference to being insulted in India by an English officer named Charles Ollivant. Strictly speaking, this could not have been Gandhi's first shock.

He was intimidated before by his own caste elders as well as insulted by an Englishman to whom he went for consultation before going to London. Still, the impact of this insult was far heavier as Gandhi had known the officer in London as a nice English gentleman. Soon he realized, however, that "an officer on leave was not the same as an officer on duty" (ibid., 125).

The incident took place when Gandhi went to see Charles Ollivant in his office to plead on behalf of his brother Lakshmidas, who was in some kind of political trouble. The sahib not only refused to listen to Gandhi, but also accused his brother of being a liar and an intriguer. When Gandhi tried to present the facts in defense of his brother, the haughty sahib showed Gandhi the door. While Gandhi was still hesitating, the officer ordered his peon to throw Gandhi out of his room. Gandhi was deeply shocked by the disparity of the officer's attitude and behavior in London versus India.

Thus, socially, intellectually, and professionally, the London-returned barrister felt like a total misfit in his own home and homeland. Having seen what the Western world could offer to stimulate his mind and accentuate his appreciation of his own culture, he expected more of himself, of his people, and of his life in India.

GANDHI'S FIRST MEETING WITH RAYCHANDBHAI OR SHRIMAD RAJCHANDRA

The only oasis during the Sahara of Gandhi's stay in India after his London sojourn was his meeting with Raychandbhai, the Jain poet-cum-diamond jeweler (or *Zaveri*) from Bombay. As Gandhi recalled in his autobiography, Raychandbhai was "a man of great character and learning" as well as a "*shatavdhani*" (one having the faculty of remembering or attending to a hundred things simultaneously). The London-returned proud barrister wanted to put Raychandbhai to the test. So he exhausted his vocabulary of all the European tongues he knew, including English, French, and Latin, and asked the poet to repeat the words. Although Raychandbhai was not literate in any of these languages, he could still repeat each word in the precise order in which Gandhi had given them to him. Even then, this amazing gift of the poet failed to cast a spell on Gandhi.

"The thing that did cast its spell over me," said Gandhi, "was his wide knowledge of the scriptures, his spotless character, and his burning passion for self-realization" (ibid., 112). Raychandbhai was a *samsari* (a married, worldly man), yet he lived like a true *sanyasin* (a man of renunciation). Though he functioned in the world, he was not of the world. Raychandbhai was the only one to have come near to being Gandhi's spiritual guru from among "the three moderns" that he mentioned in his autobiography (the others being Tolstoy and Ruskin). Yet somehow, Gandhi could not accept Raychandbhai as his guru because even though Raychandbhai was a *mahajnani* (man of great knowledge), he was still orthodox in his observance of the caste rules, which Gandhi despised. So although not officially his guru, Raychandbhai was still Gandhi's best guide and refuge in his moments of spiritual crisis. He was a "genuine seeker after truth" who inspired Gandhi to become one. Later in South Africa, Gandhi would continue to consult Raychandbhai regarding his religious doubts and deeper spiritual queries.

God-Sent Job Offer from South Africa

Just when Gandhi was contemplating how to get out of his predicament in India, he received a job offer from a South African firm owned by Dada Abdulla, a Gujarati Muslim from his own native Porbandar. Abdulla's firm in Natal was involved in a huge civil suit against a rival cousin firm and needed an English-qualified legal counselor. The one-year job contract, which included first-class sea fare both ways and a pay of 105 pounds, was too attractive to turn down.

As Gandhi mentioned in his autobiography, this time when he left his wife behind, he did not feel the pang of parting. In his words, "Our love could not yet be called free from lust, but it was getting gradually purer. Since my return from Europe ... I had now become her teacher." (130). Gandhi's remarks are worth noting for two reasons. One, he has not yet been able to rid himself of the self-image of being "a lustful husband." Two, he thought that the only way he could be a "lust-free" husband was by becoming his "wife's teacher." In the first statement one can clearly mark his deep-rooted aversion for sex, which he saw as detrimental to a husband-wife relationship. In the second statement we see how Gandhi conceives of a husband's role as that of being his wife's "teacher," and not the other way around yet. We need to keep track of Gandhi's continually evolving views of a marital relationship in order to understand the full impact of the events to come.

En Route to South Africa

Full of zest to try his luck in South Africa, Gandhi set forth on the steamer *Safari* in April 1893. No berth was available on the boat, but the sea captain allowed Gandhi to share his own cabin. Although Gandhi enjoyed his voyage, his mind was preoccupied with what was awaiting him on that mysterious, dark continent of Africa, which he would later describe as "that God-forsaken country where I found my God."

En route to Durban, Natal, Gandhi's steamer stopped at several ports—Lamu, Mombasa, and Zanzibar. As the ships were to be changed at Zanzibar, Gandhi spent a week there with other passengers. Eager as ever to see new places, the twenty-three-year-old barrister accompanied the Captain and another Englishman on an outing. Looking back at the incident, Gandhi wrote in his autobiography, "I had not the least notion of what the outing meant, and little did the Captain know what an ignoramus I was in such matters" (132). As it turned out, the so-called outing was a trip to a seaport brothel in which each person was taken to a room. Gandhi said that although he entered the assigned room, he "simply stood there dumb with shame." Although deeply ashamed of himself for not having "the courage to refuse to go," Gandhi also thanked God that "the sight of the woman had not moved him in the least." He also pondered how "many a youth, innocent at first, must have been drawn into sin by a false sense of shame. ... The incident increased my faith in God and taught me ... to cast off false sense of shame" (ibid., 133).[2]

Focusing on some of the landmark events, decisions, and actions of Gandhi during his first three years in South Africa, my aim is to examine Gandhi's self-ruminations, his dilemmas, and his painfully arrived-at positions that mark a distinctly different, new Stage 4 Individuative-Reflective Faith, to be interpreted later. For now we shall witness the process by which the once-inhibited young Gandhi finally broke out of his cocoon of shyness to assume a new identity as a self-authorized Indian attorney as well as a bold, moral, and political Indian leader who made history. As Martin Green (1993; 118) put it, "During this period of his life Gandhi changes remarkably, and becomes a leader and a man of power. ... He begins to design and implement the personality we know."

ARRIVAL IN NATAL

In the first week of his arrival, Gandhi explored Durban with his employer, Dada Abdulla. One of his first visits was to the Durban court proceedings where the Magistrate, irritated by Gandhi's huge Indian turban, asked him to remove the hat. Refusing to do so, Gandhi just walked out. Following the incident, he penned a letter of protest to the press about his right to wear his national headgear, which he said was a mark of both his national and cultural identity. The issue was publicized in the Natal newspapers, which described Gandhi as an "unwelcome visitor" from India; this was the first instance of his receiving negative publicity in South Africa, which would only get bolder and more venomous in the years ahead. During that first week in Durban, Gandhi noticed the Europeans' resentful yet condescending attitude toward the rich Indian Muslim merchants (called "Arabs") in contrast to their openly scornful attitude to the poor, indentured Indian workers, called "coolies."[3] Gandhi, the shrewd *Bania* and lawyer, could not help noticing the internal divisions, economic disparities, and confusion of identity among the local Muslims, Hindus, Parsees, colonial-born Indian Christians, and other members of the South African Indian community. Most disturbing to him, however, was the total apathy of his fellow Indians toward their own social, economic, political, and human rights, as well as their future in South Africa.

Sheth Abdulla thought of sending Gandhi to Pretoria as his legal representative for their pending lawsuit. This being a financial suit involving accurate bookkeeping of credits and debits, Gandhi felt it was "all Greek and Latin" to him. He had never learned bookkeeping in India or in England, but once he found out his ignorance in these areas, he diligently studied its intricacies from books and from Sheth Abdulla himself, who was a walking-talking encyclopedia of practical business knowledge. Now feeling confident and well-informed, the Indian barrister left for Pretoria, first class via train.

SATYAGRAHA IN THE MAKING

Despite his first-class ticket and proper European attire, the "Coolie Barrister" Gandhi was ordered by the train conductor to vacate his seat and move back to the van compartment. Gandhi refused to get out voluntarily and insisted on his right to travel first-class. Not accustomed to such resistance from a "coolie," no matter how distinguished looking, the conductor threw Gandhi out, baggage and all, on a chilly wintry night at the Maritzburg station.

Like an electric current, the shock of humiliation jolted Gandhi's mind and body. Multiple memories of past insults from authority figures flooded Gandhi's mind and he felt frozen—not by cold or fear alone, but by his helplessness in this "God-forsaken land." After reacting to the incident in his characteristic "eternal negative" style, Gandhi pondered:

> I began to think of my duty. Should I fight for my rights or go back to
> India, or should I go on to Pretoria without minding the insults, and

return to India after finishing the case? It would be cowardice to run
back to India without fulfilling my obligation. The hardship to which
I was subjected was superficial—only a symptom of the deep disease of
colour prejudice. I should try, if possible, to root out the disease and suffer hardships in the process. (*Autobiography*, 141)

In the last two sentences of the quote above, we can hear the distant
rumblings of *satyagraha* in the making; the seed idea of nonviolent resistance to racial injustice and voluntary suffering was sown in that historical
moment in Gandhi's mind.

Contrary to what is widely believed and powerfully portrayed in Sir
Richard Attenborough's motion picture *Gandhi*, this was not Gandhi's first
or last experience of racial discrimination in South Africa. As we know, in
the very first week of his arrival in Durban, he had been ordered by the
High Court judge to remove his Kathiawari turban, for which he got his
first negative publicity in the press. The Maritzburg incident, however, was
a far more vehement, brutal affront, not only on his person but also on his
dignity in a foreign land. Of course it is undeniable that this particular
occurrence had all the drama going for it—Gandhi's forced expulsion from
the train, the strange concomitance of time and place, and the victimization of a naïve young Indian attorney, all of which are overplayed by most
biographers and the media. This kind of overt dramatization, however,
misleads the largely Western audiences into thinking that Maritzburg was
a magic wand that metamorphosed the shy Indian attorney overnight into
the moral-political leader of world significance. They gasp in awe at the
genius of Gandhi but have no clue as to why he rebelled the way he did;
nor can they appreciate the developmental significance of the event (other
than political) in terms of Gandhi's evolving identity and faith.

From the faith developmental perspective, Gandhi's agonizing dilemmas, his internal upheaval, and the connection of this with similar prior
events of humiliation need to be emphasized, since they cumulatively triggered his rebellion. Maritzburg was a cross station between the life Gandhi
left behind and the life he was now to design for himself. Gandhi now
assumed a new identity not only of a political leader but also of a moral
spokesman of his community.

The question still seems to puzzle most Western audiences all over the
world—how did such a shy Indian newcomer like Gandhi gather so much
courage to fight the apartheid in South Africa? The answer lay in Gandhi's
shrewd assessment of both his educational qualifications and his moral
capabilities. Although a virtual stranger in the country, Gandhi knew that

no one at the moment was as legally qualified as he to be able to fight the apartheid system. He also knew from meeting with some of the Muslim merchants in the first week of his arrival that most of them were apathetic to the whole racial situation as long as they made money. Gandhi felt they lacked not only the knowledge but also the moral courage to fight and suffer the consequences. This is where, he thought, he could help because he was most qualified—legally as well as morally—to lead them into some kind of nonviolent rebellion (the exact ideology or the strategy of nonviolent resistance is not yet formed). "There is every reason to believe," said Erikson (1969, 166), that "the central identity which here found its historical time and place was the conviction that among the Indians in South Africa he was the only person equipped by fate to reform a situation which under no conditions could be tolerated." As Green mentioned (1993, 123), Gandhi wrote a letter to Dadabhai Naoroji[4] in 1894: "I am the only available person who can handle the question. . . . (even though) I am yet inexperienced and young and … quite liable to make mistakes." This was no arrogance, only an acknowledgement of Gandhi's eligibility and availability.

But wherefrom came the strength to resist the world's most notorious racial regime? The strength came from within him, from Gandhi's lifelong yearning for truth, which translated into a demand for political justice and assertion of human dignity. In that dark, cold, forlorn waiting room at Maritzburg, Gandhi saw the Light. He received a call of his conscience, which he called "the still small voice within me;" it counseled him to go after Truth, come what may in the days ahead. (R. K. Prabhu and Rao, 1946, 11)

More Harassment on the Way to Pretoria

Gandhi had immediately wired the general manager of the railway complaining about his ill treatment and inconvenience. Despite the manager's instruction to the station master to see that Gandhi reached his destination safely, he still had in store more racial harassment, even direct, physical assaults. During his stagecoach ride between Charlestown and Johannesburg, Gandhi's ears were boxed; he was kicked, cursed, and badly beaten by the coach driver. Again Gandhi wrote a letter of protest to the coach company, but to no avail. Next time, again at Germiston station, despite his first-class ticket, he was ordered to move back to the third-class compartment. This time, luckily for Gandhi, the only English passenger in the same compartment intervened and stopped his harassment. The racism only worsened in Pretoria, the capital of the Transvaal, where Gandhi could find boarding only in Johnston's Family Hotel owned by an American black man. Even here, he had to dine by himself at first, but later the owner apologized and invited Gandhi to join the others in the common dining room. When Gandhi described his hardships later to several Muslim Indian merchants, Sheth Abdul Gani said, "This country is not for men like you," meaning they did not mind putting up with such harassments as long as they made money. Gandhi was appalled, even pained, by the Indian traders' indifference and ignorance about their own human and legal rights in South Africa. As Gandhi wrote in his auto-biography, after making a painstaking study of the hard conditions of the Indian settlers, he realized that "South Africa was no country for a self-respecting Indian" (1948, 164). His mind was more and more occu-pied now with the question as to how he could help solve the Indian problem.

First Meeting with the Indians in Pretoria

Gandhi had to spend some time in Pretoria prior to his involvement in the legal case, so he used it in gathering more information regarding both the case and the Indian situation in the Transvaal. Although he mentioned calling "all the Indians," according to Maureen Swan (1985), they largely consisted of the business community of Muslims, a few Hindu and Parsee secretaries and clerks, and only a sprinkling of colonial-born Christian Indians. There was hardly even one indentured Indian laborer in that audience.

This was Gandhi's maiden speech in South Africa; with it he launched his public career as a dynamic, moral, and political leader of the Indian community. The way he identified himself as one of them, and the utmost sincerity with which he told the bitter truth about them and about their problem of "image" among the South African whites, set the tone of Gandhi's future theme and style of leadership. The young Indian attorney sounded like a "miniature replica" of the future pedagogical Mahatma, who insisted on the importance of sanitary habits, the intercommunity unity, and truthfulness in all walks of life including business. This was the first public platform on which Gandhi stressed the need for his people to earn their internal self-liberation before they strove for their external social, economic, or political freedom. This was the end of his shy self; this was the birth of a charismatic leader and his moral-political ideology.

First Legal Case

During his first year in Pretoria he "acquired a true knowledge of legal practice," wrote Gandhi in his autobiography. He added that, "here I also gained confidence that I should not after all fail as a lawyer. It was likewise here that I learnt the secret of success as a lawyer" (1948, 165).

Gandhi acted here only as an assistant to the major legal counselor and attorney for Dada Abdulla's firm in Durban. They had a long-standing civil suit claim for more than 40,000 pounds against another rival Muslim firm in Pretoria that belonged to Sheth Abdulla's relative, Tyeb Sheth. After having initial difficulties, Gandhi had fully investigated the case and was prepared to answer any question. Not until he presented the case in the court, however, did Gandhi see the truth behind the late Mr. Pincutt's advice that "facts were three-fourths of the law." As he put it, "I realized the paramount importance of facts. Facts mean truth; once we adhere to truth, the law comes to our aid naturally" (ibid., 167). These first lessons also proved to be lasting lessons. "Fact-finding" and "faithfulness to facts" meant following truth, and truth as justice became Gandhi's trademark in all his future battles—whether with the apartheid in South Africa, with the British in India, with his people, or even with himself.

Gandhi also realized the importance of arbitration to bring two warring parties together in hopes of a private settlement out of court. The key was to depend on facts, that is, truth, and to appeal to the better side of the adversary's heart. With this approach, Gandhi won his first legal case, which made both parties happy and part as friends. Gandhi remarked, "My joy was boundless. I had learnt the true practice of law. ... I lost nothing thereby—not even money, certainly not my soul" (ibid., 168). At this point the pragmatic *Bania*, the shrewd lawyer, and the truth-seeker all came together in Gandhi, giving us a glimpse of the multifaceted Mahatma-to-be.

Christian Contacts

During the trial in Pretoria, Gandhi met the prosecuting attorney Mr. A. W. Baker, a devout Christian who introduced Gandhi to his many other Christians friends, such as Mr. Coates, Miss Harris, Miss Gab, and the Walton family in Durban. With Mr. Baker, Gandhi attended prayer meetings at his church and became closer to Mr. Coates, who was a "frank-hearted staunch Quaker." Although Coates did not directly try to convert Gandhi to Christianity, he gave Gandhi many books to read.[5] Gandhi mentioned in *Autobiography* that although he read them with an open mind, the argument that "Jesus was the only incarnation of God and the Mediator between God and man," turned him cold; he could also not accept the Christian claim of exclusivity (170).

Gandhi mentioned an incident in which Mr. Coates, thinking of Gandhi's Vaishnava necklace of Tulasi beads to be "a superstition," offered to break it. Gandhi explained that the necklace had no mysterious significance, but since it was a sacred gift from his mother, it became a symbol of her love for him and her trust that wearing it would be conducive to her son's welfare. If the necklace wore out or broke of its own accord, he would not get a new one, said Gandhi. He could not, however, break it himself, nor would he allow anyone else to do so. Although their friendship was not affected by this confrontation, Coates continued to try to convince Gandhi that salvation was impossible without Christianity. Coates introduced Gandhi to a member of the Plymouth Brethren sect, who zealously tried to deliver Gandhi "from the abyss of ignorance"; he argued that "sin we must, and Jesus was the only sinless Son of God, who can save us all through his suffering and atoning for our sins." Gandhi retorted, "I do not seek redemption from the consequences of my sin. I seek to be redeemed from sin itself, or rather from the very thought of sin" (ibid., 156).

Gandhi noted this as a period of his religious ferment. He was now hungry for more and more books on religion. He wanted not only to read but also to compare and reflect over what he read; he had many baffling questions that needed satisfactory answers. Thinking of his friend, philosopher, and guide, Raychandbhai, who was well-versed in all world religions, Gandhi initiated a correspondence with the learned man.

Gandhi and Raychandbhai Correspondence

When Gandhi had first met Raychandbhai in Bombay after coming home from London, he had no serious interest in raising religious questions or discussions with him. This time, however, he had a burning passion for such queries because of reading religious books and coming into deeper contact with Christians. So, Gandhi wrote to Raychandbhai and asked him twenty-seven questions among which the major four were: (1) Were the *Vedas* the "the only inspired word of God"? (2) Was the exclusivity claim of Christianity correct? (3) What was the meaning of *moksha* and how can it be attained? (4) "Which was the true religion"—which could he accept and reject as false?[6]

First, Raychandbhai explained to Gandhi that "the antiquity of the *Vedas* cannot be denied. Before the Buddha and Mahavir were the Vedas. But the antiquity does not mean perfection. Later revelations may possibly be more perfect." He thus ruled out the *Vedas'* claim of being "the only inspired word of God."

Second, Raychandbhai challenged Christianity's claim of exclusivity, that it was the only religion that contained "truth" or that it was "the greatest of all religions." He endorsed Gandhi's views that Jesus was "a martyr, an embodiment of sacrifice, and a divine teacher," but he rejected that Jesus was "the only incarnate son of God" (1948, 170).

Third, Raychandbhai construed *moksha* as "one's complete deliverance from the passions of hatred and attachment and the resulting ignorance." His interpretation differed from the traditional Hindu understanding of *moksha* as freedom from the ceaseless cycle of births and deaths. Gandhi's later interpretation of the *Bhagavad Gita* as "*Anasakti-yoga*" or "the Science of Detachment" could be partly attributed to Raychandbhai's views regarding *moksha*.

Fourth, and the most significant one in relation to Fowler's Theory of Stages of Faith, are Raychandbhai's views on what is "true religion":

> Religion is not an "ism". It is not merely intellectual knowledge of or belief in any set of doctrines. It is an innate attribute of the soul. It is that which enables us to define our duties in life as a human being, and establish correct relationship with our fellows. ... It is the common heritage of all mankind.[7]

The Impact of Tolstoy

Toward the end of his first year in Pretoria (1894) Gandhi read Tolstoy's *The Kingdom of God is within You* for the first time (until now he had only known his ideas through his author friends in London). As he acknowledged in his autobiography, "the book overwhelmed me, and left an abiding impression on me." So deeply did the book move him that he added, "before the independent thinking, profound morality, and the truthfulness of this book, all the books ... seemed to pale into insignificance" (172).

Gandhi was inspired by Tolstoy's "anti-imperialistic approach" in his book, which highlighted the principles of "the infinite possibilities of universal love, inward perfection, and truth." What Gandhi believed to be true in his heart, Tolstoy expressed powerfully; this was the birth of

Gandhi's ideology of nonviolence and truth, which resonated with his own Jain ideals of *ahimsa* and the Hindu concepts of *truth* and the *unity of all life*. As Margaret Chatterjee suggested (1983), Gandhi was enthralled by "Tolstoy's vision of a transformed community built upon a transformed inner life." As was characteristic of Gandhi, once he was fired up by the truth of an idea or inspired by a book, he would not rest until he figured out how to put it into practice. As we shall see later, Gandhi would initiate correspondence with Tolstoy in 1910 and would found one of his two ashrams in South Africa in Tolstoy's name.

Tolstoy and Gandhi shared a rare affinity of spirit and a common vision. "The similarity bordering almost on family likeness in the mental and spiritual structure was so striking," said Kalidas Nag, "that both Tolstoy and Gandhi seemed to be cast in the same mould" (1950, vi). As Gandhi acknowledged in his autobiography, Tolstoy was one of the "three moderns who left a deep impress" on his life by his book *The Kingdom of God is within You* (114).

More Religious Readings

Among other spiritually nourishing books that Gandhi read at this time were *The Perfect Way* by Edward Maitland and Anna Kingsford, and Maitland's *The Interpretation of the Bible*. Gandhi's own views about Christianity were confirmed by Maitland who believed that Christianity failed, not because Christianity was false but because it had been falsified. Gandhi was strongly influenced by Maitland's moral-allegorical interpretation of the Bible, which later shaped his own allegorical interpretation of the *Bhagavad Gita*. Gandhi particularly liked Maitland's esoteric-mystical Christian approach emphasizing inner perfection, self-denial, and asceticism, which strongly endorsed his own Jain principles. Not only did Gandhi read some of the Hindu and Jain classics sent by Rajchandra, including *Panchikaran, Maniratnamala, Mumukshu Prakaran of Yogavasistha*, and Haribhadra Suri's *Shaddarshana Samucchaya*, but also the scriptures of Christianity, Islam, and Zoroastrianism (Parsee faith). This time, however, he made a detailed and deeper comparative study of what he read. He perused once again Arnold's *Light of Asia* (which he had first read in London) and compared the life of Jesus with that of Buddha. Upon the second reading, he was much more moved by the "compassion of Buddha" that extended to "all living beings," of which he said, "One fails to notice this love ... in the life of Jesus" (ibid., 160). Upon Raychandbhai's recommendation, Gandhi also read more books, such as Narmadashankar's *Dharma Vichar*, Max Muller's *India—What Can It Teach Us?*, and various *Upanishads*. He compared Washington Irving's *Life of Mohamet and His Successors* with Carlyle's "panegyric on the prophet" and *The Sayings of Zarathustra*. Another book by Tolstoy, *The Gospel in Brief, What to Do?* also made a profound impression on him.

Farewell South Africa, But Not Yet

His one-year legal mission in Pretoria having been accomplished, Gandhi proposed to return home in 1894, but God had planned otherwise. On the eve of his farewell party, Gandhi read a small paragraph in the newspaper with a caption "Indian Franchise." It referred to a bill that proposed to deprive all Indians of their right to elect members of the Natal Legislative Assembly. Gandhi wrote in his autobiography, "If this Bill passes into law, it will be the first nail into our coffin; it will strike at the root of our self-respect" (1948, 174). Everyone pressed Dada Abdulla to detain "Gandhibhai" (*bhai*: brother), who had now become indispensable to them. Yielding to their plea, Gandhi extended his stay for two more years, saying, "God thus laid the foundation of my life in South Africa, and sowed the seed of the fight for national self-respect" (ibid.).

Gandhibhai: The Dynamic Indian Leader in Natal

Between 1894 and 1896, Gandhibhai emerged as a dynamic Indian leader of rare integrity and humanity, and as a powerful spokesman of his community. In 1894 he organized the Natal Indian Congress and was feverishly busy collecting 10,000 signatures to oppose the anti-Indian Franchise Bill. He had now earned the respect and friendship of his own community members, as well as South African Europeans like the Reverend Joseph Doke (Gandhi's first biographer in 1909), Henry Polak, and Hermann Kallenbach—the latter two would later join him in his *satyagraha* from Natal to Transvaal. A huge wave of newspaper publicity spread his fame even outside South Africa to England and India as a champion of the Indians' legal and human rights.

During this period, Gandhi fiercely campaigned for Indian voting, trading, and immigration rights, as well as for better sanitary facilities for Indians living in Natal. Through his restrained yet candidly crafted "Open letters" to the press ("An Appeal to Every Briton in South Africa"), he won the white man's sympathy for the Indian cause. Drafting powerful petitions and appeals (e.g., "The Indian Franchise—An Appeal"), he sent them to the legislative assembly, to the secretary of state for the Colonies, to the British prime minister, to the Indian viceroy, and to other influential Indians such as Dadabhai Naoroji in England. Until 1894, Gandhi was a respected Indian leader among rich and elite Muslim merchants, but toward the end of 1896, he had reached out to the poorest of the poor and to the exploited Indian laborers as well.

Gandhi Meets Balasundaram

Gandhi's desire to serve the downtrodden was first fulfilled when he took the case of Balasundaram, a Tamil Indian indentured slave. As he saw the brutally beaten Balasundaram enter his office with his mouth bleeding, scarf in hand, and crying, Gandhi felt doubly humiliated. First, he was deeply hurt to see this poor man without power being abused by the one in power. Gandhi wrote in his autobiography, "It has always been a mystery to me how men can feel themselves honoured by the humiliation of their fellow beings" (192). Second, Balasundaram's ill treatment reminded him of his own past humiliations in India and in Natal. Identifying deeply with this helpless man, Gandhi wiped his tears, washed his wounds, and sent him to a doctor. He also succeeded in negotiating with his white master for Balasundaram's transfer to another employer.

"The echoes of Balasundaram's case were heard in far off Madras (the man's home in South India) and that there was someone to espouse their cause and publicly work for them gave the indentured labourers a joyful surprise and inspired them with hope," said Gandhi (ibid., 192). From this point on Gandhi began to associate service to the poor with serving God as the *Daridra-Narayana* or God incarnated in the poor.

Gandhi Visits the Trappist Monastery

Beginning in London, Gandhi had associated vegetarianism with a spiritual way of life. He had continued sending his articles to the *Vegetarian* (a Weekly) regularly, and he maintained contact with Edward Maitland and Anna Kingsford in London. It was through them that he came to know about the Trappist missionaries who were strict vegetarians, and in 1895 he visited a Trappist monastery at Mariann Hill near Pine Town, not too far from Durban. The impressions of this self-contained, self-disciplined, and deeply religious settlement remained permanently etched on his mind. The strictly vegetarian brothers and sisters supplied all their needs by their own labor, including farming and grinding grains, hauling water, and chopping wood. They did their own carpentering, shoemaking, and printing; they read, taught, and prayed throughout the day at regular intervals. But the feature that made a lasting impact on Gandhi was the residents' vows of "silence and chastity." This was Gandhi's very first exposure to such a spiritually based settlement, which operated on the principles of self-sufficiency, manual labor, brotherhood, strict vegetarianism, silence, chastity, prayers, and service. Their motto of *Ora et labora* (prayer and work) appealed to Gandhi greatly, and he would later incorporate the same into his own ashrams. Gandhi's first visit to the Trappist monastery received further reinforcement through Ruskin's and Tolstoy's books and ideas about simple living, high thinking, and the dignity of manual labor.

Gandhi the Householder

Although Gandhi was drawn to the spiritual world by making a comparative study of religions, and although he worked for the poor, he had no desire yet to give up his worldly life or attachments. He therefore settled down in his own house at the Grove Beach Villa, one of the prestigious suburbs of Natal. In keeping with his highly respectable position of a well-to-do Indian barrister and community leader, Gandhi lived in style and pomp in a fully furnished house overlooking the sea, with a garden, playground, and more. The point to note here is that even before his family joined him in 1896, he had already established a joint family residence shared by his cook, servants, colleagues, clerks, and friends, including his old childhood chum, Mehtab.

Good-Bye Mehtab

It was in this house, however, that Gandhi was made aware of Mehtab's frequent secret meetings with a prostitute during Gandhi's absence. Another friend warned Gandhi about it, but being of a trusting nature, Gandhi had refused to believe it. Once he caught Mehtab red-handed, however, he ordered him to leave the house instantly. It was when Mehtab refused and became violent that Gandhi decided to call the police. Knowing too well that Gandhi was not a man of empty words or threats, Mehtab finally admitted his wrongdoing, apologized, and begged Gandhi to still let him stay with him. But that was the end of Gandhi's friendship with Mehtab, his "negative identity." In retrospect Gandhi realized how Mehtab had come between him and his wife in the early years of his marriage. Years later, however, Mehtab changed his ways, married, dabbled in Urdu poetry, and even joined Gandhibhai's *satyagrahas*.

For Gandhi, saying good-bye to Mehtab meant saying good-bye not only to his "negative identity" but also to all kinds of fears and intimidations—whether from his caste elders, from the apartheid in South Africa, or from the British in India. He had learned to fight his own inner demons of self-doubts, fears, and dilemmas in order to find his new identity. Instead of one year in South Africa, he had now lived for three full years, during which he had been able to establish a successful and lucrative law practice as well as to earn respect from his community as their only caring and qualified leader. But now it was time to go home. In 1896, Gandhi sailed home to reunite with his family and to propagate the South Indian cause among his countrymen.

GANDHI IN INDIA

The very first project Gandhi undertook upon coming home was to write a detailed, accurate, and graphic account of the grim Indian conditions in South Africa, which came to be known as "The Green Pamphlet" because of its green cover. He finished it in Rajkot, printed 10,000 copies, and sent it to all the papers and leaders in every part of India. A summary of the same, with great exaggeration, was cabled by Reuter to England with graphic pictures of the ill-treated Indians in South Africa. The Natal newspapers further distorted these reports, because of which Gandhi would be attacked six months later on his trip back to Durban.

While in India, Gandhi launched his countrywide journalistic mission seeking the support of newspaper editors in Allahabad, Madras, Poona, Bombay, and Calcutta. They published his stories of the mistreatment of Indians in South Africa to educate the public and to earn their sympathy for their fellow Indians in a foreign land. His other valuable asset was meeting with the then most popular and powerful Indian leaders—Tilak and Gokhale; Gokhale would take the place of his "political guru" and visit him later in South Africa. Gandhi was given "a hero's welcome" upon his visit to Madras, the home of Balasundaram. He was most pleased, however, when he found an opportunity to serve the poor and to nurse the plague victims in Bombay and Rajkot. This was the first time he inspected and cleaned the latrines of the poor (the Untouchables) as well the rich in Bombay. He was more and more convinced that serving the poor and nursing the sick truly satisfied his soul. Gandhi wrote in his Autobiography, "All other pleasures and possessions pale into nothingness before service which is rendered in a spirit of joy" (1948, 215).

GANDHI AND STAGE 4 INDIVIDUATIVE-REFLECTIVE FAITH: AN EVALUATION

To paraphrase what Fowler has described, the transition to Stage 4 usually occurs in the early to mid-twenties, but for some adults, if it comes at all, it can be as late as in a person's thirties or forties. The transition can be precipitated by changes in one's primary relationships (divorce, death, or separation); it can also result from the challenges of moving, changing jobs, or by similar disruptive experiences. Regardless of the reason, this transition to Stage 4 invariably represents "an upheaval in one's life" or "unavoidable tensions." Thus, the transition can be not only painful but also protracted over years.

As we saw in the Chapter 6, Gandhi's experience of leaving home for London at the age of eighteen set off the transition from Stage 3 to Stage 4, which involved intense struggle with his caste elders, uprooting from his native Indian culture, and adjusting to a new culture, people, and lifestyle in England. The process of Gandhi's stage transition,[8] which had just begun prior to his leaving home for England, continued throughout his three years in London and extended even beyond for two more years. For Gandhi, the transitional process proved to be both painful and prolonged. Yet it also prepared him to forge a new identity as a self-confident young adult of Stage 4.

Gandhi's first three years in South Africa provide powerful evidence of all the major characteristics of Stage 4. Gandhi's first phase of coming to South Africa marked a turning point not only in his life and career but also in the forming of his new self-identity, which was inextricably connected to his people's acquisition of identity as a "single community"; Gandhi was wholly responsible for awakening their self-consciousness and their self-esteem. It was through his initiative and moral courage to take a stand, to take the risk as well as the responsibility for it, that others would later be led into nonviolent resistance against apartheid policies. Yet, without any exaggeration, Gandhi found his own identity while helping others to find their own. Gandhi needed them as much as they needed him. He, however, took the first step. It was that first crucial step that was to change his own destiny and in that process, the destiny of his countrymen in South Africa.

The Maritzburg incident provides a classic example of Stage 4 in three ways. First, in faith terminology, Gandhi displayed "a strong executive ego" by taking the reins of action into his own hands on that fateful night. By raising his head against the most formidable foe of apartheid in a foreign land, he showed not only extraordinary courage but also a capacity to take both risk and responsibility for his actions. Gandhi's willful act of defiance was to bring serious political repercussions that would endanger his life and the lives of other Indians as well. He decided to take the risk come what may, but not without critical reflection.

This brings us to the second point that his resistance to external power was not bereft of inner resistance; he went through an acute inner struggle preceding the action. This very important point is missed, undermined, or completely bypassed by the well-known movie, *Gandhi*, and by most of his biographers. Gandhi's nonviolent resistance at Maritzburg was neither so sudden nor as dramatic as shown on the screen. Gandhi, like Hamlet, faced a big dilemma: "Should he quit and go home" or "Should he stay on and fight" the ten-headed Ravana[9] of racism? His mind was raging a battle between the "internalized voices" of the "they" and the still small voice of his conscience. What would "they" say if he returned home without accomplishing anything? Would "they" not call him a coward? Arguing against the "they," his inner voice raised a question: What was his *dharma*, his moral duty? Was it not to stick to truth, to fight for justice for himself and for his people? These deliberations, together with the painful memories of his insults and humiliations by authority figures in the past, triggered a reaction that only seemed to be sudden but in reality was a well-reflected decision to stay and fight. This is the second strong example of Stage 4 "objectification and critical choosing of one's beliefs, values, commitments and actions."

Third, on that lonely, freezing night at Maritzburg, Gandhi first conceived the idea of nonviolent resistance. Although his "explicit ideology" or philosophy of nonviolent resistance was still far away, the germ idea that "I should try, if possible, to root out the disease and suffer hardships in the process," has been planted in his mind at that crucial moment in history. The full-fledged strategy of *satyagraha* will follow later, but the seed of ideology is sown for sure.

Besides Maritzburg there are several other examples of the "birth of ideology," which testify to Gandhi's distinct self-awareness of his moral mission in South Africa. In Gandhi's first meeting with his fellow Indians in Pretoria, he was deeply convinced that "he and he alone" could help mend or reform a situation as no one else could. This deeply felt yet reasoned conviction of his singular role in that time and place unleashed the powers of his tongue; he now became an uninhibited speaker. Gandhi became free of his own inner demons, doubts, and diffidence. He became a self-awakened man who made others think and who would later inspire them to fight for their human and legal rights. As Erikson observed (1969, 166), Gandhi knew he was "the only person equipped by fate" to guide and lead, to help them out of their duress and distress. In many ways he was indispensable to them because of his superior education, professional status, and command over the English language, both written and spoken.

His first public speech thus manifested all the key features of Stage 4—an "executive ego" at work, and the "critical distancing" that made his people think beyond their short-term goal of moneymaking and into their long-term future in South Africa. Gandhi's maiden speech also marked the birth of his ideology of insistence on truthfulness, cleanliness, internal unity, and duties before rights. On the Pretoria platform was born a leader—a leader who, lighting his own lamp of self-knowledge, lit others' lamps as well. And vice versa—in giving them voice, he found his own voice.

Similarly, Gandhi's first legal victory was representative of his future philosophy of a practice based on telling the truth, appealing to the better side of the adversary, and bringing the two warring parties together as friends through arbitration, mutual goodwill, and trust. This is another illustration of the formation of his explicit moral ideology based on truth both in his public work as well as his profession.

Fowler has conceded "Stage 4's ascendant strength" to be "its capacity for critical reflection on identity (self) and outlook (ideology)." There cannot be more powerful evidence of both than in Gandhi's firm refusal to be converted to Christianity, despite his well-meaning friends' covert and overt efforts to do so. He resisted his Christian friends not out of his blind adherence to his own tradition, nor because he was committed to what Fowler called his "previous assumptive value system." As shown throughout this chapter, Gandhi remained open to listen to his Quaker and Christian friends and to attend their prayer sessions, churches, and meetings; he also carefully read and reflected over the meanings of the Bible and other books to compare and contrast one with the other.

The biggest proof of the Stage 4 critical distancing and intellectual questioning, however, was found in Gandhi's long-distance correspondence with Raychandbhai. The level of his doubts and in-depth religious queries to this Jain scholar in India, and his further renewed contact with Edward Maitland, Anna Kingsford, and Tolstoy, reveal young Gandhi's intellectual reasoning and critical frame of mind of a Stage 4 person. Even after the discussions and readings, he accepted only those concepts and ideals that deep down "confirmed what he was coming to feel" as Geoffrey Ashe put it (1968, 65). As in a genuine Stage 4, he critically weighed their comparative merits and demerits and did not depend on others' views nor succumb to others' pressures.

The only deviation I find in Gandhi's Stage 4 faith development is in his refusing to break the Tulsi necklace upon his friend Coates' insistence. As discussed before, that necklace was a symbol to him of his mother's love and trust and faith, and he did not believe in breaking it—not for superstitious reasons as much as for what it stood. In so doing, Gandhi broke the norm of Stage 4, which is called "a demythologizing stage." As we will see later, Gandhi would never break the sacred symbols or images of worship, but only breathe new meaning into them or reinterpret traditions. He was not a "demythologizer" like his reformist predecessors—Raja Ram Mohan Roy or Dayanand Saraswati, but rather was a "Critical traditionalist" like Swami Vivekananda, who revived the old tradition by changing it from the inside and by introducing fresh ideas from the outside.

If the ascendant strengths of Stage 4 are the formation of one's self-authorized identity or "an executive ego," "critical distancing, questioning and reflection," and the emergence of "explicit ideology," Gandhi proved to be an eloquent exponent as well as exemplar of all these major strengths. To sum up the chapter with Judith M. Brown's insightful observations:

> More deeply, South Africa made Gandhi "an outsider" to the Indian environment in which he was to work—for all that he came to be the symbol of India and its campaign for political freedom ... Gandhi as the critical outsider, [was] a man on the margin of different worlds, as a potentially creative figure, precisely because he was not trapped in the assumptions and expectations of those with whom he worked. (1996, 22–23)

8

A Leader in South Africa, Phase II

Having now accomplished his mission of educating the public about the Indian situation in South Africa, and having also served the poor and the afflicted, Gandhi set sail again for South Africa in November 1896 with his family. During his second phase in South Africa, Gandhi reaches the pinnacle of his professional practice, prosperity, and prestige, and earns respect as a leader to reckon with among both Indians and Europeans of Natal and Transvaal. From the faith developmental perspective, Gandhi will assume all the strength, power, and authority of the Stage 4 "executive ego" at its full bloom; he will fight nonviolently not only for his own human rights and dignity but also for the human and legal rights of his people. As Gandhi's legal practice increases, so also will the range and scale of his sympathies; he will become the beloved leader and spokesman of both the rich Indian Muslim merchants and the poor indentured laborers.

In the latter part of this time frame, Gandhi was still hovering between the material and spiritual poles, although soon thereafter begins the process of Gandhi's gradual transition from a primarily "self-oriented," Stage 4 Individuative-Reflective Faith to the "other-oriented" Stage 5 Conjunctive Faith.

GANDHI TO SOUTH AFRICA WITH HIS FAMILY

So, this time Gandhi was not alone on his sea voyage to South Africa in December 1896. With him aboard the S.S. *Courland* ship were his family members—his beautiful wife, Kasturbai (twenty-six), their two sons Harilal and Manilal (nine and five years of age, respectively), and Gokuldas, the son of Gandhi's widowed sister.

Gandhi, as usual, loved to dress in style (as in his London dandy days); he wore the then fashionable Indian outfit of a black, Parsee long coat, trousers, and hat. Kasturbai, too was dressed fashionably in her embroidered silk saree worn Parsee-style. The Gandhi family was all dressed up but had no notion of what was awaiting them on board or across the sea in Durban.

Storm at Sea

"As though to warn us of the coming big storm on the land, a terrible gale overtook us, whilst we were only four days from Natal," wrote Gandhi in his autobiography (1948, 230). The storm was so violent and prolonged that everyone aboard—Hindus, Muslims, Parsees, and Christians—became alarmed and began to pray earnestly. It was "a solemn scene," said Gandhi, because all passengers forgot their differences and "became one in face of the common danger." Their prayers were answered, and after twenty-four agonizing hours, the storm subsided, the skies cleared, and the sun shined.

The moment the danger disappeared, so did the name of God from everyone's lips. This sad irony of human nature warranted a comment from Gandhi, "eating and drinking, singing and merry-making again became the order of the day. The fear of death was gone, and the momentary mood of earnest prayer gave place to Maya" [1] (ibid., 231). After eighteen days, the ship landed at the Durban port on the 18th of December. On the same day, another ship *Naderi* also arrived from Bombay with eight hundred passengers. Since Bombay was just then recovering from the plague epidemic, the passengers were rumored to have carried over plague germs with them. Therefore, both ships were quarantined for three weeks. The real reason to keep them from disembarking, however, was the government's bias against all Indians, and "a specific hostility towards Indian merchants," said Maureen Swan.[2] Another reason they kept the passengers from disembarking was the gathering of a huge, white mob at the shore; the target of the mob's fury was Gandhi, who, they were made to believe, was the chief cause of all the Indian trouble.

Mob Attack in Durban

The mood of the white mob was murderous; hooting and cursing, they were ready to attack Gandhi as soon as he disembarked from the ship. Their fury was aroused for two reasons. First, they had read exaggerated

Reuter reports of Gandhi's "Green Pamphlet," which allegedly painted a dark picture of South African whites and their inhuman treatment of the Indian population. Second, they accused Gandhi of purposely bringing with him two shiploads of unwanted "free Indians" (independent traders) who would take away jobs from white businessmen. Gandhi now knew that he was at the center of the South African hostility against Indians in general. Because it was dangerous for Gandhi and his family to disembark in full view of the mob, Dada Abdulla's white attorney advised that Gandhi's family be secretly removed to safety to Parsi Rustomji's house (a friend of Gandhi), but only after the crowds had dispersed, and under police protection, should Gandhi disembark. Gandhi decided to act, however, against the latter piece of advice; he went ahead and descended from the ship while the mob was still there. The mobsters recognized Gandhi, and separating him from the officer, they kicked, punched, pushed, and brutally beat him up. Gandhi would not have been saved but for the accidental arrival of Mrs. Alexander, the wife of the police superintendent, who stood there with her parasol shielding Gandhi from his attackers until more help arrived. Police Superintendent Mr. Alexander subsequently rushed to the scene, and while he tactfully entertained the crowd by singing along with them, "Hang old Gandhi, on the sour apple tree," Gandhi was secretly transferred to Rustomji's house and given medical treatment. Later, upon further official investigation, both charges against Gandhi—of conspiring to bring two shiploads of Indians and of defaming the whites—were dismissed. Gandhi was not only proved innocent, but he actually earned his first positive publicity in the South African press.

Recalling the incident later, Gandhi wrote in his autobiography, "The press declared me to be innocent and condemned the mob. Thus the lynching ultimately proved to be a blessing for me," as it also "enhanced the prestige of the Indian community in South Africa and made my work easier" (241). From the faith developmental perspective, Gandhi's response to this assault was qualitatively different from his response to his previous attacks when he had first arrived in South Africa. Unlike before, this time he had "a deep conviction" that "the truth will triumph in the end and his assailants will be sorry for their conduct." Gandhi decided not to prosecute his assailants, because according to him, the Natal government misled them into believing the Reuter reports, which were false, distorted, and exaggerated. Gandhi's kind gesture of forgiveness was not only his own moral victory but also that of Indians and their image. By rising above his attackers, Gandhi proved victorious on many counts. First, he testified by showing his written speeches that he had said nothing in India that he had not already said before in South Africa, and in stronger language. Second, he shamed and blamed the Natal government for circulating such false reports about him and the Indians. Third, this attack on him in broad daylight exposed to the world "who was whom"—that the whites were the culprits, and the Indians the victims. Fourth, the attack brought to the forefront the long-neglected Indian grievances and justified their cause in the public eye. Fifth, Gandhi's self-restraint and forgiveness earned him and the Indians the goodwill, respect, and friendship of many South African whites.

INTENSE INVOLVEMENT IN INDIAN COMMUNITY SERVICE

Between 1897 and 1899 Gandhi became intensely involved in fighting the Natal Assembly and the Colonial government concerning two anti-Indian legislative bills. The Dealers' Licenses Bill severely curtailed all Indian commercial activity, and the Immigration Restriction Bill required all immigrants to possess twenty five pounds and a written knowledge of English. Although the language was couched in both the bills, Indian merchants were the most obvious targets. Gandhi began penning letter after letter to major newspapers in Natal and India; he also sent petition after petition to the colonial secretary, the natal governor, the British prime Minister, and the British viceroy in India. Because of his razor-sharp logic, powerful yet restrained language, and unvarnished truth, Gandhi's letters made a strong impact both on editors and on readers, winning their sympathy and support for the Indian cause. Not only that, but because Gandhi stayed away from any exaggeration and remained true to facts, the Indian grievances received serious political hearing in the liberal British parliament. At this time Gandhi made some of his most loyal friends among Europeans, both Christians and Jews.[3] His legal practice also flourished, now covering an entire Indian community. Moreover, he managed his administrative responsibilities for the Natal Indian Congress, including fundraising, recruiting new members, and handling finances, which helped him a great deal later in India.

A "CRUELLY KIND HUSBAND"

As mentioned earlier, Gandhi had brought with him his wife, Kasturbai, and his family this time to South Africa. Although not mentioned in his autobiography, his wife was expecting their third child, due in May 1897. Nor did Gandhi say anything about her serious gynecological condition at that time, or about her reaction to that traumatic event on the very first day of her arrival in Durban.

Strangely, however, Gandhi did write in detail about one major domestic quarrel (among several others) between himself and his pregnant wife in 1897 at the Beach Grove villa house in Durban. As there was no running water in the house, each room was provided with a bedpan that required cleaning every morning. All members of the Gandhi household, including the residential guests, knew about this and usually did their own cleaning. Somehow, a newly arrived Christian clerk who was a *Panchama* (an Untouchable converted to Christianity) was either not informed or exempted from this duty. In India, this kind of latrine cleaning is assigned to the Untouchables (the lowest caste), and no higher-caste Hindu would ever imagine doing it for himself or for the family; the chance would be one in a million that someone would ever clean the human waste of an outsider, who himself is suspected to be an Untouchable. Kasturbai, being an orthodox Hindu woman, could not bear the idea that she or her husband would ever volunteer to do such work, especially if it involved cleaning the bedpan used by a *Panchama*. Because Gandhi himself cleaned the bedpans with pleasure, he insisted that his wife must do the same. Kasturbai grudgingly complied, but that was not enough for Gandhi; he demanded that she must do the work cheerfully and not resentfully. At this point Kasturbai burst into tears, and Gandhi became enraged. As he tried to push her out of the house, she begged him to compose himself by reminding him of "who he was" (in view of both his self-ideal and social image); she resisted him with all her moral might, love, and endurance. Her patient suffering and her gentle, moral appeals to Gandhi's "good self" or "noble self" made a deep, lasting impact on him. Gandhi later realized that in spite of being a loving and caring husband, he had caused his wife frequent pain by compelling her to do things against her will and beliefs. That is why he called himself a "cruelly kind husband." (Autobiography, 339)

This domestic explosion proved to be profoundly meaningful to Gandhi; he later admitted that his wife, by her patience, endurance, and gentle approach, taught him the power of truth and nonviolent resistance to tyranny. Gandhi later developed this power into his philosophy and technique of *satyagraha*. In his autobiography, he confessed that his "wife, with her matchless powers of endurance, has always been the victor" (1948, 339).

Although Gandhi publicly gave credit to his wife, in many matters of principle, he overruled her protests. As we shall see later, he would prevail over her to return some of the most precious gifts given to them on the eve of their departure from South Africa. Even later, in India, he would use his veto against his wife's refusal to let an Untouchable family live with them in the Sabarmati Ashram in Ahmedabad. Kasturbai, like most traditional Hindu women of her time, bent her will to that of her husband's; she had no choice but to acquiesce in the end. Later, however, she not only understood her husband's selfless intents and ideals of all-inclusive humanity but also joined him in his social-educational projects for women and children; she also led women's *satyagrahas* in South Africa and in India. Though not flawless, Gandhi was a loving and loyal husband who later awakened and admitted his follies; he blamed himself for most of their earlier marital disharmony. Having awakened, he deeply appreciated his wife's superior power of moral endurance, self-sacrifice, and contributions to his life.

GANDHI AS A FATHER

Gandhi saw himself as a fully involved father who loved and cared for his sons from the moment of their birth through the early formative years of their childhood. He was also proud of the fact that he self-delivered two more sons in South Africa—Ramdas, his third son (1897), and Devadas, his youngest son (1900). Not only did he deliver his boys with little outside help, he also took personal, tender care of both the mother and the infants at the time of delivery and thereafter. Looking back with great satisfaction, Gandhi wrote in his autobiography, "my children would not have enjoyed the general good health that they do today, had I not studied the subject and turned my knowledge to account" (1948, 251). His views regarding the importance of the first five years in a child's learning and growth sound amazingly contemporary as he said, "We labour under a sort of superstition that the child has nothing to learn during the first five years of its life. On the contrary the fact is that the child never learns in after life what it does in its first five years" (ibid.). Not only were the first five years important in a child's life for his or her learning and growth, but according to Gandhi:

> The education of the child begins at conception. The physical and mental states of the parents at the moment of conception are reproduced in the baby. Then during the period of pregnancy it continues to be affected by the mother's moods, desires and temperament, as also by her ways of life. After birth the child imitates the parents, and for a considerable number of years entirely depends on them for its growth." (Ibid.)

Those views were deeply ingrained in his cultural beliefs, which were supported by the ancient Indian health science of *Ayurveda*. Gandhi, as a caring and conscientious father, also believed in educating his children at home.

Formal Education of Children

Gandhi's ideas concerning his children's formal education remain controversial. He could have sent his young children (ages ranging from five to nine) to the schools for European children in South Africa, where they would have been accepted as a personal favor to him. However, Gandhi said that he would never want to send his children to such exclusive schools where other Indian children were denied admission. Gandhi also disapproved of schools run by the Christian Missionaries because of their Western bias and because they taught only in English or at the most in inadequate Tamil or Hindi. He decided, therefore, to teach his children Gujarati at home and to hire an English governess (paying seven pounds a month), but these plans fizzled out after Gandhi became more and more involved in community service. Another alternative was to send his boys to schools in India, but that was the least acceptable choice to Gandhi as he firmly believed that "young children should never be separated from their parents." Thus Gandhi ended up teaching his children at home, but only intermittently.

Gandhi knew that out of all his sons, his eldest son Harilal resented him the most for depriving him of the same higher educational opportunities that Gandhi himself had availed of as a child and as a young man. In fact, despite Gandhi's opposition to children being separated from their parents, Harilal broke away from his father in South Africa to attend a high school in Ahmedabad, where he stayed with the family of a well-known lawyer—longtime acquaintance of his father. Gandhi quotes some of his closest friends like Polak, and C. F. Andrews, who took him to task and asked him point blank: "What harm had there been, if I had given my boys an academic education? What right had I thus to clip their wings? Why should I have come in the way of their taking degrees and choosing their own careers?" (*Autobiography*, 247).

Gandhi answered that he was sorry for the way his children felt about the issue, but he was not sorry for the decision because he believed that such personal sacrifices were demanded of "a votary of truth." He was deeply convinced that he had served his children well by inculcating in them "a sense of self-respect" and "love of liberty" that no "literary education" could have given them; he never felt they were less smart for the lack of formal school education. Like his wife, Gandhi's three sons later understood their father's broad educational perspectives and his pursuit of truth at any cost.[4]

Formal education, however, was not the only issue that caused a serious rift between Gandhi and his son Harilal. As Gandhi's views changed radically over the years, he insisted on molding his sons into his own image and ideals. Although his other three sons adapted to their father's philosophy of sacrificing their smaller, personal interests in the wider interests of service, liberty, and truth, Harilal could not. Gandhi saw the "undesirable traits" in his eldest son as a reflection or "an echo" of his "own undisciplined and unformulated early life of indulgences," (ibid.) which coincided with Harilal's most impressionable years. To the contrary, Harilal believed that the early period was the the "brightest" and the "happiest" in their life, whereas the later changes were because of Gandhi's "delusion" or his "miscalled enlightenment." The father and the rebellious son drifted further and further apart and remained estranged until the end of Gandhi's life. After his wife, Gulab's, death, Harilal turned into a derelict and a drunkard; he later converted to Islam and wrote letters to newspapers under his new name of "Abdulla," alleging his father for his misfortunes. Although Gandhi could bear all this defamation and pain with detachment, Kasturbai could not; she suffered acutely until the last moment of her life; she beseeched Harilal to mend his ways and his relationship with his father, but that was not to be.

THE BRITISH-BOER WAR

Despite his strong aversion to wars and violence, Gandhi decided to get the Indian community involved in the British-Boer War[5] (1899–1902) on behalf of the British for four reasons. First, he then believed that since Indians in South Africa were British subjects, they must be loyal to the Empire, particularly at their critical hour of need. He told his fellow-Indians that if they demanded their rights as British citizens, they must also fulfill their duty by nursing the wounded in the war. Second, he also believed then that India's complete emancipation was possible only within and through the British Empire. Third, he wanted to wipe out the average Englishman's image of Indians as cowards. And fourth, he hoped that this particular good gesture of the Indians would help soften the Natal government's anti-Indian policies in the future.

Indian Ambulance Corps

Gandhi organized an Indian volunteer corps of 1100 men, of whom three hundred were "free Indians" or traders and the rest were indentured laborers. This was Gandhi's first experience of leading an army of Indian volunteers whose duties comprised carrying the wounded on their stretchers [out of the battlefield] to safety, and nursing them. Many a time they had to risk their own lives and march tirelessly for twenty to twenty-five miles a day. They stood up to their challenge, and proved themselves to be the "sons of Empire" after all, as all the Natal newspapers lauded their war efforts. Gandhi himself received a war medal for his distinguished services in the British-Boer War.

Gandhi thought that his Boer War experience was a God-sent opportunity to come closer to the indentured Indians; they saw in Gandhi their "savior," as Gandhi saw in their faces the very "face of God." He was overjoyed to see another marvel happen among his fellow Indians, who, forgetting all their religious, economic, and other differences, united as children of one motherland, India. The Boer War thus proved to be an "Indian equalizer."

WHAT PRICE PROSPERITY, POPULARITY, AND SUCCESS?

By the end of the nineteenth century, Gandhi had more than he could ever have imagined—a flourishing career, name, fame, success, prosperity, and political prestige, as well as a good family life and the respect of friends both Indian and European. And yet, as he noted in his autobiography, "I was still ill at ease. I longed for some humanitarian work of a permanent nature" (1948, 249). He was beginning to feel that his life was becoming more and more self-centered; he yearned now to make it more other-centered by doing something totally unselfish for others. With this idea in mind, even prior to his Boer War services, he had started volunteering as a nurse for two hours every morning in Dr. Booth's charity hospital. He derived deep satisfaction from nursing the poor indentured Indian patients at this hospital; this experience proved invaluable to him while nursing the wounded in the Boer War.

During this time Gandhi was continuously seeking ways to serve the sick and the poor. As if God heard his prayers, a leper once appeared at his door. Overjoyed, Gandhi offered him shelter, dressed his wounds, and nursed him day and night. Only when the leper required further regular care did Gandhi send him to a government hospital for indentured laborers. Gandhi's life goals were gradually shifting from outward to inward, from the transitory pleasures of the world to the deeper, lasting joys of the soul.

Gandhi felt that his mission in South Africa was practically over. Besides, he now wanted to make service to his motherland his major goal instead of moneymaking. So, in 1901, he went back to India with his family with the intention of settling there, but he promised his loyal friends that he would return to South Africa if and when they needed him.

To Keep or Not to Keep the Gifts

At the time of his farewell, in an overwhelming appreciation of his services, the Natal Indian community showered Gandhi with gifts, including some expensive gold (a necklace worth fifty guineas), silver, and diamond jewelry. The gift issue posed a painful dilemma to Gandhi. Torn between two desires—one for the financial security of his family, and the other for reducing, if not totally renouncing his material possessions—Gandhi spent a sleepless night debating with himself. He knew his wife's intense passion for jewelry. How could he deprive her of what she loved so dearly? But at the same time, how could he allow her to keep the jewelry if he was now wedded to a life of simplicity and poverty? Jewelry meant attachment to worldly possessions, and "non-possession" was to be one of the nine major principles of his new life. The next morning he made up his mind. The gifts must be put in a Community Trust in the care of his trusted friends. As he expected, Kasturbai severely protested, but the children sided with their father who had talked to them beforehand. Now helpless and angry, Kasturbai taunted her husband that he was "out to make sadhus (monks) of their boys." When that failed, she tearfully begged Gandhi to keep the jewelry, if not for her, then for their future daughters-in-law. But Gandhi was adamant. Kasturbai acquiesced; Gandhi prevailed.

BACK IN INDIA, 1901–1902

For the first time, Gandhi attended the Indian Congress Convention held in Calcutta in 1901, and he proposed a resolution for the rights of the South African Indians.[6] Although his resolution was unanimously passed, it was not properly discussed; Gandhi was disappointed. He was more disappointed, however, by the Congress itself, which was primarily an elite organization consisting mainly of upper-caste Hindus who cared little for the masses. He was appalled to see how the congressmen depended on Untouchables for the cleaning of their latrines and for other menial work. Unable to bear such unhygienic conditions, Gandhi took matters into his own hands, as well as the broom, and started sweeping the surroundings and cleaning the latrines himself. Orthodox Hindus were aghast to see a high-caste Hindu like Gandhi act like a *Mahabhangi*![7] But as we know, Gandhi despised and defied all such caste codes and distinctions. He had not yet developed his philosophy for the removal of untouchability, but in Gandhi's life, act always preceded philosophy, and philosophy followed the act. This act, however, was no short of blasphemy in the eyes of orthodox Hindus. As George Woodcock put it (1971, 6), "It was an act which itself constituted a revolution among caste Hindus."

Having attended the Congress session in Calcutta, Gandhi proceeded to Poona to spend time with his political mentor, Gopal Krishna Gokhale. The Gandhi-Gokhale attraction was mutual. Gandhi respected the Moderate Indian leader for his political wisdom,[8] and the veteran leader admired Gandhi's rare integrity. Gandhi observed Gokhale at close quarters, and the latter initiated his junior protégé for his future leadership role in India.

After leaving Gokhale and Poona, Gandhi ventured to undertake a train journey by third-class to all the major holy places through the length and breadth of India. His idea in traveling by third-class was to know firsthand how the underprivileged masses in India lived, and the kinds of hardships they suffered. Visiting the famous Kashi Vishvanath temple in Benaras, Gandhi felt disgusted by the filth of the place and by the greed of the *pandas* (priests). On his way to the renowned Kali temple in Dakshineshvar, he saw rivers of blood caused by the lamb sacrifice to be offered to Mother Kali. Deeply pained by such violence even on holy ground, Gandhi would later write in his autobiography, "This cruel custom must be stopped," and added, "To my mind, the life of a lamb is no less precious than that of a human being" (1948, 290).

GANDHI'S FAITH ON TRIAL

The most trying ordeal of Gandhi's move to India was his son Manilal's near-death illness due to typhoid. Refusing to give any Western medicine or nonvegetarian food to his son, Gandhi insisted on treating him with his hydropathical remedies, and put his son on a diet of skim milk and orange juice only. One night as the ten-year-old Manilal's fever surpassed 104 degrees, Gandhi underwent an excruciating conflict. His faith was on trial, and the holy name of *Rama* was continuously on his lips and in his heart. Gandhi sat up all night praying and applying wet sheet packs to Manilal's iron-hot body. The next morning, seeing profuse perspiration pouring through every pore of his son's body, Gandhi knew the fever was finally breaking. Reflecting later, he wrote in his autobiography, "Who can say whether his recovery was due to God's grace, or to hydropathy, or to careful dieting and nursing? ... But I was sure that God had saved my honour, and that belief remains unaltered to this day" (305).

Whether Gandhi was right or wrong in treating his son only with his home remedies remains debatable; the pertinent point for us to note, however, is his changing faith perspective—his shifting of gears from self-reliance to God-reliance. Although he continued to do his human duty with utter sincerity, he surrendered the fruits of his action to God in the spirit of *nishkama karma* (detachment) as propounded in the *Gita*.

Deciding now to settle in Bombay, Gandhi opened his law office in Santa Cruz; unlike before, he was able to build a lucrative law practice there. During his stay in Bombay, Gandhi ended up buying from an American agent an insurance policy worth Rs. 10,000 for his family. Though he thought that life insurance implied fear and want of faith in God, he was ensnared by the American's smooth selling tactics. The agent succeeded in creating a horror picture of his penniless wife and children after his death, which made Gandhi feel guilty about getting rid of his wife's ornaments. Gandhi finally succumbed to the temptation, but not for long.

To South Africa Again, 1902–1906

Upon receiving an urgent cable from his colleagues, Gandhi returned to South Africa alone for one year in 1902. Although he rushed to the Transvaal to represent the Indian grievances before the visiting British colonial secretary, he was refused entry into the Transvaal by the newly established Asiatic Department. Gandhi knew then that the issue was going to drag on for an uncertain length of time, so he decided to ask his family to join him in South Africa. He applied to the Transvaal Supreme Court to practice as an attorney in Johannesburg, and to his surprise, his application was granted. He soon opened his law offices in Johannesburg.

HOVERING BETWEEN TWO POLES

The years between 1899 and 1904 were marked by Gandhi's ambivalence and oscillations. He leaned toward the pole of renunciation while still holding on to the pole of his worldly desires. He canceled the insurance policy that he had bought in Bombay after having second thoughts about it in South Africa.[9] As he put it, "Up to now there had been in me a mixed desire. The spirit of self-sacrifice was tempered by the desire to lay by something for the future" (ibid., 320). Similarly, he could not decide whether to keep his house and his prosperous lawyer's identity, or to give them up and live in austerity. He kept hovering between the temporal and the spiritual poles until 1904, after which his self-transformation began to take a concrete shape.

The Weekly *Indian Opinion*

Launched by Gandhi in 1904, the weekly *Indian Opinion* was first published in the English, Gujarati, Hindi, and Tamil languages; later, however, only the English and Gujarati versions remained. *Indian Opinion* was operated on a volunteer basis by Albert West, Chhaganlal Gandhi (Gandhi's cousin), and Polak. Mansukhlal Naazar was the paper's first unsalaried editor, but since Gandhi wrote most of the editorials, he soon took over the editorship. Gandhi's gift of journalism showed in every word he used with economy and restraint, in every argument he backed by facts, and in every editorial that was thought provoking. He wrote on the importance of self-reliance, duty before rights, communal unity, truthfulness and honesty in all walks of life. He covered inspiring life stories of great leaders like Lincoln, Mazzini, Elizabeth Fry, and Nelson, as well as the lives of saints like Meerabai and Narsimh Mehta. In addition, Gandhi introduced the Readers' Column, which provided a powerful public platform that served the community well. To Gandhi, "service to the community was the sole aim of journalism." As he put it in his autobiography, "*Indian Opinion* in those days like *Young India* and *Navajivan* today was a mirror of part of my life. Week after week I poured out my soul in its columns, and expounded the principles and practice of Satyagraha" (1948, 348).

The Black Plague in the Coolie Locations

Gandhi held the municipality's "criminal negligence" responsible for the spread of the Black Plague in the coolie locations. Living in abject poverty, the indentured Indians were huddled together in shanty homes with no latrines, clean water, sunlight, or fresh air. Actually, it was not the coolie locations but one of the gold mines in the vicinity of Johannesburg that was responsible for a sudden outbreak of the pneumonic plague, considered more fatal than the bubonic plague. Gandhi, his physician friends (Dr. Godfrey, Dr. Booth), and other colleagues spent days and nights of vigil, nursing hundreds of plague patients and endangering their own lives. Here again Gandhi treated the patients with his "earth treatment," and was happy to have saved two out of three patients. Daily he bicycled tirelessly for miles in order to supply medicine and other life necessities to his patients, who were later moved to another military-like camp location. Gandhi's supreme satisfaction came not only from nursing the plague victims, but also from wiping their tears, giving them the will to live, and sustaining their faith in God. Gandhi's critical articles about the municipality's "criminal negligence" generated wide public sympathy for the indentured Indians, and earned them the government's financial aid as well.

Serving the poor and nursing the sick was only one way of drawing closer to God, thought Gandhi. He wanted to get rid of the life of ease and comfort to which he had become accustomed, so he began to conduct more rigorous experiments in self-austerity.

Increasingly Strident Self-Experiments

Gandhi now began to drastically cut down his dependence on servants and others—for housework as well as personal work. As a student in London, Gandhi had experimented in simple living, but at that time it was strictly for economic reasons. This time, however, "self-help" and "simplicity" were his self-chosen ideals; spiritual self-restraint was now his aim. In South Africa, as he came under the influence of Tolstoy and Ruskin, he began to implement their ideas of simplicity, self-restraint, and austerity for spiritualizing his life. He had experimented with nature-cure, "earth and water treatment" (as during his son Manilal's illness), and the application of mud baths and massage for health. He was now turning to palate control as an essential part of *brahmacharya*. He tried to give up all cooked food and sustained himself on a diet of only sun-baked fruits and nuts. He even gave up milk because of his belief that "man need take no milk at all, beyond the mother's milk that he takes as a baby." Only later, after a life-threatening illness, did he reluctantly switch to goat's milk after his Doctor's insistence.

His articles on dietetic experiments as part of *brahmacharya* were later compiled in a book form, *A Guide to Health.*

The most significant point here is that Gandhi saw "an intimate connection between diet and *brahmacharya*, and between the mind and the body." He wrote in his autobiography, "concupiscence of the mind cannot be rooted out except by self-examination, surrender to God, and lastly, grace" (1948, 402). The beginnings of the Mahatma "fasting to death" can be seen.

Unto This Last

Henry Polak, who shared Gandhi's ethical-spiritual and journalistic interests, gave John Ruskin's book *Unto This Last* to Gandhi, which he read during his long train journey from Johannesburg to Durban. The book cast such a magic spell on Gandhi that he finished it overnight. Not only that, but he determined to change his whole life in accordance with the ideals propounded in the book. What Gandhi wrote about Polak, that "he had a wonderful faculty of translating into practice anything that appealed to his intellect," applied to Gandhi himself. This was the book that stirred him deeply and "brought about an instantaneous and practical transformation," said Gandhi (*Autobiography*, 365); it converted him from a *grihasthi* (householder) into a *vanprasthi ashramvasi* (commune-dwelling spiritual seeker). Ruskin's ideas—the dignity of manual labor, total self-reliance, and communal living in the midst of nature—fired up Gandhi and resulted in the founding of his first ashram at Phoenix. As Gandhi put it, "I discovered some of my deepest convictions reflected in this great book of Ruskin, and that is why it so captured me and made me transform my life" (ibid.).

The question is: Did Gandhi correctly interpret Ruskin's views in *Unto This Last*? Gandhi seems to have correctly grasped Ruskin's first principle "that the good of the individual is contained in the good of all" (Gandhi translated it as *Sarvodaya* or "The Welfare of All," also the title of his book). However, his second derivation that "a lawyer's work has the same value as the barber's, inasmuch as all have the same right of earning livelihood from that work," does not seem to be exactly what Ruskin meant. Although Ruskin suggested that a laborer serves his country with his spade, just as a lawyer does with his brain, at no point did Ruskin say that the work of both "had the same value." It is possible, as Louis Fischer observed, that just as "Gandhi read his deepest convictions into the

Bhagavad Gita, so also he wove his own notions into Ruskin" (1950, 69). Regardless, the profound influence of Ruskin's book on Gandhi and the metamorphosis of his life are far more important from the perspective of his faith development.

The Phoenix Farm Settlement

Gandhi established in 1904 his first spiritually motivated community on a farm in Phoenix, a town near Durban. The Phoenix Farm was a direct, logical consequence of what Ruskin had only visualized and propounded in his book *Unto This Last*. The move marked Gandhi's first major shift from the cozy and comfortable life of a prosperous lawyer to the life of a self-converted laborer living on a farm, producing all his needs, and sharing the fruits of his labor with others. From farming to carpentering, from hauling water to chopping trees, from shoemaking and cooking to teaching and printing as well as publishing the *Indian Opinion*, the Phoenix Farm became a sort of "miniature republic under Gandhi's spell," as Geoffrey Ashe put it (1968, 86). A mixed Indo-European population lived there in a natural, spiritually heightened environment. Even though Gandhi could not always be there physically, his presence was still palpable as its spiritual patriarch (later *Bapu*).

During this time Gandhi reread and reflected over some of his old favorites like the *Gita* and the *Upanishads*. He also read more books, such as Swami Vivekananda's *Rajyoga*, Patanjali's *Yoga Sutra*, and others. He pasted his favorite verses from the *Gita* on his bathroom wall, and tried to learn by heart two verses a day. He thus memorized all eighteen chapters of the *Gita*, which he acknowledged as "an infallible guide of conduct." Its principles of *a-parigraha* (non-possession), *sama-bhava* (equability), and *an-asakti* (action performed without attachment) gripped his heart, mind, and soul; he endeavored to emulate the same into his everyday life. After comparing the original Sanskrit version of the *Gita* with its various translations, he came up with his own interpretations of the Gita as "the science of non-attachment" or "Anasaktiyoga." For all his troubles, he turned to this dictionary of conduct.

The Zulu Rebellion and Gandhi's Volunteer Services

In his autobiography Gandhi said, "the Boer war had not brought home to him the horrors of war with anything like the vividness that the 'rebellion' did" (1948, 386). Why did he think so? Because, as he explained, the so-called rebellion was "no war but a man-hunt"; it was a savage act of the white races' manslaughter of the native Zulus, who had refused to submit to their over-taxation by the whites. Gandhi once again organized an Indian Volunteer Corps who served as stretcher bearers, carrying the wounded away from the battlefield and nursing them. His heart bled with compassion for the Zulus, who were only inadvertent victims of the horrors of war. While marching for many long miles, thirsty and bone-tired, Gandhi fell into deep thought; he began to reassess his life so far.

Gandhi's Soul Searching

Witnessing the Zulu war violence, Gandhi underwent a conversion of heart, similar to that of Prince Siddhartha on the eve of his renunciation before becoming Buddha (the enlightened one).[10] This traumatic experience served as an eye-opener and a soul-searcher. Gandhi began to contemplate the meaning of life and death; he shuddered at the sight of such colossal violence inflicted by one human race upon another. Reflecting on his life, Gandhi found it to be too far removed from what his soul really yearned for—"to have more and more occasions for service of this kind." He craved peace, not war.

Gandhi asked himself: How could he find time to do what really mattered to him? From deep within rose his "still small voice" or the inner voice; it urged him to stop procreating, and to renounce his present comfortable, self-centered life in order to live a life of service to mankind and self-sacrifice for peace. Gandhi reflected, "I could not live both after the flesh and the spirit. Without the observance of *brahmacharya*, service of the family would be inconsistent with service of the community" (ibid., 387).

THE VOW OF *BRAHMACHARYA* AND ITS MEANING

Gandhi's deep soul-searching resulted in his vow of *brahmacharya* at the age of thirty-seven in 1906. *Brahmacharya* (*Brahma*: God or Truth; *charya*: conduct) meant to Gandhi a search for Truth through "not only sexual restraint but control of all the senses and nonviolence in thought, word, and deed." The thoughts of observing *brahmacharya* were already percolating in Gandhi's mind ever since he met Raychandbhai in India. Although

a married man, Raychandbhai was known to have controlled and con-
quered all his passions including the sexual; he was Gandhi's earliest role
model of a family man who lived in the world (*sansara*), but like a monk
(*sadhu*).[11] Gandhi's inner wish to live like a celibate was further reinforced
by Patanjali's *Yogasutra*, and Vivekananda's book on *Rajyoga*. Both texts
emphasized *brahmacharya* through self-purification for God or Self-
realization; it meant total self-control over one's diet, speech, thoughts, emotions, and sensual pleasures, including the sexual. As Gandhi put it, "a
perfect *brahmachari* (celibate) is near to God (*Brahman*) and those wishing
to attain God must practise *brahmacharya*" (*Navajivan*, 1928).

In the Hindu tradition, renunciation requires self-purification (both
external and internal), and self-purification can only be attained through
various *tapasya* (spiritual disciplines). Because *brahmacharya* signifies an
all-comprehensive self-restraint, it is the most difficult as well as the most
revered of all self-disciplines. *Brahmacharya* aims at conversion of sexual
energy into spiritual energy through conservation of the life-generating
seminal fluid. Thus, it is not a negative act of self-denial but a positive spiritual striving for freedom from all bondage (*Moksha*). For this reason, sexual indulgence is considered wasteful in the Hindu tradition and not sinful
as in Christianity. Moreover, it is a widespread Indian social and religious
belief that the observance of *brahmacharya* enhances one's physical, mental, and spiritual (*alaukik*) powers as well.

Various other personal and cultural factors also contributed to Gandhi's
abhorrence for sex while yet in his mid-thirties. As previously discussed,
his sexuality was first marred by his early adolescent marriage for which he
severely criticized his father. His being sexually involved with his pregnant
wife at the time of his father's death further intensified his guilt and shame
complex. Gandhi internalized his culture's bias against sex, if it was not for
procreation. He associated violence in war with sexual violence in bed—of
the male over the female.

What was Gandhi's motive in taking the vow of *brahmacharya*? As
Gandhi admitted, his immediate motive was to curtail the size of his family through voluntary sexual restraint. He was striving since 1900, but to no
avail. As his will was not strong enough to maintain self-control, he needed
to take a formal vow of celibacy as a spiritual prop. His vow thus meant
more to him than a means of family planning; it was his sacred compact
with God, whereby he sought divine assistance for the success of his mission. His deep faith in the efficacy of the vows can be attributed to his
pious mother Putliba, whom we saw in previous chapters keep the hardest
of the hard vows. To Gandhi, "Self-restraint was the very keystone of the

ethics of vow-taking," and the "taking of vows was not a sign of weakness but of strength" (Iyer 1986, 2:103, 106).

TRANSITION FROM STAGE 4 TO STAGE 5 CONJUNCTIVE FAITH

An "egocentric worldview" maintained by the well-demarcated logic and an "explicit ideology" of Stage 4 begins to crumble when a person becomes aware of the "hollowness" of things or activities. It is when one begins to realize that life is too complex to be divided into two simple camps of "black and white," and when one knows that many polar tensions in life do not always have clear-cut solutions.

The earliest telltale signs of a major internal upheaval in Gandhi's life were first visible around the time of the Boer War (1899) continuing through the Zulu Rebellion (1906), the year in which Gandhi made his biggest breakthrough by finally taking the vow of *brahmacharya*. Gandhi's inner turmoil was reflected in his introspective thought patterns, painful dilemmas, and ambivalent decisions. Reaching the heights of success, prosperity, and fame, he began to feel dizzy and uneasy; he did not want moneymaking to become his sole goal in life. He now yearned to turn his life around by turning inward. His frequent changes of mind and mood made him act in self-contradictory ways, such as buying an insurance policy and canceling it right after, furnishing and living in a house and then getting rid of it to live in an ashram, and so on. From the stage transition perspective, Gandhi's self-contradictions and oscillations at this time suggest a deeper, internal awakening; he now saw the need to focus more on the service-oriented activities rather than on self-centric ones.

No more satisfied with the Stage 4 kind of logical explanations or clear-cut theories, Gandhi began to see the complexities of life, the reality of death, destruction, disease, violence, and injustice. He now wanted to experiment with truth, and live by it in all its various forms and aspects; his pursuit of truth was not other-worldly, but this-worldly. Although Gandhi worshipped God as Truth (absolute), he also saw God in the poor, the exploited, and the rejected masses of humanity. From an egocentric life of material gratification and self-exaltation, Gandhi moves on to a more self-humbling, service-oriented, and God-centered life in Stage 5.

9

A Satyagrahi in South Africa, Phase III

In this last act of Gandhi's South African drama, *satyagraha* occupies center stage. Gandhi remains in the limelight, though, not because others do not matter, but because he is the main character as well as the director. Gandhi is the spiritual genius who masterminded *satyagraha*, the first mass-scale nonviolent revolution in human history, considered to be the "moral equivalent of war." As Geoffrey Ashe said (1968, 67), "The South African drama has only one fully realized character, under a constant spotlight. Gandhi is the master spirit, while most of his companions, with all their zeal and goodwill, are simply names."

Let us first understand the political circumstances that propelled Gandhi to conceive the principle of *satyagraha*, which preceded the actual nonviolent campaign. After the Zulu Rebellion, Gandhi was so deeply shaken by the violence and victimization of the innocent Zulus that he determined to devote himself totally to the cause of human service. In order to serve humanity better, and to get rid of his own carnal nature, Gandhi took the *brahmacharya* vow right after the Zulu Rebellion. As Louis Fischer observed (1950, 73), "Less carnal, Gandhi became less self-centered. He seemed suddenly lifted above the material. A new inner drive possessed him. ... A new Gandhi faced the South African government." He was now ready to fight the new Botha-Smuts government.[1]

Much to Gandhi's dismay, despite the Indian volunteer services in both wars (The Boer and the Zulu), the newly established responsible government did not relent its harsh laws or attitude toward Indians. "If anything, the position of the Indians deteriorated," said Robert A. Huttenback (1971,

127), because the new government was no longer obstructed by protests from London and Cape Town. It proceeded, therefore, to enforce republican legislation with extraordinary zeal.

"THE BLACK ACT"

Mr. Lionel Curtis of the newly created Asiatic Department drafted the Asiatic Law Amendment Ordinance. Gandhi saw in it "nothing except hatred of Indians." Striking at the very root of the Indian problem, the law put greater restrictions upon Indians' entry into the Transvaal; because of its dark, sinister nature, Gandhi called it "The Black Act."

According to the proposed ordinance, the old Indian permits and registrations were valid no more; all Indian men, women, and even children above the age of eight would not only have to reregister but also give their fingerprints or thumb impressions as primary marks of identification. Having reregistered, the Indians would also have to carry with them the new registration certificate at all times, and produce it upon demand. Every Indian who failed to apply for new registration before a certain date would forfeit his or her right of residence in the Transvaal. Moreover, anyone who failed to produce the certificate upon demand could be arrested without a warrant, fined, imprisoned, and even deported if the court decreed so. Under the pretext of preventing illegal immigration, the government enforced fingerprinting, thereby, treating all Indians as potential criminals. The whole South African Indian community was incensed; the Muslims, however, were more vociferous since this law allowed the police to inspect their houses at anytime, which invaded their women's religiously sanctioned seclusion. Gandhi strongly felt that if the Indians meekly allowed this ordinance to pass, it would spell absolute ruin for them in South Africa. Calling it "a question of life and death," Gandhi wrote (1928, 101), "it was better to die than submit to such a law," although he had no concrete plan yet about the way to put a stop to it. He decided to call a small meeting of all the prominent Indians of Johannesburg. As he explained to them the ordinance word by word, he saw they were as shocked by it as was he. The Muslim sentiments ran high and strong; in a fit of passion one of them said, "If anyone came forward to demand a certificate from my wife, I would shoot him on the spot and take the consequences" (ibid.). Determined to put a united Indian front against the Black Act, the Transvaal Indians held a huge public meeting to vent their wrath and decide their line of action.

BIRTH OF THE *SATYAGRAHA* PRINCIPLE

On September 11, 1906, thousands of Indians gathered at the Jewish Empire Theatre in Johannesburg to oppose the Black Law. Prominent Muslim businessmen delivered fiery speeches; the environment was electrifying and the mood, explosive. In order to seek justice and protect their women's honor, the Muslims were ready to kill or be killed. It was when Gandhi listened to Sheth Haji Habib's impassioned appeal to "pass a resolution in the name of God," that he said, (ibid., 103), "I was at once startled and put on my guard. Only then did I fully realize my own responsibility and the responsibility of the community." Gandhi confessed that until he heard the Muslim leader, he himself had not understood all the implications of the resolutions, nor had he known the possible conclusions to which they might lead. "I only knew," said Gandhi, "that some new principle had come into being" (ibid., 109). Since he had recently taken the vow of *brahmacharya*, he wanted everyone to be fully aware of the sanctity of pledge-taking, and of the irreversibility and self-responsibility before making a solemn commitment.

As a trusted adviser and a servant of the community, Gandhi saw it as his duty to fully explain to his people the novelty and the solemnity of passing this resolution. The element of novelty was that, unlike any other resolution before, the resolution they were about to pass this time was a grave one. Why was it a grave resolution? Because, the name of God was invoked in it; God was to be their holy witness to it. Gandhi said (1928, 104), "An oath in the name of that God or with Him as witness is not something to be trifled with. If having taken such an oath we violate our pledge we are guilty before God and man."

The gravity of the issue tied in with the solemnity of pledge-taking in God's name. To Gandhi it signified taking a solemn vow, an unbreakable vow, which he knew firsthand even as a child. He wanted to explain to his people, therefore, the full significance and the inviolateness of taking a vow—what kind of preliminary training it required, what kind of sacrifices they might have to make, and what kind of consequences they might have to suffer. Gandhi first clarified the definition of a vow: "If we resolve to do a thing and are ready to sacrifice our lives in the process, we are said to have taken a vow" (ibid.). Resolving to do anything requires strength of will, and the taking of a vow helps strengthen the will. Accustomed from his early childhood to taking vows, Gandhi testified that because of his adherence to those vows he was able to overcome many a temptation and come out unscathed from many a crisis. He gave an example of his own saintly mother who was a living, breathing, inspiring role model in the taking and keeping of the hardest vows; moreover, his childhood was nurtured by the mythological stories of "Truthful King Harishchandra," "Shravana," and "Prahalada," each of which reinforced the sanctity of the pledged word. Gandhi suggested that "one may take easy and simple vows to start with and follow them with more difficult ones" (ibid.).

According to Raghavan Iyer (1986, 2: 7), "For Gandhi, the English term 'vow' carried with it all the meanings of the original Sanskrit term *vrata* (a solemn resolve or spiritual decision) and *yama* (a spiritual exercise or self-imposed restraint)." The *yamas* that Patanjali prescribed in his *Yogasutra* include truth, nonviolence, celibacy, control of the palate, non-stealing, and non-possession. The *yamas* are to be observed with the *niyamas* or ancillary exercises of cleanliness, contentment, purificatory rituals for the body and mind (*tapas*), spiritual study, and the dedication of every action to the Lord. Thus, we can see that a vow is not to be taken lightly; it requires "self-restraint (*tapas*)" which is "the very keystone of the ethics of vow-taking," says Iyer (ibid.). These preliminary spiritual exercises are intended to awaken one's conscience through the power of the vow. Iyer observed, "Gandhi sought to socialize the individual conscience rather than internalize the social conscience," (ibid., 8). Herein lay Gandhi's originality. Instead of the society or religion commanding an individual to obey what is right and wrong, it was the inner voice—the God-inspired conscience—that showed an individual the right path course of action. Thus, Gandhi utilized the traditional spiritual discipline of vow-taking not only for his own inner transformation, but also "for the wider purpose of the transformation of society," as Margaret Chatterjee pointed out (1983, 68).

In addition, Gandhi raised two more points in his speech before the impassioned crowd in that historic meeting. First, Gandhi brought up a theme dear to his heart: "Personally I hold that a man, who deliberately and intelligently takes a pledge and then breaks it, forfeits his manhood" (1928, 105). We may note that the theme of manhood runs like a refrain throughout Gandhi's life, beginning with his early adolescent years when he wanted to be as strong and manly as Mehtab. If physical prowess and muscle power defined manhood during his adolescence, moral courage and the soul power comprised real manhood to the middle-aged Gandhi; it was the kind of manhood that inspired him to take a pledge in God's name, and even to die for a principle. The second noteworthy point raised in Gandhi's speech is that this was the first time he referred to the "inner voice," saying that "Everyone must search his own heart," and "only if the inner voice assures him that he has the requisite strength to carry him through, then only should he pledge himself and then only will his pledge bear fruit" (ibid.). He emphasized thereby the spiritual import of taking this pledge which is not like casting a political vote, but to follow one's own inner voice.

Having explained to his people the moral implications and self-responsibility involved in taking a pledge in God's name, Gandhi also wanted to alert them to the serious consequences of committing to this vow. He explained to them in detail what was the worst that may happen in the present struggle. They might have to go to jail, do hard labor, go hungry or be forced to eat unpalatable food; they may have to suffer the insults, floggings, and assaults. They might even die in jail due to disease or torture, or they might lose their job, family, or property. Even if they joined today, they might drop out tomorrow, as the struggle could drag on and on for an unpredictably long time.

It was at this point that Gandhi said, "But I boldly declare, and with certainty, that so long as there is even a handful of men true to their pledge, there can be only one end to the struggle, and that is victory." (1928, 106). Even though this idea as well as the phrasing of the words strikingly resemble those of Henry David Thoreau in his essay on "Civil Disobedience," [2] Gandhi maintained he had not read Thoreau's essay until after the *satyagraha* was well advanced.[3] His claim is verified by the fact that he had borrowed Thoreau's book from the Volksrust jail library where he was serving his second term after having launched *satyagraha.*

As mentioned earlier, even Gandhi was taken by surprise when this moral principle came into being. Gandhi himself had no clear concept of what that new principle entailed, except for knowing intuitively that if it was to be taken as a pledge in God's name, it could not be violent. He also did not know what name to call it by, how it would develop, or in which direction it would take them. The only thing Gandhi knew for sure was that his inner voice had spoken to him and that it was the voice of God; he had full faith that God would show him the way from darkness to Light and lead him from untruth to Truth.

INDIAN STRUGGLE VERSUS PASSIVE RESISTANCE

During its initial phase, the Indian struggle was often mistaken as passive resistance. When Mr. Hosken, a European sympathizer of the Indian movement, introduced it for the first time to the public as "passive resistance" or as "a weapon of the weak," Gandhi was startled, because nothing could be farther from truth. On the spur of the moment, he had to explain the fundamental difference between the Indians' struggle and the other two passive resistance movements—that of the British non-conformists under Dr. Clifford's leadership, and the women suffragist movement in England. It was while explaining to Hosken what the Indian struggle was *not*, that Gandhi began to see what it *was*, and how fundamentally different it was from the others in three ways. First, Gandhi said (1928, 112), "The suffragist movement did not eschew the use of physical force. Some suffragists fired buildings and even assaulted men." In contrast, "brute force had absolutely no place in the Indian movement in any circumstance" (ibid.). Second, even though the Indians were politically weak without any franchise, they were stronger in spirit; they possessed "soul-force pure and simple." Third, there is no scope for love or goodwill toward the enemy in passive resistance; in the Indian struggle, however, there is absolutely no place for hatred or ill will toward the adversary. In order to differentiate the Indian movement from passive resistance, Gandhi now needed to find an appropriate name for it.

The Naming of *Satyagraha*

Gandhi arranged a naming contest and invited all his colleagues to help him find the most meaningful name for the Indian movement in South Africa. Out of more than one hundred entries, Gandhi originally selected his cousin Maganlal Gandhi's suggestion for the Sanskrit compound name *sadagraha* (*sada*: good; *agraha*: adherence); later, however, he replaced the first part of the name *sada* with *satya* (truth). *Satyagraha* was thus the final choice of a name that symbolizes the quintessence of Gandhi's philosophy, namely, the power of truth based on nonviolent courage and self-suffering; it highlights the spiritual origin and intent of *satyagraha*.

Three Cardinal Principles of *Satyagraha*

Time and again Gandhi stressed that *Satyagraha* was "not a weapon of the weak" nor was it meant to be used by "cowards." A *satyagrahi*, or the wielder of *satyagraha*, must first have an unflinching faith in the supreme value and power of truth, both Absolute and relative. The whole structure of *satyagraha* is built upon the three pillars or principles of *truth, nonviolence*, and *voluntary self-suffering*.

A *living faith in God or Truth* is the number one prerequisite in *satyagraha*; the name itself means "adherence to Truth." A *satyagrahi* must wholeheartedly believe in the ultimate triumph of Truth, in the saving power and grace of God. Only if a *satyagrahi* has an unflinching faith in God, can he or she suffer blow after blow, insults, and tortures without hatred or retaliation. Such undying faith alone makes one capable of non-violence, love, and forgiveness. Gandhi regarded, therefore, a living faith in God as indispensable in *satyagraha*. In his own words:

> He or she must have a living faith in nonviolence. This is impossible without a living faith in God. To bear all kinds of tortures without a murmur of resentment is impossible for a human being without the strength that comes from God. (Diwakar 1948, viii)

Until 1931 Gandhi used the terms "God" and "Truth" interchangeably to indicate one and the same ultimate Reality. Later, however, he found that the very concept of God created a stumbling block in his encounters with atheists; most did not object, however, to Truth as a goal or as a method of inquiry into the mystery of the universe. As Chatterjee put it, (1983, 58), "A stage came in Gandhi's life when he found the formulation 'Truth is God' preferable to 'God is Truth.' The word Truth is not substituted for God but serves to elucidate what 'God' means for Gandhi."

Gandhi did not systematically define Truth as a metaphysical concept, nor did he have any mystical experience of God as Shri Ramakrishna had through *Samadhi*, an ecstatic union with God through deep meditation. He was not a philosopher-monk like Swami Vivekananda, nor a yogi like Raman Maharshi. He was primarily a *Karmayogi*, whose domain was action; his field of action was human service through politics and social reforms. Yet Gandhi was also a true *bhakta* at heart (a man of prayers), whose every thought, impulse, and action was "profoundly God-centered and man-oriented" as Judith Brown phrased it (1989, 90). His approach to truth was intuitive-ethical rather than metaphysical-intellectual; it was this-worldly, not other-worldly. Gandhi's frequent references to his inner voice spoke of the living presence of God in every human heart. He yearned to see God not in a cave, cloister, or a temple but in the faces of the poor, the downtrodden, and the outcasts. He founded *satyagraha* based on his faith in God that "we are all sparks of the divine and therefore, partake of its nature." Since we are all rooted in God, we cannot but be interconnected. God is our common origin, our true self, and our fundamental link with one another.[4]

Nonviolence or Ahimsa (*a*: non; *himsa* or *hinsa*: violence) is the second prerequisite in *satyagraha*. According to Gandhi, truth and nonviolence were invariably intertwined in theory and practice. If truth was the end or goal, nonviolence must be the means. The means must be compatible with the end; they must symbolize or further the goal, and the goal must be advanced through the media of adequate means. If the goal in *satyagraha* was to fight for justice, peace, or a transformed relationship, the means must also be nonviolent and peace promoting. This is where Gandhi's *satyagraha* differed from other passive resistance movements. Truth and nonviolence would have to continue to interact in a dynamic-creative process. Joan Bondurant wrote in *Conquest of Violence* (1965, xiii):

> Point not the goal until you plot the course
> For ends and means to man are tangled so
> That different means quite different aims enforce
> Conceive the means as end in embryo.

What connection did Gandhi see between truth and nonviolence? Why was he adamant about nonviolence as the only means to fulfill and advance the goal of truth? Gandhi worshipped God as Truth, the unchanging Reality beyond time and space, an all-pervading cosmic presence that is both transcendent and immanent. A single spirit pervades the whole universe, all life is one, interlinked and sacred. Our roots are in God, we are all potentially divine and partake of the divine nature, which is unconditional love, nonviolent love, forgiving love. Thus Gandhi interpreted nonviolence not as a passive virtue of noninjury but as an active principle of unconditional, universal, compassionate love. He wrote in *Navajivan* (November 4, 1928), "Nonviolence means universal love; it implies compassion for all living beings and the resultant strength to sacrifice oneself."

Herein lay Gandhi's creativity. From childhood he had been exposed to this fundamental Jain tenet of *ahimsa* as nonviolence or noninjury. He revitalized the same concept, however, turning it into a formidable soul power or a positive and active principle of love. Later, after reading other world religions, his faith was reaffirmed that love by its very nature was nonviolent, unconditional, life transforming, and as expansive as the skies. Agape in Christianity, *karuna* or compassion in Buddhism, ahimsa in Jainism and Hinduism—all mean universal love, which is the very essence of God. Gandhi thus saw not only a viable connection between *satya* and *ahimsa* but also brought these metaphysical principles down to the ethical plane, making them the very foundation of his *satyagraha* in South Africa and later in India. Gandhi wanted "to identify with everything that lived." In order to "see the universal and all pervading Spirit of Truth face to face," said Gandhi in his autobiography, "one must be able to love the meanest of creation as oneself." He added that such "identification with everything that lives is impossible without self-purification" (1948, 615).

Tapasya or Voluntary Suffering is the third quality invariably connected to *satya* and *ahimsa*. A *satyagrahi* relies upon his or her faith in truth, moral courage, and inward strength of the soul. He or she is a crusader of truth, a soldier of nonviolence, and an epitome of self-endurance. Just as vow-taking keeps one focused on the goal, *tapasya* (rigorous physical, mental, and moral exercises) enhances the inner resilience of the spirit. Indian mythology is replete with stories of *tapas*. In the Hindu pantheon, Lord Shiva is the very incarnate of yogic powers acquired through austerities, meditation, control of the mind and senses, and inner concentration on the Self. A *satyagrahi* practices *tapas* not for personal, material, or even spiritual powers but for becoming the fittest instrument of God in the moral warfare. Gandhi wrote, "Real suffering bravely borne melts even a heart of stone. Such is the potency of suffering or *tapas*. And there lies the key to *Satyagraha*" (1928, 17). Gandhi believed in the healing, transforming, and redemptive power of voluntary suffering.

DEPUTATION TO LONDON IN 1906

To go back to where we left before our exposition of *satyagraha*, the Transvaal Indians unanimously agreed to exhaust all constitutional means to oppose the Asiatic Ordinance. Per Gandhi's advice, they decided to send a deputation to England to meet with the secretary of state for the Colonies, Lord Elgin, and with Lord Morley (then Mr.) of India. Gandhi wanted to bring extra pressure through veteran Indian leaders like Dadabhai Naoroji and Sir Muncherji Bhownuggree, who exerted considerable influence in the British Committee of the Indian National Congress. Because the Indians of Transvaal were divided on religious, economic, and educational bases, the biggest hurdle Gandhi faced was in selecting the right persons who would best serve the interest of all Indians. After heated debates, finally only Gandhi and H. O. Ali were selected as representatives of the Hindus and the Muslims, respectively.

In addition to these two groups, there was a third group involved—colonial-born Indian Christians, whose leaders were William Godfrey and Joseph Royeppen, both London-educated barristers. According to Swan (1985, 11), both these young leaders played "an active role in the politics of the new Natal elite as well as the passive resistance campaign in the Transvaal." They were extremely resentful, therefore, when no one from their group was selected to go to London. So, Godfrey, Royeppen, and C. M. Pillay (another Indian Christian) conspired against Gandhi and wrote strong letters of protests to England. Their protest jeopardized the success of the Gandhi-Ali delegation to London.

We notice a gulf of difference between Gandhi the young law student who was in London during the late 1880s, and Gandhi the mature leader who visited his favorite city in 1906. Between then and now an astounding inner growth had taken place in his personal development; he had emerged from his shy cocoon self to become not only a successful, prosperous Indian lawyer but also a highly respected, moral-political leader of the South African Indian community.

Despite turning all the right keys, that is, meeting with the right leaders, drafting perfect petitions, holding personal diplomatic sessions with Lord Elgin, and addressing the House of Commons (and having tea with Mr. Churchill), Gandhi's high hopes regarding the outcome of the Indian delegation crumbled, and the Asiatic Ordinance was passed. Only after returning to Johannesburg did Gandhi find out that he and Ali had been made scapegoats of the imperial government's "crooked policy." Feeling betrayed, Gandhi said, "Elgin made an outward show of friendliness to Indians while at the same time he really and secretly supported the newly formed Responsible Government." [5]

This was the last time Gandhi used his strategy of seeking justice through rational appeals, formal delegations, and parliamentary procedures. Realizing the futility of this approach, he said, "Up to the year 1906 I simply relied on appeal to reason. ... But I found that reason failed to produce an impression when the critical moment arrived in South Africa" (1928, 90). Whenever the outer skies turned dark, Gandhi turned inward for Light; his disillusionment with formal political maneuvers was more a result of his inner self-awakening, deepening perspectives, and changing priorities in life. "*Satyagraha* in South Africa came into being," said Gandhi (ibid.), as "the moral equivalent of war." It emanated from and evolved as a means to seek political justice for South African Indians. To Gandhi, the means and the end were two sides of the same coin of *satyagraha,* the earliest phase of which he was about to launch with his fellow *satyagrahis.*

REFUSING TO REGISTER

Under Gandhi's leadership, thousands of Indians anxiously awaited July 1, 1907, the deadline for the new registration. With boundless enthusiasm the volunteers picketed at every place to dissuade any Indian who went to renew his permit. They were clearly instructed, however, not to be rude or violent to anyone who still opted to get the permit. Not only that, the *satyagrahis* were even supposed to escort anyone who was afraid to go to the permit office and to bring him or her back safely. Most important, at no time and under no aggravating circumstances, should they retaliate. Gandhi stressed:

> They must behave to the police too with due respect. If the police abused or thrashed them, they must suffer peacefully; if the ill-treatment ... was insufferable, they should leave the place. If the police arrested them, they should gladly surrender themselves." (1928, 134)

First Prison Experience

Along with hundreds of other Indians including the Tamils, Muslims, Christians, and also the Chinese, Gandhi, too, was imprisoned for disobeying the law. In spite of his initial maladjustments to the bland and half-cooked jail food, the lack of privacy, inadequate latrine facility, and other hardships, Gandhi not only survived his first jail term but actually thrived on it. Initially, as he confessed, Gandhi was quite afraid to live in a prison, not knowing the outcome of the issue or the length of time to which the movement could drag on. His misgivings and fears were countered, however, by other thoughts in which he recalled his own words of advice to fellow *satyagrahis*, that they should "consider the prisons as His Majesty's hotels, and their suffering consequent upon disobeying the Black Act as perfect bliss!" He found courage in his own words, which, he said, "acted upon him as a bracing tonic." With plenty of leisure, he resumed his religious readings; his spirits soared once again. He managed to borrow from the prison library books by Ruskin, Socrates, Plato, Tolstoy, Huxley, Bacon's essays, and Carlyle's book *Lives*. He read and reread the *Bhagavad Gita*, the *Q'uran*, and the *New Testament*. Gandhi even looked forward to going back to jail again, because only in jail could he cleanse his soul and take a spiritual bath.

GANDHI–SMUTS ENCOUNTERS

Gandhi's principled confrontations with his arch political opponent, General Jan Christian Smuts, began from this period onward as he served a series of terms in the Transvaal prisons in Johannesburg and in Volksrust. Gandhi and Smuts had much in common. Both barristers from England,[6] they were master politicians, hard negotiators, and great patriots. Moreover, both were avid readers, able writers, and men of high moral integrity. Each tried to outmaneuver the other in the political game of chess; their motives and methods, however, were totally dissimilar. They did not see eye to eye on racial issues including the treatment of Indians, nor on the means or tactics. At the time of Gandhi's departure, Smuts said sarcastically: "The Saint has left our shores, I sincerely hope for ever." Much later, however, the same Smuts attended Gandhi's seventieth birthday celebration in India, and said: "I am not worthy to stand in the shoes of so great a man; ... men like him redeem us all from a sense of commonplaceness and futility and are an inspiration to us not to be weary in well-doing" (Radhakrishnan, 298).

By eventually showing his reverence for Gandhi, and by admitting that he failed during the Indian struggle to recognize his previous antagonist's exceptional spiritual stature, Smuts proved the point of *satyagraha*, that Truth shall always triumph in the end. Gandhi succeeded after all, in "turning a foe into a friend." Fischer observed (1950, 118), "Part of Gandhi's effectiveness lay in evoking the best Gandhian impulses of his adversary."

Gandhi–Smuts Agreement

While Gandhi was in jail, Mr. Albert Cartwright, a newspaper editor and sympathizer of the Indian movement, tried hard on behalf of Gandhi to arrange for a meeting between him and the Smuts government. Cartwright's efforts yielded fruit. On January 30, 1908, while still in jail, Gandhi met Smuts for the first time to discuss the Asiatic Ordinance. According to Gandhi, Smuts accepted the final draft of an agreement in which he assured Gandhi that he "will repeal the Asiatic Act as soon as most of the Indians underwent voluntary registration." In consultation with his coworkers inside and outside jail, Gandhi signed the agreement. Soon thereafter, Smuts not only released Gandhi but also paid his railway fare to Johannesburg.

Not all were happy, however, with Gandhi for his agreeing to the "Indians' voluntary registration." Some were apprehensive of Smuts breaking the promise. They also felt that Gandhi "played into the adversary's hands, and surrendered the most powerful weapon ... for resisting the Act." (1928, 158–159) Gandhi reminded them at this point about the essence of *satyagraha*:

A *satyagrahi* bids good-bye to fear. He is therefore never afraid of trusting the opponent. Even if the opponent plays him false twenty times, the

Satyagrahi is ready to trust him for the twenty-first time, for an implicit trust in human nature is the very essence of his creed." (1928, 159)

"Implicit trust" in the enemy is one of the basic assumptions in *satyagraha*. A *satyagrahi* should never lose his or her faith that even the most hardened human heart is capable of conversion—of being moved by an opponent's genuine gestures of love and suffering for truth.

An Assault on Gandhi

Mir Alam, a Pathan (Muslim native of Afghanistan, India's northwest frontier), accused Gandhi of "selling out to General Smuts" and refused to go for registration or to be fingerprinted. He swore "with Allah as his witness" that he would kill Gandhi if he went or led others to get the registration certificate. Remaining unperturbed, Gandhi said, "To die by the hand of a brother rather than by disease or in such other way, cannot be for me a matter of sorrow." He only prayed to God, he added, that "even in such a case I am free from the thoughts of anger or hatred against my assailant" (1928, 163). What a prophetic irony! His words spoken in 1907 proved tragically true some forty years later, although Gandhi's assassin was not a Muslim but a Hindu!

Gandhi, a born Hindu, addressing his Muslim coworker as a "brother" gives us the first clue to his expanding vision and inclusive humanity. Not only that, but Gandhi was prepared to absorb Mir Alam's intense animosity. Mir Alam carried out his threat and attacked Gandhi on his way to the registration office, causing him severe head injuries. Gandhi fell unconscious to the ground with the words "He Rama" on his lips, as he had always wished. Gandhi was rescued from the scene by a kind Baptist minister, Rev. Joseph Doke, who, along with his wife and little daughter, Olive, nursed him at his home. Olive daily sang for Gandhi his favorite hymn of "Lead, Kindly Light." Rev. Doke and Gandhi cherished a lifelong friendship, and Doke wrote the first biography of Gandhi in 1909.

Bonfire of Certificates

General Smuts betrayed Gandhi; he did not repeal the Black Act. His breach of trust added fuel to the fire of the Indian *satyagraha* in South Africa. Thousands of Indians joined together in Johannesburg to burn their registration certificates rather than submit to the degrading Black Act. The leaping flames of the bonfire peaked sky-high, turning more than

2000 cards to ashes. Gandhi was the first to throw his certificate into the huge cauldron, which was set ablaze in full public view. This was the first demonstration of Gandhi's dramatizing genius—his "rare gift for picking on symbols," to use the phrase of Chatterjee (1983, 3). The placing of a gigantic cauldron in the middle of a busy street, the long twisting and winding lines of *satyagrahis* walking silently but steadily toward the cauldron, and the throwing of their certificates one by one into the fire—all created a powerful impact on the viewers. Gandhi's symbolic act spoke louder than words or violent protests. Later in India (in 1930), with a mere pinch of salt he will bring the great British Empire down to its knees! This symbolic bonfire of certificates was compared to the Boston Tea Party by most European reporters, who were profoundly impressed by the Indians' disciplined display of nonviolent courage under Gandhi's leadership.

The ink had not even dried from the Black Act when another Transvaal Immigrants Restriction Bill was passed in 1908. It prohibited even those Indians who passed the educational tests from entering the Transvaal. This new immigration bill met with further nonviolent protest under the leadership of a Parsee, Sorabji Shapurji Adajania. Gandhi's eldest son Harilal, now twenty years old, also joined; he was imprisoned along with other *satyagrahis*.

Second Jail Term

Gandhi, too, was arrested and confined to two months of hard labor in the Volksrust prison. He served as a cook, a teacher, and a toilet cleaner for all his seventy-five fellow jail compatriots. It was during this second jail term that Gandhi borrowed from the Volksrust prison library Thoreau's essay on "Civil Disobedience." He was overjoyed. In Thoreau's independent frame of mind and in his bold declarations, Gandhi found a strong affirmation of his own ideas of a principled, moral resistance to the government's arbitrary laws. He disliked, however, Thoreau's term civil disobedience because his idea in *satyagraha* was not just to disobey the law to remedy an outer situation, but to change the enemy's inner attitude of hostility; he therefore coined his own term, *civil resistance*. During his third jail term in Pretoria, Gandhi immersed himself in reading Ralph Waldo Emerson's essays, which elated his spirits all the more. He was thrilled to know that both Thoreau and Emerson had read the *Bhagavad Gita* and the *Upanishads*, and that they were indebted to both. Gandhi, who had already memorized all eighteen chapters of the *Gita*, was now striving self-consciously to follow its precepts; he was performing his day-to-day activities with calmness and detachment.

Soon after his release from jail, Gandhi went to London again in 1909 to raise British consciousness regarding the South African Indian situation. Gandhi's approach was far different this time in three respects. First, instead of relying totally on formal speeches and meetings, Gandhi now used a more personal, direct approach through private meetings with both British and Indian key power holders. He found a supporter in Lord Ampthill, (who also wrote a warm Introduction to Gandhi's first biography by Rev. Joseph Doke). Second, this time Gandhi was wiser as he personally had borne the cross of suffering for truth; he had endured the hardships of jail as well as the pain of political disappointments. Third, he met this time with prominent Indian patriots like Veer Savarkar, Shyamji Krishnavarma, and others, who were secretly involved in terrorist activities for India's freedom from the British raj.[7] Gandhi's book *Hind Swaraj* was based on his discussions with them.

HIND SWARAJ OR THE INDIAN HOME-RULE

Written by Gandhi during his return voyage from London to South Africa, *Hind Swaraj* is one of his earliest seminal works, which was first published as a pamphlet in the Gujarati edition of *Indian Opinion* in November 1909. (It was prohibited in India by the government of Bombay.) The book was inspired by several heated discussions in London with the scholarly Indian patriots Shyamji Krishnavarma, Veer Savarkar, and others, who endorsed a violent overthrow of the British Raj in India. Gandhi detected that while they vehemently opposed the British rule in India, they still loved the English parliamentary system and the educational and industrial institutions; they also liked some other aspects of the modern, Western civilization. Although Gandhi respected their patriotism, he did not condone their views or violent tactics.

The book, written in 1908, in dialogue form, represents the perspectives of both the editor (Gandhi) and the reader (the revolutionaries) about *swaraj* (*swa*: self; *raj*: rule). Here, however, we shall discuss only Gandhi's concept of *swaraj*. In its Introduction, Gandhi described the intent and the theme of the book:

> It teaches the gospel of love in the place of hate. It replaces violence with self-sacrifice. It pits soul force against brute force. ... The booklet is a

severe condemnation of "modern civilization." ... if India adopted the doctrine of love as an active part of her religion and introduced it in her politics, Swaraj would descend upon India from heaven." (*Hind Swaraj*, xxiii–xxviii)

Behind Gandhi's severe condemnation of modern civilization lay his larger vision of "a total man living in an ideal state of *swaraj*"; it was "a state of freedom from all bondage both external and internal." To Gandhi *swaraj* meant more than political freedom from the British rule; he envisioned it as an ethico-spiritual human quest for self-knowledge, self-conquest, and self-transformation. Gandhi believed that true *swaraj* was incompatible with hate, violence, greed, disharmony, and all harmful or destructive states of mind. He held that India must resist all kinds of exploitation—economic, social, political, and even ideological; he refused to put "self-interest at the centre of man's existence." Thus, Gandhi's "condemnation of modern civilization" sprang from what Ramashray Roy described as "man's relationship with the outer world ... characterized by an organismic vision emphasizing inseparable unity, harmony, and non-injury" (1985, 44).

THE GANDHI–TOLSTOY CORRESPONDENCE

During April 1910, Gandhi had sent a copy of *Hind Swaraj* to Tolstoy, his spiritual mentor, who was near death at that time. With deep reverence, Gandhi explained to Tolstoy how he had endeavored to implement Tolstoy's ideas of "love and peace" in his *satyagraha* movement in South Africa; Gandhi also sent Tolstoy a copy of Rev. Doke's biography of him. Tolstoy, in his "Letter to a Hindoo," praised Gandhi's "work in the Transvaal as most fundamental and important of all the works now being done in the world, wherein not only the nations of the Christian, but of all the world, will unavoidably take part." According to Green (1993, 199), "This was Tolstoy's last long letter, and it is appropriate that it should have been addressed to Gandhi."

TOLSTOY FARM

Named after Tolstoy, this farm was Gandhi's personal homage to the memory of his spiritual mentor; it breathed Tolstoy's spirit and his ideas of "peaceful and constructive co-existence." Hermann Kallenbach, a German-Jewish architect who was Gandhi's close friend and follower, donated this fertile land of more than one thousand acres near Johannesburg. Gandhi established here his second spiritual community in South Africa (the first being the Phoenix Farm in 1904), and moved there with a family consisting of his wife, their four sons, his nephews, and many other friends, relatives, and coworkers. Living here, Gandhi intensified the dietetic and palate control experiments that he had begun earlier in the Phoenix Farm. At the Tolstoy Farm, however, in addition to other self-austerities, Gandhi introduced fasting for the first time, not for health but for doing penance. He went on a vicarious, penitential fast for the moral lapses of some adolescent boys and girls living on the farm. Gandhi served as a patriarch, a general manager, a cook, a farmer, a carpenter, a shoemaker, and also as a sanitary worker who dug outdoor latrines for everyone. He continued to publish his weekly *Indian Opinion* and conducted experiments in "co-education" on the farm.

THE FATHER AND THE SONS

Gandhi's relationship with his eldest son, Harilal, which was damaged early on, now went rapidly downhill. Harilal, twenty years old, returned to South Africa without education, without money, and with a family in tow.[8] As mentioned earlier, Harilal joined *satyagraha*, was arrested, and was detained in the same jail (Volksrust) as his father. In jail, Harilal pleaded with his father yet again to send him abroad for higher education. Gandhi's answer was an "eternal no"; he neither believed in it nor did he want Harilal to desert his family. Gandhi wrote long letters from jail to Harilal's wife, Gulab (pregnant for the second time), admonishing her for not observing self-restraint in her marriage; he also advised her about a proper nutritive diet during pregnancy and the advantages of breastfeeding her baby. Harilal, at the age of twenty-three, broke off from his father again and vanished from Johannesburg, abandoning his family. Gandhi and Kasturbai took care of Gulab and the family, but unfortunately, Gulab died later in Ahmedabad during the 1917 influenza epidemic. Harilal remarried, but the marriage failed; Harilal's life now began to disintegrate to an extent that the father and the son lost each other forever.

Gandhi's relationship with Manilal, his second son, was also strained at this point. From the Volksrust jail, Gandhi wrote letters to Manilal (seventeen years old) about the futility of formal education. Gandhi advised his son to read Emerson, Ruskin, Mazzini, the *Bhagavad Gita*, and the *Upanishads*, which all confirmed his own view that education did not mean knowledge of the letters but character building. He also advised Manilal to keep up with his studies at home and to practice the virtues of chastity, poverty, and manual work.

Despite his love and genuine concern for Manilal's proper education and growth, Gandhi failed to recognize his adolescent son's needs, dreams, and ambitions. The moral injunctions of his scrupulous father were hardly music to the ears of the seventeen-year-old Manilal. At the threshold of young adulthood, Manilal was the least thrilled at the prospects of observing chastity or poverty. Just as with Harilal, Gandhi failed to get into the heart and the mind of young Manilal. As Fischer observed (1950, 93), "Married at thirteen, Gandhi never had a boyhood and therefore never understood his boys."

GOKHALE WITH GANDHI IN SOUTH AFRICA

Gandhi's political mentor, the veteran Indian leader Gopal Krishna Gokhale,[9] visited South Africa during the mounting crisis of the Indian *satyagraha* in 1912. Although Gokhale knew that General Smuts had broken his promises to Gandhi about the removal of the Black Act, the three-pound tax, and other Indian immigration restrictions, he wanted to exert his influence as an unofficial spokesman of the Indian Congress, and as a friend of Gandhi. However, Gokhale met with the same fate as Gandhi, and his negotiations with Botha and Smuts, which had looked promising in the beginning, failed in the end. Yet Gokhale's visit to South Africa proved beneficial in three ways. First, his noncontroversial position as an unofficial spokesman of the Indian Congress helped raise the moral credibility of the Indian struggle; it added authenticity to the Indian demand for justice. Second, his active participation in political negotiations helped focus world attention on the gravity of the Indian situation in South Africa. Third, it was Gokhale who recognized as early as 1909 Gandhi's high spiritual caliber both as a leader and as a person:

> Men of all races and creeds would recognize in him one of the most remarkable personalities of our time, but it was only those who had the privilege of knowing him intimately, knew the pure and indomitable spirit that dwelt in that frail-looking frame which glorified whatever it touched. (*Indian Opinion*, November 9, 1912)

Last Phase of *Satyagraha* in South Africa

As if the earlier anti-Indian acts were not enough, the Transvaal government added yet another insult to the injury; in conjunction with the Supreme Court decision in Cape Colony, the government declared that only Christian marriages were accepted as legal. No other law hit Indians as hard or as low as this one; it rejected the sanctity and legality of all Indian marriages. As Vincent Sheean put it, "this made all Indian wives concubines, and their children bastards" (1955, 81). The Indian women were now aroused to join the *satyagraha*; they picketed in the mines, factories, and farms to recruit thousands of Indian laborers as *satyagrahis*.

Three innovative features of this *satyagraha* set it apart from the rest and established a precedent to be followed by the other *satyagrahas* in the future. The number one outstanding feature was the involvement of women of all ages and stages; the sight of young women, mothers, and mothers-to-be marching fearlessly at the forefront, inspired thousands of men to sacrifice their all in this moral warfare. The women's voluntary suffering and exemplary courage proved to be the biggest incentive for those who were initially reluctant to join the *satyagraha*. Kasturbai herself took the plunge now, leading the "Sisters of the Tolstoy Farm" across the Transvaal borders.

The second novel feature of this *satyagraha* was its mass involvement. People at the grass roots level—the New-castle miners, the farm laborers, the factory workers, and the poorest of the poor indentured Indians—marched hand-in-hand with rich Muslim merchants and colonial-born educated young men. Gandhi called it an " 'army of peace' consisting of Christians, Jews, Hindus, Musalmans or anything else." (1928, 298)

Third, under Gandhi's leadership, the political protest assumed a divine dimension as the masses marched along singing *bhajans* (hymns), cheerfully bearing their "cross of suffering" for truth. Thousands were arrested, and the jails were overfilled. As the news spread, the world conscience was awakened. The South African government was shamed, and finally, on June 30, 1914, the Indian Relief Bill was passed and signed.[10]

Gandhi and Stage 5 Conjunctive Faith: An Evaluation

The final phase of Gandhi's stay in South Africa proved to be the most enlightening one from the faith developmental perspective. During this period he discovered both the mission of his life and the means to achieve it in and through his invention of *satyagraha*. The fact that the birth of *satyagraha* immediately followed his final taking of the "vow of *brahmacharya*" was no mere coincidence, nor was it an accident. Gandhi said that "the principle called *satyagraha* came into being before that name was invented." However, the way he was startled by Sheth's suggestion of oath-taking in the Empire Theatre meeting confirms that he had not consciously planned even that principle. He was taken totally unaware, and yet he had felt the truth of the idea of *satyagraha* in the deepest layers of his psyche. This stage-typical dialectical tension between "an unconscious preparation" and "a lack of self-conscious planning" is explained by Gandhi, who interpreted *satyagraha* as a *dharma-yuddha* (righteous struggle). As he said (1928, xiv), "It comes unsought; and a man of religion is ready for it." However, "a struggle which has to be previously planned is not a righteous struggle. In a righteous struggle God Himself plans campaigns and conducts battles" (ibid.).

Here is Gandhi's own testimony that to him *satyagraha* was not just a political campaign or a mere technique of conflict resolution. It was, rather, a *dharma-yuddha* or a spiritual-ethical warfare fought for truth and by truthful means alone of nonviolence and self-suffering. It was a gradually ripened fruit of Gandhi's deepening spirituality and widening sympathies that display major characteristics of Stage 5.

Gandhi's emphasis on oath-taking as a solemn commitment to self and God rather than as a mere formality of passing a resolution was yet another reflection of his deepening spirituality. This spiritual dimension of the Gandhian *satyagraha* is often missed by most biographers and filmmakers; it is his deeper underlying intent that distinguished *satyagraha* and raised its stature above a mere political movement both in South Africa and later in India. Gandhi's originality lay in maintaining a fine dialectical tension between the two—the spiritual and the political dimensions—in *satyagraha*, which actually enhanced the strength of each separately and together.

Moreover, the creative way in which Gandhi fused the two traditional Indian concepts of *satya* and *ahimsa* and used them interconvertibly in his *satyagraha* substantiates Fowler's point that "there must also be in Stage 5 a new reclaiming and reworking of one's past." To Gandhi, the concepts of truth and nonviolence were as old as the hills. He activated those passive, old principles, however, in ways that were at once creative and pragmatic. In Stage 5 terminology, Gandhi "reclaimed" and "reworked" the familiar in unfamiliar ways in his *satyagraha*.

Another characteristic that Fowler associates with Stage 5 is that one "knows the sacrament of defeat and the reality of irrevocable commitments and acts" (1981, 198). Gandhi's return to South Africa from both his London visits (in 1906 and in 1909) was marked by "a stab in the back" by the British. Only later did he learn that he was deceived and betrayed, and that all his previous petitions, arduous efforts, and persuasions had failed. However, the way in which Gandhi coped with his defeat and with his adversary's betrayal gives another proof of his deepening spiritual outlook. With a sanguine resignation of mind and with detachment in the true spirit of the *Gita*, Gandhi continued with caution but without losing his trust in the enemy's potential for goodness; he never forsook his faith in the human ability to respond to another human's love and suffering.

Gandhi's attitude and behavior in jail exemplified his God-centered vision of life as well as a deepening "interiority of perspective-taking" both for himself and others. Although he suffered severe physical hardships, his spirit soared. He even came to consider human suffering as a "perfect bliss" in which one lives closer to God. In Gandhi's philosophy of truth, self-suffering had a redeeming value; he experienced it first in jail that suffering for Truth alone softens the heart of the enemy; it also makes one capable of bonding with other fellow *satyagrahis* as copilgrims on the path of Truth.

Two examples of Gandhi's inclusive humanity and his widening perspective-taking ability, which highlight another central feature of Conjunctive faith—its "orientation to the 'stranger',"—bear repeating. As Fowler elucidates the point, "this stage strives to unify opposites in mind and experience. It generates and maintains vulnerability to the strange truths of those who are other" (1981, 198). The first instance substantiates Gandhi's trusting attitude and love for his arch political enemy, General Smuts. Since Gandhi was committed to his ideal that "one must live at peace with both friend and foe," he risked being "vulnerable" to Smuts' crooked policy ("strange truths"). Gandhi was never afraid of trusting the opponent despite his frequent breaches of trust. He maintained his faith in Smuts' capacity to respond to love and suffering. He wanted to test the truth of what he knew deep in his heart, that "real suffering bravely borne melts even a heart of stone" (1928, 17). His faith was eventually confirmed. Although Gandhi could not entirely change Smuts' policy or laws, he could still win his enemy's heart, and earn his respect, which was akin to reverence. Gandhi said an "implicit trust in human nature was the very essence of his creed" (1928, 159); the word *creed* stands for his deep inner conviction that basic trust is the very foundation of all human relationships. It is compatible to Fowler's conception of "faith as relational," which means, "I trust, I commit myself, I rest my heart upon, I pledge allegiance" (1981, 16). Gandhi even went a step beyond by putting his trust in his enemy's ability to respond to the gestures of love.

In the second instance, we see Gandhi remaining open to the "strange truths" of not only his enemies, but his would-be assassin as well. In spite of knowing ahead of time that Mir Alam was most likely to carry out his threat, Gandhi still dared to go to the registration office, and risked "vulnerability" to death. He continued to call his Muslim fellow *satyagrahi* "a brother" even after he attacked him. Gandhi proved true to his own deepest conviction that "all men are brothers" regardless of who they are and where they come from, and regardless of whether they hold the same beliefs or belong to the same religion, region, caste, community, or nation. These two examples of Gandhi's inclusive humanity and his widened perspective-taking ability substantiate Fowler's statement regarding Stage 5 that "Ready for closeness to that which is different and threatening to self and outlook, this stage's commitment to justice is freed from the confines of tribe, class, religious community or nation" (ibid.).

Similarly, the book *Hind Swaraj*, which Gandhi introduced as his "Gospel of love in place of hate," represents the heart and soul of his all-embracing humanity and enlarged world vision. Here for the first time he differentiates his conception of a "true *swaraj*," which is more internal than external, more spiritual than material, and more inclusive than exclusive. Those who dismiss this book as Gandhi's unrealistic and bitter criticism of the modern, Western civilization, fail to see this fine underline of Gandhi's emerging global vision of the brotherhood of mankind subsisting on love and not hate.

This period of Gandhi's life most powerfully exhibits another hallmark quality of Stage 5 in which the "symbolic power is reunited with conceptual meanings." We find here a strong resurgence of ("reclaiming and reworking") his own unconscious tendencies as well as his social unconscious—the myths, ideals, traditions, and so on, which acquire new meanings now in both his personal and political life. In the personal context, Gandhi returns to his roots with a renewed enthusiasm and deeper appreciation of his parental and cultural traditions. His self-austerities on the Tolstoy Farm now included a self-imposed fasting for penance, which is different from religious fasting. Gandhi's use of fasting as a means of self-purification and self-penance for his own and others' moral lapses begin from this period onward. Similarly, his mother's dietetic disciplines, her moral restraint and self-denials that lay deep in Gandhi's unconscious were now reclaimed to influence not only his life but others' as well.

The huge bonfire of certificates proved to be the most symbolic-dramatic display of the Indian "social unconscious" aroused by Gandhi; it was the first visual proof of the power of the human spirit ignited by God or

Truth. Moreover, as thousands of men, women, and children marched relentlessly yet happily singing hymns along the Transvaal border, and as many suffered, starved, and even died for the sake of truth, something elevated the Indian movement from a political to a spiritual level. In terms of Stage 5, it showed what human beings could do when moved by the "depths of unrecognized voices of inspiration and guidance," as Fowler put it (ibid.).

Without any reservation, I reaffirm that during this last phase of his stay in South Africa, Gandhi exemplified most powerfully and symbolically all the major qualities and strengths of Stage 5. Through his *satyagraha* in South Africa, he himself was transformed into a *satyagrahi*, a truth-seeker, who would continue his journey of faith in India. To conclude with Brown's succinct analysis (1989, 94), "During his South African years Gandhi's inner life was transformed, as was his outwardly visible life. ... But it was the inner changes which were the most significant because they undergirded the outer ones."

10

India Welcomes Home Her Mahatma

The Gandhi who had gone to South Africa in 1893 was an awkward, unsure, unsuccessful young man in search of career, money, success, name, and fame. The Gandhi who was heading home in 1914 was a middle-aged man of forty-five, self-confident, successful, affluent, and a famous leader of Indians in South Africa. Material fulfillments, however, left him unfulfilled at the deepest core of his heart and soul. Driven no more by worldly ambition, Gandhi was now driven by his faith in God or Truth.

Although many people now knew Gandhi for his *satyagraha* in South Africa, few people knew him as a *satyagrahi* or truth-seeker. Gandhi saw himself neither as a politician nor a saint, but only as a seeker after truth; everything that he undertook from that moment on was an experiment with and exploration of truth. As Brown observed (1989, 74), "It was for his experiments with truth, his inner turmoil and its results that he would have wished to be remembered, rather than his political achievements. To him the latter was ephemeral: the spiritual quest was of eternal and universal significance."

Our objective is to explore the inner world of Gandhi, hence, I shall analyze the complexities of Gandhi's character and paradoxes, including his doubts and dilemmas, ambivalences and polar tensions. I will argue that most of his seeming and real paradoxical traits were held together because of his deepening faith in God, which manifested itself in his ever-widening sympathies for the afflicted of the world. Gandhi said he found his order in the midst of disorder. The center of his equilibrium was located inside—in his "irrepressible optimism" and trust in the basic human goodness of all people, even the hard-hearted. His optimism was rooted in his ever-increasing faith in God as Truth and Nonviolence as Love.

Before continuing further on Gandhi's faith developmental journey, I would like to reemphasize that my primary focus in this chapter is not on Gandhi the politician or saint, but on Gandhi the spiritual seeker after Truth. Gandhi's search of Truth, however, was not bereft of his sociopolitical involvement; I shall, therefore, cover pertinent political and other events only insofar as they reflect the inner process of Gandhi's faith development.

After having spent two decades in South Africa (1893–1914), Gandhi was longing to go home and serve his motherland, although he had no specific plans yet in this regard. Afraid that he would feel like a stranger in his own country, Gandhi wanted to consult his political guru, Gokhale, who was going to be in London for his medical treatment. On his way to India, Gandhi heard that Gokhale was detained in Paris because of the sudden outbreak of World War I. Gandhi decided to go to London anyway and wrote to Gokhale, expressing his supreme wish to "be at his side as a nurse and attendant" at this time, and to "to learn at his feet" upon his return to India.

LOYALTY TO THE BRITISH OR TO NONVIOLENCE?

World War I posed a painful dilemma to Gandhi: Should he participate in the war as a loyal British subject? Or must he adhere to his moral commitment to nonviolence? If we recall, Gandhi had faced a similar dilemma twice in South Africa, but he had resolved it then by organizing an Indian Ambulance Corps. That decision was taken, however, prior to the advent of *satyagraha,* when he had made no firm commitment yet to nonviolence. Between then and now, however, his inner life and outlook had changed. After much consideration, Gandhi decided in favor of raising an Indian Ambulance Corps in London to support the British in World War I. Why? What was his rationale?

Gandhi justified his humanitarian help to the empire for several reasons. First, he said that "the retention of British connection was a sine qua non for India's progress" (Desai, 1968). Second, he said England's need should not be turned into our opportunity. Third, since all Indians were still protected by the British, they were in no status to resist participation unless they surrendered their citizenship or went to jail prior to the war. Fourth, if Indians did not resist the English during peacetime, they should not do so at Britain's hour of need. Fifth, all who participate in war, regardless of whether as soldiers or as volunteers nursing the wounded in battle, cannot be absolved from the guilt of war.

Thus, Gandhi the idealist yielded to Gandhi the pragmatist. Just as in South Africa, he began to organize his own volunteer Indian army for supporting the empire during its hour of crisis. This time, however, he encountered many unforeseen difficulties, one of which was his constant struggle with the British Colonel R. J. Baker, who forbade Gandhi to select his own corporals. Because of this continuous interference from and tussle with British authority, Gandhi decided to resign from the corps. Another big obstacle was Gandhi's failing health on account of extraordinary stress, exhaustion, and pleurisy, which compelled him to stay in bed for several weeks. His physical breakdown might have been a symptom of the unresolved conflict between his conscious and unconscious mind; his conscious decision to be loyal to the British was rejected by his unconscious as being disloyal to the principle of nonviolence. Thus the political activist Gandhi was unwittingly at war with Gandhi the pacifist.

The roots of Gandhi's wartime dilemma lay deeper, however, in his ambivalence toward the British.[1] In *Hind Swaraj*, he expressed dichotomous feelings toward them from the editor's perspective (himself then as pro-British) versus that of the readers (against the British). Gandhi was now beginning to see the gulf of difference that lay between the British in England and the British in India. He admired the British democratic principles of liberty, justice and fairness, but on the other hand, he resented their "sahib mentality" toward the natives of India.

Arrival of a Strange New Leader in India (1915)

Gandhi was detained in London because of his illness, but as soon as he regained some of his strength he headed home with Kasturbai and arrived in Bombay on January 9, 1915. Prominent Indian leaders had planned a gala reception in honor of the homecoming hero of South Africa. All were eyes and ears to see and hear this man; they had read so much about him but never had met him in person. Sheean said (1955, 93), "Gandhi was extremely known for his work in South Africa, yet he was himself unknown to most of them."

Their expectations were either too high or the reality was too disappointing, but all the sophisticated leaders of India felt embarrassed to see Gandhi—a meek-mannered, diminutive of a man dressed in his rustic

Kathiawari cloak, huge turban, and dhoti. As Fischer put it (1950, 127), "The Indian nationalists had expected a new giant, a lion of a man who might lead them to independence.... (but) they were disappointed." They felt even more frustrated to hear him speak. Because of his earlier bout with illness, Gandhi's voice was so weak it was hardly audible. As if that were not enough, Gandhi insisted on speaking in Hindi or Gujarati only, which further turned off the largely English-speaking leaders like Mohammed Ali Jinnah,[2] Pherozeshah Mehta, Srinivasa Shastri, and others. At another reception organized by the Gujarati community, Gandhi not only spoke in Gujarati but also prodded other Anglicized speakers like Jinnah to do the same. Recalling the incident twenty-seven years later, Gandhi said that Jinnah had hated him ever since he made him (Jinnah) speak Gujarati. Jinnah was not alone, however, in his resentment of Gandhi; there were some other Westernized Indians, too, who disapproved of this plainspoken man in his peasant garb and peasant mentality. This was only the beginning; Gandhi would become even more outspoken in the days ahead, but not yet, as he had promised Gokhale (when the latter visited South Africa in 1912) that he would observe political silence for one year in order to get reacquainted with his country and countrymen at close range.

Gandhi spent a few more weeks in Bombay, during which the British government awarded him the *Kaiser-i-Hind* ("Lion of India") gold medal for his distinguished humanitarian services during the wars. Afterward, Gandhi headed to Poone (in Maharashtra State) to pay his respects to his beloved *Rajyaguru* (political adviser) Gokhale, whose health was now rapidly failing. Gokhale, who as early as 1909 had seen Gandhi's great potential as a future leader of India, rolled out the red carpet to welcome him home. The other members of his Servants of India Society, however, like M. R. Jaykar and Srinivasa Shastri, were only lukewarm, if not hostile, to this strange little man, who went scavenging their premises, cleaning up their latrines, and taking away their servants' work. Most of them were Western-educated intellectuals and reformers, who were "working to improve society from within, but by constitutional means," observed Green (1993, 165). Like Gokhale, they moved with caution and believed in slow but steady reform; they disapproved of Gandhi's method and manners, and above all, his "radical views." Gandhi also disliked their intellectual snobbery and hypocrisy. He wondered why they would not allow someone without a higher education to join their society? And why they kept servants if they believed in uplifting the poor? Naturally, their styles clashed and views differed. Brown said (1989, 98), "They made it plain that they disapproved of Gandhi's anarchical views, both political and social." After Gokhale's demise in 1915, Gandhi distanced himself from the Servants of India Society and its members.

From Poone, Gandhi went with Kasturbai to see his immediate families in Rajkot and Porbandar. It was a sad visit as both his older brothers, Karsandas and Lakshmidas, had died recently and entrusted to Gandhi the responsibility of their bereaved families.

Touring India by Train

Gandhi decided to use the first year of his political silence meeting the grassroots people of his motherland; he wanted to experience for himself how the poor lived and the hardships they suffered. He thought, what could allow closer contact with the poor than by traveling third-class via train?[3] Though Gandhi already knew about the hardships of third-class passengers in general, until he met a tailor named Motilal, he had no idea about the heavy customs duty that passengers were forced to pay at the Viramgam station. As was Gandhi's style, he personally investigated the matter upon reaching Rajkot, and he sent letters to the railway authorities and the state governor about the high-handedness of the bureaucrats and the unreasonable custom duties. He also chided the passengers for their apathy and unhygienic habits.

When there was no response from the railway authorities, Gandhi approached Lord Willingdon and Lord Chelmsford (Viceroy); through his persistence and their intervention, the Viramgam customs were finally abolished. Although a small victory, this unpublicized mini-*satyagraha* was symbolically similar to Gandhi's Martizburg experience in South Africa. Now Gandhi was free to go to Bengal to visit Gurudev (Great Guru) Tagore at Shantiniketan.

Visiting Tagore's *Shantiniketan*

Rabindranath Tagore,[4] the Bengali Nobel poet laureate (1913), called Gandhi a "Mahatma"[5] and Gandhi called the poet "The Great Sentinel." Both revered each other deeply, but they also fought verbal-ideological battles from time to time. Though poles apart in their personalities, appearance, talents, and ways of thinking, the two contemporaries were ardent nationalists and humanists whose hearts bled for the poor, rural folks of India. Senior to Gandhi by eight years, Tagore greatly contributed to India's cultural regeneration in the twentieth century. Each served the motherland in his own unique way—Tagore by his muse and music, and Gandhi through his active social and political service. To borrow Fischer's poetic prose:

> Gandhi was the wheat field and Tagore the rose garden. Gandhi was the working arm, Tagore the singing voice. Gandhi the emaciated ascetic with shaven head and face, Tagore the large, white-maned, white-bearded aristocratic intellectual with a face of a classic, patriarchal beauty. Gandhi exemplified stark renunciation; Tagore felt "the embrace of freedom in a thousand bonds of delight." (1950, 128)

Tagore and Gandhi were also severe critics of each other. Tagore disapproved of Gandhi's advocacy of bonfires and boycotts of British goods and institutions as potentially violent, whereas Gandhi considered Tagore's aesthetic approach to be too far removed from the real, bread-and-butter issues of the poor, who need to eat before they can sing. In *India of My Dreams*, Gandhi said (1947, 14), "For the poor the economic is spiritual; their only God is their bread." He saw God in the faces of the poor—the peasants, the Untouchables, and the starving millions of his motherland.

When Gandhi visited *Shantiniketan* (*Shanti*: peace; *niketan*: residence), Tagore was away from this educational-aesthetic institution that he had founded in the rural Bolpur region near Calcutta in West Bengal. The entire *Shantiniketan* community, however, consisting of musicians, singers, artists, and academics, gave Gandhi and his group a hearty welcome; the Phoenix people had already arrived there by previous arrangement. During the time that Gandhi was there, "he turned the whole place upside down," said Fischer (1950, 129). The very first change he introduced was to relieve the servants from their daily tasks and distribute them among the residents of the community. Thus, he turned singers into sweepers, artists into cooks, and professors into janitors. The hands that once played on the *Veena* (stringed instrument) now chopped wood; poets who took pride in their poetry were now proud of their handmade pieces of pottery. Little by little, Gandhi instilled in them the pure delight of doing things by hand, doing work as worship, and appreciating the dignity of manual labor. The result of Gandhi's experiment was marvelous for as long as it lasted, but after his departure, the *Shantiniketan* residents returned to their old aesthetic delights of singing, painting, and music-making.

FOUNDING THE SABARMATI ASHRAM

Gandhi established his first ashram in India on the banks of the river Sabarmati in the outskirts of the industrial-historical city of Ahmedabad, Gujarat, his own home-state in west India. The Sabarmati Ashram, also called the *Satyagraha Ashram*, was founded in 1915 on the same principles of work ethics as his previous two ashrams in South Africa. In selecting his location, Gandhi showed both practical foresight and spiritual insight.[6]

This was the ashram where "Gandhi grew to full stature as the leader of the nation," said Fischer (1950, 129). From here Gandhi launched his first nationwide salt satyagraha (in 1930), which catapulted him to international fame. This was also the place that first tested Gandhi's mettle as a truth votary who, despite severe protest, welcomed an Untouchable family to live in his ashram. He thereby risked the wrath of orthodox Hindus, including his own wife and close associates who threatened to leave him, but Gandhi remained true to his principle of treating all human beings as "Children of God."

Gandhi, like his childhood hero "Truthful King Harishchandra," suffered for truth but did not forsake his principles. He was boycotted from both inside and outside his family. The enraged orthodox Hindus withdrew all their financial and social support to the ashram, leaving Gandhi to fend on his own. At this crucial hour, however, help arrived mysteriously from a wealthy anonymous donor—later recognized to be Sheth Ambalal Sarabhai. Orthodox Hindus saw his acceptance of Untouchables in his ashram as "blasphemy"; it was both an act of religious violation and a social defiance. As Sheean put it (1955, 96–97), "This episode, which may seem small, in retrospect, was not small at the time. ... It was not done. ... From this time onward it was understood in India that he meant what he said."

GANDHI'S BENARES SPEECH

Finishing his one year of political silence, Gandhi accepted Annie Besant's invitation to speak at the inauguration of the Benares Hindu University Central College in February 1916. Among all his earlier speeches upon coming home, this was the most outspoken one, which signaled the arrival of a new leader who was a reformer, a revolutionary, and a spiritual seeker— all in one. As earlier in Pretoria, South Africa, Gandhi emphasized truthfulness and advised his fellow Indians to be self-critical before criticizing the government. This time, however, his tone and manner of speaking were far more vehement, and his mood markedly rebellious. He spared no one from criticism—not the Maharajas, nor the government officers, not even the students and religious leaders. He was bold. He was outspoken. He was deeply caring, yet unsparing. Determined to expose the hypocrisy of Westernized Indians and shake off their sycophancy, Gandhi declared, "I am also an anarchist, but of a different type." The Raja-Maharajas squirmed in their seats, and some left; some asked Gandhi to sit down. Annie Besant felt embarrassed; the students, however, cheered loudly and said, "Go on, Gandhi, go on."

Gandhi meant to upset the applecart but not to annihilate it. As Woodcock observed (1971, 96), "Gandhi remained anarchistic rather than anarchist." In his first truly public speech in India, Gandhi forewarned his people of what kind of leadership they should expect from him. Without fear, and without a false sense of shame, Gandhi spoke about his unique vision of *swaraj* (*swa:* self; *raj:* rule), which meant not only political independence from the British, but a radical reordering of the Indian society from both within and without. He aimed at total transformation of individual and society—a transformation that was not only economic and political but also internal and spiritual. No leaders before Gandhi had ever talked like this. It was a moment of rude awakening for all—including those who had initially walked out on him, but later joined him. Moreover, at this meeting, many idealistic young men like Vinoba Bhave, Mahadevbhai Desai, Pyarelal, and others came under Gandhi's spell and became his most trusted disciples.

CHAMPARAN: THE FIRST *SATYAGRAHA* IN INDIA

If at Benares the Indians first heard Gandhi's "anarchical views," in Champaran (Bihar, North India), they first saw him as a leader in action. Until Champaran, the intelligentsia had never been exposed to Gandhi's style of working from the grassroots level, nor had they ever been led into a principled, nonviolent revolution.

Gandhi himself had never seen nor heard about Champaran—a small, remote village in the foothills of Himalaya near Nepal. However, as with most other previous involvements, this, too, came to him unsought. Margaret Chatterjee's observation (1983, 96) that "Gandhi felt himself to be addressed by events" is true insofar as he himself did not volunteer to be in places or situations that were totally new to him. Yet, having been put in such situations, he chose to lead, driven by his inner striving for truth and justice.

During the annual convention of the Indian National Congress in Lukhnow (North India) in December of 1916, Gandhi met a farmer named Rajkumar Shukla. Like many other Indian peasants, Shukla was poor, illiterate, and living on bare bones. He was persistent in trying to persuade Gandhi to go with him to Champaran to help the peasants resolve their chronic suffering and the injustice of the landlord system in Bihar. The peasants of Champaran were trapped in what is called a "*tinkathia* system" in which the landlords compelled them to grow indigo in three *kathas* (one acre) out of twenty. Like the indentured Indian laborers in South Africa, they slaved from dawn to dusk and were abused by their landlords who flogged them, starved them, and kept them in debt. The peasants desperately needed someone to listen to their problems and represent their cause. Shukla followed him everywhere and never gave up until Gandhi agreed to go with him to Bihar and investigate the case himself.

Gandhi proved to be a different kind of leader, one who personally visited the villagers of Champaran in their shanties and huts. Instead of riding in a jeep, he went walking for miles and miles under the scorching northern sun. Keeping no distance, Gandhi freely mixed with villagers, listened to their problems, ate what they ate, and spoke their language; as a result there was an instant rapport between him and the peasants. He identified with the poorest peasants just as he had identified with BalaSundaram in South Africa. In Gandhi's own words (1948, 504), "It is no exaggeration, but the literal truth ... that in this meeting with the peasants I was face to face with God, Ahimsa and Truth."

In Champaran, Gandhi first introduced his mini-scale experiments in "constructive programs" such as women's education, sanitary reforms, health care for villagers, and so on. Further, it was in the Champaran law courts that Gandhi first pled guilty before a magistrate, saying that "I submit without protest to the penalty of disobedience ... in obedience to the higher law of our being, the voice of conscience" (*Autobiography*, 506). The magistrate had never met the likes of Gandhi who would proudly admit violating a man-made law in order to obey a superior law of his "conscience"; nor had he seen anyone courting punishment for doing so. Baffled by this stranger and his even stranger ways, the magistrate ordered the case to be dropped. Gandhi made extensive inquiries of case after case of exploitation of peasants by the planters, produced compelling evidence, and negotiated a mutually agreeable sum to be paid to the peasants by the planters. Thus, Champaran marked the first triumph of Gandhi's *satyagraha* in India, inspiring hope and faith and instilling self-confidence in his people for a better future.

The Champaran *satyagraha* was also remarkable in other ways. The "Mahatma-mania" began from this place and time onward, spreading all across India. From remote corners came the *darshan-seekers* (desiring a "holy glimpse") of the *Mahatma* (Great Soul); touching his feet, they put the "holy dust" over their foreheads. Champaran was also the place where Gandhi first met his future compatriots, such as Rajendra Prasad Babu (lawyer) and Acharya Kripalani (professor), whose lives were transformed by coming in close contact with the Mahatma.

THE KHEDA *SATYAGRAHA* IN NADIAD

The Patidar (or Patel) peasants of Nadiad in the Kheda district of Gandhi's native Gujarat were unable to pay the government their land revenues because of severe failure of their crops from drought and famine in 1917–1918. The government had employed every severe measure—from confiscating and selling the peasants' cattle to "attaching" standing crops to their land to claim extra revenues on them. Since all petitions for tax exemption had failed, they now turned to Gandhi for help.

The highlight of this *satyagraha* was Gandhi's use of a local Gujarati tradition as an effective, symbolic method of protest against injustice. As in Champaran, here, too, Gandhi worked mostly with the illiterate masses at their level of understanding. He had an especially difficult task at hand to keep up the peasants' morale for many long months with no happy end in sight; he had to persuade them to starve rather than submit to the government's tyranny. Gandhi argued that the government's "attachment of crops" was nothing but an immoral act of looting the poor. At this crucial point he resorted to an old local tradition in which, under the leadership of Mohanlal Pandya, the *satyagrahis* removed a whole crop of onions that was wrongly attached to their field. Thus, what was familiar to the farmers was re-employed as a well-orchestrated technique of *satyagraha*.

"The significant contribution of Gandhi lay not in any revival of traditional forms or method," wrote Joan Bondurant (1965, 5), "but in a transformation of traditional concepts in such a way that only the symbols remained familiar—for the symbols were made by Gandhi to stand for a quite different set of values." This was Gandhi's way of making ordinary people achieve extraordinary tasks; he also prepared them to suffer serious consequences of their civil disobedience. In the Kheda *satyagraha*, Gandhi worked with brilliant local lawyers like Vallabhbhai Patel (later his loyal follower and a leader), and others like Mohanlal Pandya (called "the Onion-thief"), Shankarlal Banker, and Indulal Yajnik. Most important, Gandhi taught peasants "to first get rid of their fear of the officials and to fight with civility."

RECRUITING FOR WAR VERSUS NONVIOLENCE

Even though Gandhi's influence was very high in his own home region because of his recent *satyagraha* (1918) in Kheda, Gujarat, he was still unable to recruit his people for the British in the war. Astonished by Gandhi's plea to enlist them in war, the people asked him defiantly: "You are a votary of Ahimsa, how can you ask us to take up arms? What good has Government done for India to deserve our co-operation?" (*Autobiography*, 545).

Gandhi argued along the same line as he did earlier in London at the time of World War I: All able-bodied sons of the empire must volunteer their service in the army and thus be loyal to the government. This was not the time for them to bring up their grievances, or to count the misdeeds of the British rule in India. In addition, he also gave them hope that by "rendering voluntary help to the Government in its time of trial, distrust will disappear, and the ban on possessing arms will be withdrawn. ... and if we serve to save the Empire, we have in that very act secured Home Rule" (*Autobiography*, 546–548). At the same time, he spoke on behalf of his people as a special guest at the government's War Emergency Conference (from which prominent leaders like Tilak, Mrs. Besant, and the Ali brothers were excluded). Also, in his letter to the Viceroy, Gandhi said that though he strongly urged his people to give their "ungrudging and unequivocal support to the Empire," he certainly hoped that India would soon become "the most favored partner of the Empire" and would be given a Dominion status.

When his people were reluctant to enlist in the army despite his arduous efforts, Gandhi interpreted it as a sign of their cowardice rather than commitment to peace. He wrote in *Young India* (August 11, 1920): "I would rather that India resort to arms in order to defend her honour, than that she should, in a cowardly manner, become or remain helpless witness to her own dishonour."

In his letters to H. L. S. Polak and C. F. Andrews, Gandhi tried hard to defend his wartime ideology by arguing, "although nonviolence is superior to violence, where there is only a choice between cowardice and violence, I would advise violence" (*Nonviolence in Peace and War*, 1: 1). Yet, as in 1914, his unconscious revolted against his consciously taken decision. Fischer (1950, 161) observed, "The political Gandhi was thus caught in the ineradicable conflict between nationalism and pacifism. ... In this dichotomy lay the tragedies of Gandhi's life." This unresolved inner conflict plus the stress and strain of recruiting people in the army resulted once again in a serious illness. He suffered this time from severe dysentery, and fissures, for which he had to be operated. The doctors advised him to be on complete bed rest for months or until he fully regained his health and energy.

Even while recuperating from his operation, Gandhi subsisted only on goat milk.[7] Although "very weak," he "could not have been happier," he said, as when dieting or fasting. He added, "My experiments in dietetics were dear to me as a part of my researches in *ahimsa*. They gave me recreation and joy" (*Autobiography*, 557).

THE AHMEDABAD *SATYAGRAHA* IN 1918

This was the first labor versus capital dispute in Ahmedabad, which culminated into a *satyagraha* under Gandhi's leadership.[8] The overworked and under-paid mill workers were demanding a wage increase to cope with inflation, but the mill owners—Ambalal Sarabhai and his sister Anasuya Sarabhai—were either impervious to their demand or unable to grant it because of economic depression and foreign competition.

This *satyagraha* is particularly noteworthy for Gandhi's first use of fasting for a public cause and also as a spiritual deterrent of abuse of the powerless by the powerful. Another important feature was Gandhi's use of a strike as not only a technique of public protest but also as a method of internal self-cleansing.

There is nothing particularly striking about "striking" as a political or social tactic. Many labor unions and other groups around the world commonly use it to protest against injustice or to express grievances. Before Gandhi entered the picture, however, the disgruntled mill workers had already gone on strike to compel their employers to increase their wages. When their enthusiasm was lagging, they went to Gandhi, who advised them to take a pledge in the name of God—which is called "*Ek Tek*" in Gujarati. Gandhi himself had first been inspired in South Africa to take an oath in the name of God, which to him was as sacred as taking a "vow" and "making an unbreakable commitment to God." Taking a pledge meant abiding by the truth of their demand, suffering for truth, and using pledge as a means of self-control. Gandhi's idea of strike was rooted in self-assertion for both truth and self-control. A striker was, therefore, a *satyagrahi,* who must not only exercise self-restraint in the face of all provocation but also extend goodwill and cooperation toward the adversary.[9] When the strike dragged on for weeks with no end in sight, some of the workers began to lose hope, some quit, and some threatened to use violence. Without work or income, their families were also losing patience. The strikers' morale was at its lowest and there was no ray of hope. It was at this dark moment that "the light came to me," said Gandhi, "unbidden and all by themselves the words came to my lips ... unless the strikers ... continue the strike till a settlement is reached or till they leave the mill, I will not touch any food" (*Autobiography,* 526).

That was the origin of Gandhi's first public fasting. As he said, it came to him unbidden in a moment of sudden illumination from within. It was the prompting of his conscience, or what he called his "still small voice," which he equated with God. Its effect was like a bolt of lightning. The strikers were in tears, they were ashamed of their lapse, and they begged to fast with Gandhi.

If the strikers felt so guilty about Gandhi's fasting for them, how did the mill owners feel? Were they embarrassed? Or did they feel blackmailed? Ever since Sheth Ambalal Sarabhai had donated money to Gandhi's Sabarmati ashram, he considered Gandhi to be a part of his family. Ambalal's sister, Anasuya Sarabhai, actually felt sympathy for the strikers but was unable to meet with their demands on account of hard economic times. Because of his closeness with the Sarabhai family, Gandhi realized that his fast was "not without a grave defect" (1948, 527); he was afraid lest his fast may influence their decision in resolving the conflict. At the same time Gandhi felt that he must side with the truth, which was on the side of the mill workers.

The Sarabhai family, however, felt more aggrieved than embarrassed or blackmailed when they heard about Gandhi's fast because they loved him dearly and respected him greatly. Eventually both parties reached a happy compromise with Gandhi as a peacemaker. As he put it, "the net result was that an atmosphere of goodwill was created all around," (ibid., 528) and it survives to this day. Gandhi was thus successful in bringing labor and management together. His three-day fast set a precedent for other such fasts to come in the future; this *satyagraha* had a lasting, positive effect, as it gave birth to the Textile Labor Association.

Spiritual Practices

How did Gandhi stay tuned to God in the midst of all the chaos surrounding him? What was the secret of his well-known serenity of mind? Unlike what most people believe, Gandhi was neither born with this quality, nor did it come easily to him. As Louis Fischer put it, Gandhi's "Mahatma-calm was the product of training" (1950, 61). Although he was brought up in a religious home environment by a "saintly mother" and aspired to be "as flawless as mother," he still had to strive and struggle for self-control (over anger, sex, palate, etc.) through rigorous *sadhana* (spiritual disciplines) and *tapashcharya* (self-austerities).

Rising daily at 4 a.m., he prayed, recited, and reflected over his favorite verses from the *Gita*, and conducted his early morning group prayer session, which included select passages from the scriptures of major world religions. Gandhi spent the rest of the day writing and replying to hundreds of letters from around the world, taking long walks, spinning his daily quota of yarn, cleaning latrines, and getting busy with his various "constructive programs," which included the removal of untouchability, public health and education, promotion of village industries, sanitation, communal harmony, and others. Morevoer, an endless row of visitors—political dignitaries, ministers, and journalists—interrupted him. Still, Gandhi found time to pray, to play and laugh with children, to help deliver a calf, and to nurse the sick.

Inner Voice: The Voice of God

The fountainhead of Gandhi's inexhaustible energy was his faith in God, to whom he turned for resolving all his problems—internal and external; he listened to his Conscience, his "Inner Voice" or the "Voice of God." Note here that Gandhi's concept of *conscience* is drastically different from that of Freud. Conscience to Gandhi represents all the *sattva gunas* or ennobling qualities—love, light, purity, nobility, unselfishness, nonviolence, and others. In Freud's view, conscience is guilt-ridden and self-chastising; it is full of id and ego, which represent the *tamas gunas* or dark and evil thoughts—guilt, shame, selfishness, violence, and similar negative emotions. The first is God-illumined, whereas the other, God-alienated.

Gandhi believed that only those who are pure at heart could hear God's voice; pure conscience is therefore a prerequisite for receiving insight and strength from God. However, pure conscience is not possible without self-purification. When Gandhi was asked how he could be sure that the inner voice he heard was not "a hallucination" or "an echo of his heated imagination," he answered in *Harijan* (October 7, 1939) that "there was a possibility of self-deception," but he also clarified that "this listening to God presupposes the fitness to listen, and the fitness is acquired only after constant and patient striving and waiting on God" (ibid.). To acquire such purity of heart, the mind must first be controlled, slowly and gradually, through regular spiritual *sadhana* and practice of the *yamas* and *niyamas*.[10] It requires incessant efforts and vigilance to purify the mind, to lift it toward God through prayers and meditation, and through dedicating all activities to God or performing them without attachment.

GANDHI INSPIRED TO OPPOSE THE ROWLATT ACT

Before Gandhi entered national politics in 1919, all of India was ignited by an anti-British extremist zeal.[11] Reacting in sheer fear and panic, the British government appointed a commission, presided over by Justice Rowlatt, to investigate all seditious activities; the recommendations of the commission, approved by Rowlatt in July 1919, became a law notoriously called "The Rowlatt Act." This by far was one of the most repressive British acts, which introduced extreme and severe measures in which any Indian could be arrested anytime on even the slightest suspicion of terrorist involvement; he or she could be imprisoned without the right to appeal and without open trial. It enforced wartime measures in the absence of war.

Thinking of launching a nationwide civil disobedience against the Rowlatt Act, Gandhi formed a special *Satyagraha Sabha* (*sabha*: meeting) in Ahmedabad and carefully chose his *satyagrahis* for this truth campaign. While he was still groping for the right way to lead this *satyagraha*, he had a dream that showed him the way:

> The idea came to me last night in a dream that we should call upon the country to observe a general *hartal*. Satyagraha is a process of self-purification, and ours is a sacred fight, and it seems to be in the fitness of things that it should be commenced with an act of self-purification. (*Autobiography*, 562)

His inner voice had spoken again; it had shown him the way. All Indians should observe a general *hartal* (nationwide strike) as a protest against the Rowlatt Act. All work must stop; schools, courts, offices, shops, and other activities must be suspended for a day. Gandhi wanted people not only to close their businesses but also to observe the day with fasting and prayer. This was another example of Gandhi's use of a familiar protest tactic like a strike as a sacred symbol of fighting for human dignity and freedom. To him, *hartal* was a day of quiet contemplation, a day of self-purification.

This nationwide *hartal* took India by storm, but it was a spiritual storm, which was peacefully observed on March 30, 1919, in Delhi, and on April 6 in Ahmedabad, Bombay, Madras, Calcutta, and elsewhere. Not only the Hindus but also the Muslims of India observed the fast and prayed all day. It was the first time in Indian history that the Hindus and the Muslims joined forces to fight their common enemy; they were united like blood brothers. If the British chased the Hindus, the Muslims would shelter them in their mosques, and vice versa. The Hindu–Muslim fraternization in 1919 was phenomenal, but unfortunately, it did not last long on account of the newly developing Muslim separatism, to be discussed later.

Despite a strong start, the movement degenerated into violence because of rumors of Gandhi's arrest by the government. Even before Gandhi's actual arrest on his way to Delhi, the inflamed mobs lost all control. Violence erupted like a volcano; India turned into a blazing inferno.

A Himalayan Miscalculation

"A rapier run through my body could scarcely have pained me more," said Gandhi in response to this widespread violence (Natesan 1922). His heart bled; he felt deeply ashamed to know that his own people in Ahmedabad had burned down buildings, cut off telegraph wires, stopped trains, and killed trapped policemen. He called off the *satyagraha* and announced that the whole campaign was a "Himalayan miscalculation" on his part. (1948, 575)

A Himalayan blunder called for Himalayan atonement. He first confessed his grave error publicly and then did penance by observing three days of fasting and prayers. He held himself to be entirely responsible for the people's lack of restraint for two reasons. First, he had failed to explain to them that "a *satyagrahi* obeys the laws of society ... of his own free will" because it is "his sacred duty to do so." (ibid.) Only an honest and law-abiding citizen is qualified to judge which particular laws or rules are good and just and which are not. Therefore, it is as much his sacred duty to obey the former (just) laws, as it is to disobey the latter. Second, Gandhi felt he had overlooked the limitation of the masses to understand the deeper implications of civil disobedience. Before starting civil disobedience on a mass scale, he admitted, he should have known his people's limitation and their lack of training in how to adhere to the fundamental principles of *satyagraha* under extreme provocation.

Gandhi's discomfiture was his critics' delight. This was his first political crisis in India that tested the strength of his faith, but in the end he stood the test. He wrote to the Viceroy, "My faith in *satyagraha* remains undiminished." He never regretted making a confession, because, he said, "I have always held that it is only when one sees one's own mistake with a convex lens, and does just the reverse in the case of others, that one is able to arrive at a just relative estimate of the two" (ibid.).

Holding Gandhi to be chiefly responsible for the widespread violence, the government imprisoned him and imposed a martial law (military enforcement usually invoked in a state of national emergency). The government confiscated all the suspected incendiary literature including Gandhi's book *Hind Swaraj*, the *Bombay Chronicle*,[12] and similar material. All civil liberties and freedoms of speaking, writing, printing, gathering or distributing anti-government literature were denied. A heavy curfew was imposed, and what was felt as the worst humiliation of all, for the crimes of the few, many innocent civilians—men, women and children were forced to crawl like worms on their bellies.

THE JALLIANWALLA BAGH (AMRITSAR) MASSACRE

In the Jallianwalla Bagh (garden) in Amritsar (Punjab, north India), British soldiers ruthlessly gunned down, without any prior warning, hundreds of civilians protesting the martial law. Since then it came to be called the "Jallianwallah Bagh Massacre."[13] The news of these heinous murders spread fast, and the British reign of terror in India was now exposed to the world. Gandhi conducted his own independent inquiry into the matter to find the truth, and his detailed report falsified the British version of the event in the Hunter Commission Report. This was Gandhi's moment of rude awakening. His romantic vision of British rule was shattered; he saw it for the first time for what it was—not a benevolent but "a Satanic Government." His report was based on truth and nothing but the truth. It revealed "what inhumanities and barbarities it is capable of perpetrating in order to maintain its power" (*Autobiography*, 585).

THE KHILAFAT (CALIPHATE) CAMPAIGN

Another incident in 1919 further eroded Gandhi's trust in the British. He joined the Indian Muslims in their Pan-Islamic protest against the British, who had denied the Sultan of Turkey (after the war treaty) his right to continue to be the *Khalifah* (religious head) of the entire Muslim population around the world. Gandhi had trusted the British government to be fair and just, but the arbitrary way in which the government curbed the Muslim demand and sentiment, proved it to be otherwise.

Many Hindus were irked by Gandhi's stand on a strictly Muslim issue like *Khilafat*; they wanted to know why Gandhi, who claimed to be a *sanatani* (true) Hindu, supported Muslims in *Khilafat?* Apart from his personal association with the Muslims in South Africa and his childhood friendship with Mehtab, Gandhi was motivated at present by two major factors. First, it was the voice of his political-tactical wisdom that prompted him to seek Muslim support for resisting the British. Second, and more significant, Gandhi aimed at the larger goal of establishing Hindu–Muslim unity. His vision was broadening; his human sympathies were expanding; he felt now "truly brotherly" toward Muslims, Christians, and people of all other faiths. In his words, "Hinduism is nothing if not tolerant and generous to every other faith" (*Young India*, December 15, 1927).

A BRITISH LOYALIST TURNED REBEL

All these British atrocities during the years 1919–1920—the Rowlatt Act imposition, the Amritsar massacre, and the Khilafat agitation—contributed to the conversion of Gandhi from a British loyalist to a British rebel, but a rebel for truth and nonviolence. At the 1920 Indian Congress sessions at Amritsar and Nagpur, Gandhi was given the stewardship for conducting the national movement for Indian independence. He was recognized by all as an "uncrowned king of India," who, without any political position or portfolio, ruled over the hearts and souls of his fellow Indians; he wielded the maximum moral, spiritual, and political influence over them. In the 1920s Gandhi was India and India, Gandhi. Yet to him, politics was only a means to an end for serving God through serving His children. What he had been striving for was "self-realization, to see God face to face, to attain *moksha*" (spiritual liberation or salvation). "For me the road to salvation lies through incessant toil in the service of my country and of humanity," said Gandhi, "because I want to identify with everything that lives." [14]

THE NON-COOPERATION MOVEMENT OR *ASAHAKARA*

The Gandhian *satyagraha* now enters a technically perfected form called "Non-cooperation." The original Gujarati word for it is *asahakara* (*a*: non; *saha*: together; *kara*: action). Gandhi called "non-cooperation, the highest form of cooperation," because in its essence it meant refusing to cooperate with a law or action that violates fundamental human rights, dignity, and truth, as well as refusing to cooperate with those responsible for such violations. Gandhi stressed that "non-cooperation meant self-purification, self-reliance, sacrifice, and courage" (Desai 1968, 2:11). The three major facets of non-cooperation were: peacefulness, self-restraint, and sacrifice for human service (*yajna*). Gandhi called "non-cooperation the *dharma* of self-restraint at its highest" (ibid., 3:122).

Non-cooperation is different from civil disobedience. Joan Bondurant explains the latter as "a direct contravention of specific laws" that includes non-payment of taxes, jail-going, and carefully undertaken fasting, which rules out the "majority of hunger-strikes undertaken without previous preparation and without adequate thought" (1965, 37). Non-cooperation, on the other hand, does not involve direct confrontation with state authority or breaking of a specific law; it involves the withdrawal by individuals of their support or allegiance to various government or public institutions. This includes relinquishing titles or privileges, or withdrawing membership, participation, or attendance in government-operated schools, courts, and all official agencies. Although sometimes the methods may overlap (such as a boycott), non-cooperation remains largely symbolic, peaceful, and self-restrained. Major symbolic devices of the Gandhian style non-cooperation (in addition to striking, and spiritual fasting) were: boycotts, *swadeshi* (home-grown products), hand spinning, and the adoption of *khadi* (hand-spun cloth).

Boycott as a method of opposition against the British had been commonly used since 1905, even before Gandhi came into the picture. This time, however, the spirit of patriotism swept over the entire country and the mood of the people was joyous; their joy, contagious. Huge bonfires consuming the finest of the fine British garments and goods leaped to the skies, emblazed the streets, and illumined every Indian heart with nationalistic pride and zeal. I should mention here that not all supporters of Gandhi looked on "bonfires of British goods or cloth" as nonviolent non-cooperation. Rabindranath Tagore, who himself had relinquished his British title of knighthood as a gesture of non-cooperation, was distrustful of "the evil in human nature." According to Louis Fischer (1950, 291), "Tagore feared that when Gandhi lit bonfires of foreign cloth he would kindle unconscious emotions in men." Romain Rolland, the great French writer and biographer of Gandhi (1924), agreed with Tagore, as did C. F. Andrews. Gandhi respected their opinions but believed that humans were capable of nobler emotions and actions and could be trusted with such nonviolent expressions of their non-cooperation. Under Gandhi's leadership, therefore, the "*Swaraj* demanding" peace protesters paraded the streets day and night. There was a total boycott of all English institutions including schools, offices, law courts, and public facilities; their Indian-operated counterparts replaced them. The monstrous British machine was thus brought to a screeching halt.

Swadeshi is "that spirit in us which restricts us to the use and service of our immediate surroundings to the exclusion of the more remote," said Gandhi.[15] A gospel of the Gandhian era, *swadeshi* galvanized the whole nation in several ways. First, it fostered economic self-reliance through the hand-spun yarn and *khadi* clothes, and through the promotion of Indian handicrafts, homegrown products, and village industries. Second, psychologically, it restored Indian self-esteem by eradicating their fear of the British. Third, *swadeshi* served as a cultural symbol that enabled Indians to appreciate their own country, culture, language, and religion. Fourth, in Gandhi's hands, it acquired a spiritual dimension, inspiring people to serve and sacrifice for the larger good of the whole nation.

As just mentioned, hand spinning was an indispensable missile in the armory of Gandhi's *swadeshi* movement for India's freedom, as well as for his own spiritual salvation. For centuries the villagers in India had been using *charkha*—an old-fashioned spinning wheel. It was rediscovered for Gandhi by one of his loyal female followers, a Gujarati widow named Gangaben Majmundar.[16] Hand spinning served not only as an economic means of independence but also as a spiritual symbol of service to mankind. Gandhi said, "I feel convinced that the revival of hand-spinning will make the largest contribution to the economic and the moral regeneration of India." (1947, 48–49).[17] Although many Westernized Indians sneered at the spinning wheel, to Jawaharlal Nehru (Gandhi's political heir), "it was the livery of India's freedom," and to Gandhi, "a gateway to my spiritual salvation" (Fischer 1950, 231).

Khadi (Gujarati) or *Khaddar* (Hindi)—hand-spun coarse cloth—became a trademark of the Gandhi era. Gandhi considered spinning a duty and a sacrament; he taught it to himself first and then to others. Taking pride in spinning a daily quota of yarn himself, he made it mandatory for all his ashram residents, and later, for the Congress as well. The *Khadi* attire became an emblem of the Congress; it was a sacred symbol of simplicity, self-reliance and patriotism. As Fischer put it, "Gandhi was trying to bridge brain and brawn, to unite city and town, to link rich and the poor. ... it was an act of love, another channel of communication. It was also a method of organization" (ibid.). The white *Khadi* cap in particular, which Gandhi wore until 1921, came to be known as the "Gandhi cap"; it became an identification mark of every Congressman and a badge of nationalism as well. Wearing this cap meant following Gandhi; it was supposed to mean adopting his principles as well. Brown said, "Gandhi caps became the hallmark of the radical and patriotic" (1983, 162).

GANDHI ADOPTS THE LOINCLOTH

When Gandhi tried to explain to the villagers the importance of wearing *khadi,* he heard them tell this naked truth: "We are too poor to buy *khadi.*" Only then did he realize that millions of his fellow Indians had nothing more to wear than a mere loincloth, which was "four inches wide and nearly as many feet long." From that moment on Gandhi divested himself of his vest, cap, and full *dhoti,* and adopted a loincloth. Gandhi said, "it was a sheer necessity, but in as far as the loincloth also spells simplicity, let it represent Indian civilization" (1950, 59). Gandhi's adoption of the loincloth was not only a patriotic mark of sympathy for the poor but also a spiritual landmark of personal advancement on the journey to Truth. Moreover, each of the devices he used in the *asahakara movement* suggested Gandhi's rare gift of using powerful symbols to achieve political ends. Whatever Gandhi introduced in politics was an expression or extension of his expanding spiritual vision; as he said, "I can not conceive of politics as divorced from religion." (Harijan, February 10, 1940, 445)

The non-cooperation movement was in full swing. Every street and corner of India vibrated with the sounds of "Vande Mataram" ("Salute to Mother India") and with "Mahatma Gandhi ki jay" ("Hail to Mahatma Gandhi"). At the very climax, however, came the anti-climax, when sudden violence erupted in *Chauri Chaura* (in the United Provinces). It so happened that the police manhandled some of the demonstrators; the constables even opened fire on the rioters until, running out of ammunition, they retired to their *Thana* (police headquarters) for safety. The enraged mob, according to

Fischer's report (1950, 197), "set fire to the *Thana*. The self-imprisoned constables had to come out for dear life, and as they did so they were hacked to pieces and the mangled remains were thrown into raging flames."

Gandhi was inconsolable; he suffered physically and psychologically. Although his faith in nonviolence was not shaken, his faith in the masses' ability to absorb his message and teachings was dampened. Gandhi decided to suspend the non-cooperation movement at its very height. To his disappointed younger colleagues, like Jawaharlal Nehru, Subhash Chandra Bose[18] and others, Gandhi explained in one of his articles in *Young India*: "The drastic reversal of practically the whole of the aggressive programme may be politically unsound and unwise, but there is no doubt that it is religiously sound" (February, 11, 1919).

Again Gandhi made himself vulnerable to his critics, who dubbed him as "an unworldly mystic miscast in politics" (Ashe 1868, 230). Unscathed by their hostile attacks, Gandhi remained serene. Taking full responsibility, but not regretting his decision to launch the movement in the first place, he decided to undergo personal cleansing to become a fitter instrument of God. He did penance by fasting for five days. In suspending the non-cooperation movement at its peak, Gandhi remained true to his inviolable commitment to nonviolence and truth. He proved thereby wherein lay his priorities.

THE GREAT TRIAL OF 1922

Although Gandhi immediately suspended the non-cooperation movement to curb the violence at Chauri Chaura, the government seized this opportunity to arrest him. Gandhi's famous court trial on March 18, 1922, in Ahmedabad, apart from its political significance, became a landmark event for two reasons. First, in this trial, Gandhi finally and officially resolved his ambivalent attitude toward the British. Second, he also witnessed here the transforming power of nonviolence in action.

Gandhi explained to Judge Broomfield why "from a staunch loyalist and cooperator" he turned into "an uncompromising disaffectionist and non-cooperator."[19] (CWMG Vol 26, 381) He was convinced, he said, that the British Government in its totality had done more harm to India than any previous system. Also, he made his historical statement: "non-cooperation with evil is as much a duty as is cooperation with good." Pleading guilty, he asked for the severest penalty. (ibid.)

The judge actually bowed to the defendant and asked for his forgiveness before sentencing him to six years of imprisonment. This was unheard of in British India. In this unprecedented case, a British judge openly acknowledged Gandhi as being in an altogether "different category from any person" he had tried or was likely to try. With reverence he added, "In the eyes of millions of your countrymen, you are a great patriot and a great leader. Even those who differ from you in politics look upon you as a man of high ideals and of noble and of even saintly life." (ibid., 385) Having announced his verdict, the judge bowed to the defendant again. Thus, "conversion, the aim of *satyagraha*, had begun," observed George Woodcock (1971, 70); "it was an incident that demonstrated Gandhi's power to arouse the better nature of his opponents." The Mahatma and his method had begun to spell a charm.

YERAVDA JAIL (POONE) FROM 1922–1924

Gandhi was happy as a lark in the Yeravda Jail in Poone in Maharashtra State. In addition to reading extensively on history, biography, and major religious traditions,[20] Gandhi wrote letters, and practiced spinning daily for four hours. In a letter to his esteemed Muslim friend Hakim Ajmal Khan, Gandhi wrote: "Hindu Muslim unity must be our creed to last for all time and under all circumstances, and this unity," he believed, "is unattainable without our adopting nonviolence as a firm policy." Gandhi also emphasized that "nothing can possibly unify and revivify India as the acceptance by all India of the spinning wheel as a daily sacrament and the khaddar (or khadi) wear as a privilege and a duty." (Collected Works, Vol 26, 355–356) To Gandhi, spinning was his rosary, his prayer, and his meditation on the Supreme Being. The four hours of spinning were for him "the most profitable and sacred time" during which, he claimed, "no impure thought haunts me. (ibid.) His jail-term was cut short in 1924 as he developed acute appendicitis for which he was taken to Sasson Hospital in Poone for an emergency operation. For convalescence, Gandhi stayed at a friend's house on the Juhu Beach, near Bombay.

During the time Gandhi was in jail, the Indian skies were overcast with dark clouds of communal tension and political chaos. The non-cooperation movement had fizzled, and the Congress party had split into two groups. The first group, the *Swarajists* (pro-change), consisted of Motilal Nehru (the father of Jawaharlal Nehru), C. R. Das, Vitthalbhai Patel (the brother of Vallabhbhai Patel), and other professional elites. They wanted to depart from the Gandhian-style politics of boycotts, strikes, and other types of civil disobedience. Like the Communists of that era, this progressive group demanded Dominion Status for India; they were more ambitious to get inside the British parliamentary power structure. The other group, who was for no change, included Jawaharlal Nehru, Sardar Patel, C. Rajgopalachari, and others. They did not want to part from the Gandhian approach, even though as insiders, they, too, criticized Gandhi whenever he suddenly reversed his policies. To both groups, however, the most pressing problem of the time was the Hindu–Muslim hostility exploding in Moplah (north) and Kohat (northwest frontier), with riots that shook up India.

GANDHI FASTS FOR TWENTY-ONE DAYS

To appease the warring Hindus and Muslims and to revive their friendship, Gandhi undertook a penitential fast for twenty-one days. Introducing his prolonged fast as "both a penance and prayer," Gandhi said, "My penance is the prayer of a bleeding heart for forgiveness for sins unwittingly committed" by both the Hindus and Musalmans. (Tendulkar, 1951, Vol 2, 150) The fast was a spiritual symbol of peace and a social duty to the highest cause of brotherhood between Hindus and Muslims. With an eye for drama, Gandhi fasted while staying at the house of his Muslim friend, Mahomed Ali. Both Hindus and Muslims prayed together once again for the life of the Mahatma, and the riots eased for the time being. Gandhi ended the fast after twenty-one days with Vinoba Bhave reciting from the *Gita*, the Ali brothers reading from the *Q'uran*, and C. F. Andrews singing Gandhi's favorite Christian hymn, "Lead, Kindly Light."

THE VYKOM *SATYAGRAHA* (1925)

While still feeling weak from his prolonged fast and not yet up on his feet, the Mahatma was summoned to lead a *satyagraha* on behalf of the Untouchables of Vykom, a southern village in Travankore. Orthodox Brahmins stopped them not only from entering the temple that happened to be in their district but also from using the road leading to the temple. George Joseph, a Christian disciple of Gandhi, had first escorted an Untouchable along the forbidden road. He was harassed by the Brahmins and arrested by the police. Soon, however, many volunteers took up the cause, but the Brahmins were unyielding and would not allow even the shadow of an Untouchable to pollute their temple or the area around it. At this point Gandhi was called upon to help. Gandhi led the Vykom *satyagraha* and inspired the Untouchables "to literally stand for truth" despite the heavy rains and floods that rose to their waists, "until the stony hearts of the Brahmins melted," as Richard Gregg put it (1959, 20). After sixteen months, the Brahmins finally relented. Whether their hearts melted or not, the temple doors and the road leading to it were now open to the Untouchables. (Later, under Ambedkar's leadership, the Untouchables will have the legal right to enter and worship in any temple anywhere in India.)

GANDHI'S SILENT YEARS AND "CONSTRUCTIVE PROGRAMS"

From 1925–1927 Gandhi observed political silence for his own spiritual regeneration and for the national—social and moral—reconstruction from within. This was also the time when the magic of the Mahatma took on divine dimensions; he came to be worshipped alongside the images of Lord Rama, Krishna, and Buddha. Gandhi expressed his horror of such idolatry and claimed to be no more than "an erring mortal, a weak aspirant ever failing, ever trying."(Harijan, September 14, 1934, 244) He felt burdened by the title *Mahatma*, which clung to him like an albatross around the neck of an "Ancient Mariner" (referring to Coleridge's poem). He was agonized to see people worship him rather than following his principles. In 1925, Gandhi founded the All-India Spinners' Association. In the same year, Madeleine Slade (Mirabehn) joined Gandhi's ashram and became his disciple; Gandhi also wrote his autobiography at this time. Gandhi got feverishly busy again, traveling on foot and by train (third-class) through every remote province of India to raise funds for his "constructive programs," to increase the sale of *Khadi*, and to spread the "gospel of the spinning wheel." The moral Mahatma and the business-like *Bania* came together in Gandhi with no conflict. He introduced to people his "five constructive programs" as "five virtues": (1) equality of the Untouchables, (2) spinning, (3) sobriety (no use of alcohol or opium), (4) Hindu–Muslim friendship, and (5) women's equality.

Gandhi had overstretched himself again. The constant touring, talking, and walking from village to village proved to be too strenuous for fifty-eight-year-old Gandhi, and his health collapsed from exhaustion and high blood pressure. Gandhi suffered a minor stroke in 1927 but had no desire for resting, as his country was in big political turmoil from 1928 to 1930. Turmoil was brewing inside his own family also, between the father and his two older sons.

BAPU AND HIS OLDER TWO SONS

"Gandhi's spirituality had a painful side," said Geoffrey Ashe (1968, 255). His relationship with sons Harilal and Manilal had been troubled for many years. Now, however, it was deteriorating even more, either because Gandhi was too demanding of these two sons or because they were more rebellious than their younger brothers, Ramdas and Devadas. According to Robert Payne (1969, 381), "Ramdas and Devadas had been obedient to him all their lives, and were the best of his sons."

As we know, Harilal was totally estranged from his father and ended up as a drunkard and a derelict. Manilal, though not as openly rebellious as Harilal, had his own story of silent suffering and unhealed hurts; it was not until the last two years of Gandhi's life that the father and the son were reconciled.[21]

Stern with himself, Gandhi was even sterner with his sons. Tender to other children, *Bapu* was harsh to his own. He loved his sons dearly, but on his own terms. He wished they would adopt his moral principles and live an austere, spiritual life.[22] This was the ambivalent side of *Bapu*—on the one hand, he was a very loving father who wanted a friendly relationship with his sons, while on the other hand, he was a stern and domineering father.[23]

THE BARDOLI *SATYAGRAHA* OF 1928

As mentioned earlier, India was in turmoil from 1928–1930. In 1928 Gandhi was needed again to revive the peasants' *satyagraha* in Bardoli (near Surat in Gujarat), which he had to suspend six years ago due to the unexpected outburst of violence in Chauri Chaura. Now, however, he decided to assist Sardar (Captain) Vallabhbhai Patel,[24] the hero of this *satyagraha* in Bardoli. Patel's matchless organizational skills, robust common sense, and shrewd strategy, combined with Gandhi's inspiring guidance and hold over the masses, worked like a miracle. Together, they led eighty-eight thousand peasants in demanding a tax deduction from the government. The Bardoli *satyagraha* proved to be "flawless"; it was a resounding success. Gandhi convinced the nation and the new Viceroy Irwin that *satyagraha* worked, and that it was not only bloodless but also a practical, long-term solution to all human conflicts. In the months and years after, Gandhi was called upon again to fight even bigger battles with the British.

Between 1928 and 1930, the political situation in India was worsening because of the imperial government's repeated betrayals of Indian trust and its increasingly offensive, arbitrary policies. One such insulting gesture was the Simon Commission (headed by Sir John Simon), which consisted of an all-white committee of British parliamentarians who came to India to investigate the situation and to help the British decide on India's future. Most Indian leaders, including Gandhi, boycotted the Simon Commission, because by selecting an exclusively white committee, the British broke their promises of increasing Indian participation in the government of their own country. Then in 1928, Lala Lajpat Rai, a fiery Punjabi leader and patriot known by the honorific title of "the Lion of Punjab," died of *lathi* (wooden stick) wounds at the hands of the British. In 1929, Assistant Police Superintendent Saunders was assassinated in Lahore, and the suspect, Bhagat Singh, was hanged and honored as a hero or *shahid* (martyr). Another popular Indian leader, Subhash Chandra Bose's call to "Give me blood and I give you freedom," fired Indians up to die for their freedom. The year 1929 was crucial and the British were getting alarmed.

The whole country was convulsing with anti-British terrorist activities, and Gandhi was trying his hardest to persuade Viceroy Irwin that the government could stop all the bloodshed by granting India its legitimate demand of freedom. In their meeting, Gandhi reiterated his demand for India's full and immediate Dominion Status to be guaranteed at the upcoming Round Table Conference in London in 1930. Irwin, however, would give no such promise.

It was the end of 1930. No Indian plea for freedom had worked, nor was there any sign or hope of the British letting go of their hold on India. Therefore, the All-India Congress, at its historic December 1930 annual convention in Lahore, unanimously authorized Gandhi to be "the stage director" to enact the most spectacular national drama for India's freedom. As Louis Fischer put it (1950, 262), "Everyone realized that Gandhi would have to be the brain, heart and directing hand of any civil disobedience movement, and it was therefore left to him to choose the hour, the place, and the precise issue."

DANDI-KOOTCH OR THE SALT MARCH OF 1930

Before embarking on this nationwide *satyagraha*, Gandhi had forewarned Viceroy Irwin in a letter about the Indians' rising discontent against the government's salt monopoly and salt taxation. He wrote, he "meant no harm to a single Englishman," but nevertheless must oppose the British rule, which was "a curse," and which had "progressively exploited and impoverished his people by imposing taxes on even an everyday item of necessity like salt." (Collected Works, Vol 48, 362) Only when the viceroy ignored Gandhi's letter and refused to see him, did Gandhi set his giant wheel of *salt satyagraha* in motion. It was his most dramatic, successful *satyagraha*.

On March 12, 1930, the sixty-one-year-old Mahatma, staff in hand and barefoot, led seventy-eight *satyagrahis* on a march from his Sabarmati Ashram to the Arabian Sea coast in Dandi. The marchers, singing *bhajans* (hymns) and chanting slogans in the name of God, walked nonstop, covering two hundred miles in twenty-four hours; hundreds and thousands joined them on their way in this sacred pilgrimage for truth and freedom.

Just as he had alerted the viceroy beforehand, so also he had instructed his *satyagrahis* before leading them on this historic march. "Everyone should understand," said Gandhi, that "the only stipulation for civil disobedience is perfect observance of nonviolence in the fullest sense of the term." (Collected Works, Vol 49; April 3, 1930)

Among many dramatic features of the *salt satyagraha*, the most outstanding stroke of Gandhi's strategic brilliance was his selection of "salt" as both a theme and as a means of protest. Gandhi knew that everybody needed salt, whether rich or poor; thereby, the *salt satyagraha* had a nationwide appeal and impact. By selecting "salt," Gandhi proved to be not only a pragmatic leader but also a psychological mind reader of the poor—their needs, their problems, and their daily struggle for living. Among all the leaders of India before and after him, Gandhi was probably the only one in complete sync with the masses; his fingers were on the pulse of the poor. Gandhi was also a dramatist who knew exactly how and when to put on the best show, and what would create the maximum impact at a minimum cost. The first two (how and when) show his histrionic talent; the last one (regarding cost) proves his natural *Bania* shrewdness. But above all, as Margaret Chatterjee observed (1983, 3), "Gandhi had this rare gift for picking on symbols." In this superbly staged "drama on the seashore," Gandhi brought the lofty principles of truth and nonviolence down to earth, making them tangible in the form of "a pinch of salt"—which everyone could grasp in their hands. Gandhi led the *satyagrahis* in literally collecting salt from the sea, thereby defying the government as well as demonstrating India's self-sufficiency. He thus lifted the mundane to the level of the spiritual, and made the spiritual accessible to all.

Erik Erikson, Earnest Jones, and Victor Wolfenstein have analyzed the deeper psychological motives in Gandhi's use of salt as a means of protest in this *satyagraha* against the British that made the world gasp in admiration and awe. Erikson acknowledges that "Gandhi's choice of the salt-tax has always impressed me as a model of practical and symbolic action" (1975). He also notices "Gandhi's shrewdness ... to focus on the infinite meaning in finite things—a trait which is often associated with the attribution of sainthood" (1975, 155–156). Erikson goes on to discuss Wolfenstein and Jones' review of "the unconscious sexual meaning of salt" in Indian folklore, religion, and superstition—all of which have salt "characteristically represent semen—the male, active, fertilizing principle." If salt represents human semen in Indian folk culture, and "if it had this unconscious meaning for Gandhi," then, in the context of the Salt March, suggest Erikson and Jones, "Gandhi's taking of salt from the British can be seen as reclaiming for the Indian people the manhood and potency which was properly theirs." (Erikson, ibid., 156) What these Western psychologists have not mentioned, however, is that in the Indian cultural and religious context, the human semen is considered too powerful an energy to be wasted; it must therefore be controlled, conserved, and converted into a spiritual force or powerhouse for God-realization. As discussed previously, the major problems with such Freudian interpretations are that they are too far-fetched, out of place, and therefore, ill fitting in the Indian context.

The salt march riveted the attention of the world to India and Gandhi. More than any written or spoken word, "one small pinch of salt" brought the mighty British Empire down to its knees to work out a solution. The "little old man in the loincloth," whom Churchill ridiculed as "the naked fakir of India," ruled the heart of not only India but also the world. While the *salt satyagraha* was still underway, Gandhi was arrested the morning of May 5, 1930, from his temporary ashram at Camp Karadi, a mango grove midway between Dandi and the sea. Gandhi surrendered himself to the district magistrate and the district superintendent of police, and they escorted him courteously to his destination—the Yeravda Central Jail, Poone.

GANDHI AND CONTINUATION OF STAGE 5 CONJUNCTIVE FAITH: AN EVALUATION

In reviewing Gandhi's ongoing self and faith developmental journey in terms of Fowler's criteria of Stage 5 Conjunctive Faith, recall that Stage 5 is "a complex, dichotomous and multidimensional faith" that seeks to probe deeper into the meaning of life, accepting the many-sidedness of truth and the coincidence of opposites and contradictions in self, others, and in life itself. Stage 5 includes the conscious as well as the unconscious, the symbolic as well as the conceptual, the depth (inner sensitivity) and the breadth (wider perspective-taking) dimensions, while maintaining a dialectical balance between the antithetical aspects of one's life and personality.

Deepening Search for Truth and Increasing Inwardness

Gandhi was not a mystic, nor was his search for Truth metaphysical or even intellectual. He was not an academic, a scholar, or even a systematic philosopher. Although Gandhi believed in the *Advaita Vedanta* (non-dualistic) philosophy of Hinduism, he was still a *bhakta* at heart—a man of prayers and inner contemplation, whose every breath, thought, and action was rooted in and dedicated to God. Earlier he used to say "God is Truth," but later he switched to say, "Truth is God." As mentioned earlier, Gandhi preferred the latter statement in order to communicate better with atheists who objected to the very concept of God. More important, Gandhi uses Truth not as a substitute for God, nor to suggest that God was lesser than Truth, but as Margaret Chatterjee explained, it was simply "to elucidate what God meant to him" (1983, 58). Gandhi himself explained in the introduction of his autobiography, "I worship God as Truth only," and continued:

> I have not yet found Him, but I am seeking after Him. ... As long as I have not realized this Absolute Truth, so long must I hold by the relative truth as I have conceived it. That relative truth must, meanwhile, be my Beacon, my shield, my buckler. (1948, 6)

Seeking the Absolute through the relative truth makes Gandhi a *karmayogi*, who performs all work as worship, without desire or attachment, yielding the fruits of action to God. Each of Gandhi's *satyagrahas* can be seen as his way of serving God through action and selfless service to humankind. As Gandhi said, "My devotion to Truth has drawn me into the field of politics, and I can say without slightest hesitation and yet all humility, that those who say that religion has nothing to do with politics do not know what religion means!" (Radhakrishnan 1944, 14). Gandhi wanted "to identify with everything that lives"; in the language of the *Gita*, he wanted "to live at peace with both friend and foe."

Gandhi's deep identification with every living being and his all-embracing love reflect the "epistemological humility" and inner awakening to the depth of reality, which are characteristic features of Stage 5. It is accepting the limitations of one's ego and opening up to the deeper inner voices, which suggest moving beyond the self-aggrandizing "executive ego" and its "dichotomizing logic" of Stage 4. Gandhi's acceptance of his "Himalayan miscalculations" (1948, 575) and his awareness of his faults, his withdrawal of political movements at their climax because of spiritual considerations, and his ability to maintain peace of mind in the midst of all the chaos surrounding him, all reflect the humility, spiritual maturity and wisdom as well as detachment associated with Stage 5.

We find further evidence of Stage 5 deepening qualities of Gandhi's faith in his rigorous spiritual disciplines and self-austerities that included the observance of various vows, such as truth, nonviolence, non-possession, non-stealing, spinning, silence, prayers, and "fasting for self-purification." In *Harijan* (August 7, 1933), he explained the difference between "fast for the body" and "the inner fast." He accepted that fasting has been "an integral part of the Hindu religion and that thousands of Hindus fast even today on the slightest pretext." However, Gandhi also pointed out that "like everything that is good, fasts can also be abused. The mere mortification of flesh is not spiritual fasting which is an intense form of prayer. . . . and a yearning of the soul to merge in the divine consciousness." In *satyagraha*, fasting should be undertaken only as a last resort and not without proper training. True fast is meant to awaken the conscience of the enemy, not to coerce his will. "Fasts are part of my being. . . . what the eyes are for the outer world, fasts are for the inner," he said in *Harijan*; "fasts are for my spiritual self-purification" (August 7, 1933).

Widening Sympathies and Perspectives

The more inward Gandhi turned in search of Truth, the wider spread the wings of his compassion for all living beings. All of Gandhi's *satyagrahas* simultaneously testify to his deepening sensibilities and enlarging sympathies; the closer he came to God, the more compassionate he became, like Buddha—the Enlightened. Gandhi was a seeker after Truth who found his *moksha* (liberation) right in the middle of the *sansara* (world) and not by retreating to a forest or a cave. All such distinctions, however, between the inner and the outer world do not apply to Gandhi because he did not think of life as divided into several compartments cut off from one another, but as interconnected. He saw "God's universe as an indivisible whole" and therefore, "all creatures as interlinked." (Harijan, November 21, 1932)

Gandhi's *satyagrahas* exemplified the outreach of the human spirit as much as his deeper yearning for Truth. He was actively involved in a wide

range of human issues, such as the social and religious (Vykom), economic
(Ahmedabad), and the human rights of the poor and exploited (in
Champaran and Kheda). In terms of Stage 5, his search for truth "led him
in the direction of a deepened quality of spirituality in which," says
Fowler, "one hungers for ways to relate to the otherness in self, God and
fellow humans" (1987, 74). Just as Gandhi reached out to the lowliest of
the Untouchables and to the poorest of the peasants, he also joined his
Muslim brothers (in Khilafat) in a largely Hindu India. Personally running
the risk of being an outcast himself, he allowed an outcast family to live
among the high caste Hindus in his ashram. Gandhi's *satyagrahas* and his
bold, moral stand for the Muslims and Untouchables of India are the finest
examples of the "outreach of the human spirit as directed by God."

Moreover, Gandhi dared to be a different kind of leader who was not
afraid to tell the truth. His bold speech at Benares ruffled many a silk
feather of the Raja-Maharajas; his strange dress, manners, diet, and
practical-spiritual approach to politics turned off many a Westernized
leader. By confessing his "Himalayan miscalculations," he made himself
vulnerable to his enemies. Most of all, his closeness to the Untouchables
and Muslims created a huge controversy. Here was a leader who not only
told the truth, but lived by it. An unconventional leader, Gandhi invited
controversy, sometimes putting his own life in danger. In terms of Stage 5,
Gandhi was "ready for closeness to that which is different and threatening
to self and outlook"; he exemplified what Fowler described as "the Stage's
commitment to justice that it is freed from the confines of tribe, class, religious community or nation" (1981, 198).

"THE COINCIDENCE OF OPPOSITES" IN GANDHI AND STAGE 5

At this point I would like to elaborate on one of the hallmark qualities of
Stage 5 Conjunctive Faith, the "*coincidentia oppositoritum*" wherein "all
opposites and contradictions meet and are reconciled."

"Maintaining a dialectical tension between polarities" is the predomi-
nant style of meaning-making in Stage 5, which also "involves the integra-
tion" of those polar tensions into one's life, self, and outlook. Fowler
prefers to call it "dialogical knowing" in which the "knower and the
known" engage in "a mutual speaking and hearing"; the knower "seeks to
accommodate her or his knowledge to the structure of that which is being
known before imposing her or his own categories upon it" (1981, 185).

For this to happen, the conscious self must develop a "humbling awareness" of the multiplex structure of reality and of the power of the unconscious. And this kind of "humility" requires "what the mystics call detachment," which characterizes Stage 5.

Among several unmistakable polar tensions that one faces in midlife, Fowler specifically mentions those of "being both old and young and of being both masculine and feminine." Further, he mentions "integrating the polarity of being both constructive and destructive and the polarity of having both a conscious and a shadow self" (1984, 65).

Some aspects of Gandhi's personality that appeared to be contradictory were actually integral parts of the whole man in whom opposites stayed side by side. What others perceived to be confusing or inconsistent about Gandhi was in fact perfectly clear and consistent in view of his uncompromising commitment to truth and his larger-than-life vision.

Saint or Politician?

Many critics of Gandhi—both British and Indian—were puzzled: Was Gandhi a saint or a politician? Not able to figure out the enigmatic man, they turned hostile, even bitter, to Gandhi. Even some of Gandhi's closest friends and followers, like Nehru and Sardar Patel, found it difficult to accept Gandhi's two simultaneous roles; they were angry with Gandhi when he withdrew the politically sound and successful Non-cooperation Movement (1919) for nonpolitical considerations. They, too, fumbled for an answer—was *Bapu* a saint or a politician?

Ironically, Gandhi was neither; he was only a seeker after Truth, who chose politics to serve God through human service. Gandhi himself saw no dichotomy between politics and religion; to him both were only means to an end in his search for Truth. He believed Truth to be one, yet many-sided; it was as multidimensional as life itself. "I do not regard my life as divisible into so many watertight compartments. ... it is one organic whole," said Gandhi in *Harijan* (November 21, 1932); he further added, "all my activities spring from the same source, namely, my passion for and vindication of truth and non-violence in every walk of life, be it great or small."

Gandhi's commitment to truth required that he first be true to himself and admit his "Himalayan" blunder of launching the movement without adequate preparation. He refused to compromise his commitment to truth and nonviolence just for appearing to be consistent. Many criticized him, but there were a few who recognized his integrity. As Geoffrey Ashe observed: "Here and here alone in the human record is a revolutionary who could have launched his revolution, yet refused because it would be the wrong sort of revolution. The Mahatma ... was willing to fail" (1968, 230).

Though Gandhi was deeply involved in politics, he was not hungry for power, position, or prestige. "Ironically it was precisely because he was not a career politician," said Judith Brown (1983, 389), "that he had such a long career in politics." Although he could be "a master tactician" when the occasion demanded, he detested the usual political games, power struggles, and backstabbing.

Gandhi's purpose in entering politics was "purely religious," as he told his Christian missionary friend, John S. Hoyland. To resolve the "puzzle of saint/politician," Gandhi put it lightly in *Harijan:* "Most religious men I have met are politicians in disguise; I, however, who wear the guise of a politician, am at heart a religious man." Having made that statement, however, Gandhi spelled out in his interview with Will Durant that he believed in "religion not in a conventional but in the broadest sense," and in a religion that "helps me to have a glimpse of the Divine essence" (*Harijan* April 13, 1940). Like his spiritual mentor Raychandbhai, Gandhi believed in that religion which underlies all religions—it was the religion of humanity that transcended all religions—Hinduism, Islam, Christianity, and all others. As H. N. Brailsford said, "the key to the puzzle of Gandhi is to grasp as a single harmonious personality Gandhi the tactician and organizer and Gandhi the saint" (1949, 155).

"*Sanatani* Hindu" or "Non-Conformist Hindu"?

Gandhi asserted he was a "*Sanatani* Hindu" who believed in the eternal principles of Hinduism and in the Hindu scriptures, such as the *Vedas*, the *Upanishads*, and the *Bhagavad Gita* (1950, 7–10). He also accepted the *Varnashrama dharma* (caste system, but only in its *Vedic* sense), and believed in "protecting the cow" but only as a symbol of the animal world. He was not against idol worship, although he did not worship any. Gandhi maintained that "he was proud to belong to that Hinduism which was all-inclusive," and which "stood for tolerance of all religions." He refused to take the words of any scripture for granted if they failed the test of reason. He wrote:

> Hinduism, not being an exclusive religion, enables the followers ... not merely to respect all the other religions, but it also enables them to admire and assimilate whatever may be good in the other faiths.

Non-violence is common to all religions, but it has found the highest
expression and application in Hinduism. (ibid., 6)

The traditional Hindus were incensed, however, by Gandhi's nonconformist stands on the eradication of untouchability and for his kinship with
the Muslims, as we discussed earlier. Yet, in spite of their venomous attacks
(ending in his assassination later on), Gandhi maintained a polar tension
between the two apparent contradictions—being true to the essence and
spirit of Hinduism versus being a nonconformist reformer who endeavored
to purge Hinduism of all its impurities. As B. R. Nanda observed (1994,
248), "Gandhi could take all these liberties with Hinduism, because he was
an insider." A devout Hindu, Gandhi was not blind to the pitfalls of
Hinduism. To repeat Bhikhu Parekh (1989a): "Though Gandhi valued his
tradition, he was not a traditionalist."

Apart from some of the apparent contradictions in Gandhi, there were
also some real or built-in polarities in Gandhi's personality and outlook,
which indicate the "coincidence of opposites" in Stage 5 faith. These were
the opposite traits that stayed side by side in Gandhi or were assimilated
into his personality in a way so as to complement one another.

Union of the Male and Female

Bapu (father) was also a *Ba* (mother) to not only his grandniece Manubehn
Gandhi, who wrote the book *"Bapu, My Mother"* (1949) but to many of his
close women and men associates like Rajkumari Amrit Kaur, Mirabehn,
Nehru, Mahadevbhai Desai, and countless others. As Rajkumari Amrit
Kaur said, "We found in him not only a Bapu—a wise father, but what is
more precious, a mother" (Green 1993, 211). Sometimes Gandhi even
"out-mothered" some birth mothers by the way he cared, comforted,
nursed, and took detailed interest in women's diet, health, and daily activities, and by advising them regarding their personal intimate problems. He
had a way of connecting with women, in making them aware of their
own superior spiritual powers of love, endurance, forgiveness, and more.
Women, too, found a true friend in Gandhi; they looked up to him, and
opened up to him as to a mother. Gandhi maintained regular correspondence with many of his women friends and followers all over the world.

Gandhi himself enjoyed "mothering" and doing such activities that
traditionally are allotted to women, such as spinning, nursing, cleaning
chores, and attending to the minutia of household management. His true

inner joy came from such feminine spiritual practices as observing vows, fasting, nursing, and self-sacrificing love, just like his mother, Putliba, and his wife, Kasturbai. Most important, Gandhi saw women as the best *satyagrahis* or as the self-suffering "soldiers of nonviolence." In his words:

> Woman is incarnation of ahimsa. Ahimsa means infinite love, which means infinite capacity for suffering. And who but woman, the mother of man, shows this capacity in the largest measure? Let her translate that love to the whole humanity. ... she can be the leader of satyagraha.[25]

Side by side with these feminine tendencies, however, were some equally powerful male traits in Gandhi, such as having a "strong executive ego" (an "I am in charge" mentality), a drive for action, and pugnacity to fight for principles. Gandhi's most distinctive contribution—*satyagraha* itself—was a fruitful union of both feminine and masculine traits. In Gandhi's mental make-up were present some of the finest feminine Indian ideals of "conquering by self-suffering love" and "self-restraint," and their opposite male prototype behaviors related to "power," "pugnacity," "self-assertion," and the "fighting instinct." As H. N. Brailsford observed:

> Gandhi's originality lay largely in the fact that female tendencies were at least as strong in his mental make-up as male, ... and this polar opposition between violence and self-suffering is really a contrast between male and female patterns of behaviour. ... the male fighting instinct in Gandhi made him a rebel and a reformer. (1949, 168)

Fusion of the Symbolic and the Practical

The way Gandhi impregnated political tactics with symbolic, spiritual meanings in his *satyagrahas* was highly original. His use of devices such as *hartal,* prayers and hymn-singing, fasting, boycott, spinning, *khadi* wearing, and *swadeshi* all illustrate the Stage 5 characteristic of fusion of the symbolic with what is conceptual.

Besides these, we found many other examples of Gandhi's rich use of symbolic actions. He freely used his gift of dramatizing events in symbolic ways to win the masses and to maximize the impact on onlookers and the enemy. With an eye for drama, he translated abstract religious principles into simple, symbolic actions that even an ordinary peasant could grasp and carry out. For example, in Kheda, he used a well-known peasant practice of making a whole crop disappear for teaching the farmers a new principle of civil resistance or "suffering for truth and justice." Similarly, by utilizing an everyday household item like salt as a nonviolent weapon in the 1930 *satyagraha*, Gandhi displayed a rare ingenuity for transforming a simple object into a symbolic act that was at once practical and spiritual.

Man of Contemplation and Action

Gandhi was a man of action, but almost all his major actions were preceded by terrific struggle and introspection. For example, it was after he had spent a whole night in agony, cogitating about how he should oppose the Rowlatt Act, that the answer had come to him in "a dream." That "dream" signified his own "Voice of Conscience" or "the Voice of God" that spoke to him and showed him the way. Similarly, his dilemma of war versus nonviolence, and his loyalty to the British versus rebellion, indicated his unconscious search for solutions that were spiritual yet practical. The preceding mental agony and reflection, the dream, the inner voice were intuitive messages from his unconscious that were acted out by the conscious. Gandhi was simultaneously a man of vision and action, a man of principles and practical wisdom.

"One of the secrets of Mahatma Gandhi's strength was just holding in a living balance strongly marked antithesis," observed the Reverend E. Stanley Jones (1983). He mentioned other polarities that Gandhi balanced well in his personality, life, and faith:

> He was a meeting place of the East and West, and yet he represented the soul of the East; he was an urban man who became the voice of the peasant masses; he was passive and militant, and both at the same time; he was ascetic and the servant, he was mystical and practical. ... , the man of prayer and the man of the spinning wheel. He combined the Hindu and the Christian in himself. ... He was serious and playful, he was the person who embodied the cause, the cause of India's freedom. (1983, 7)

Constructive and Destructive

There were darker elements and shadowy substances in Gandhi of which he was largely unaware or could not control. According to Fowler (1987, 73–74), "No polarity can perhaps be as painful as that of knowing that one is not only a constructive and well-meaning person but that one is also and often without intending it—a destructive person." He elucidates the point thus: "In interdependences, of which we may only gradually and partially become aware, our very beings impinge on others in ways that bring them pain or bring us benefit from the diminishment of their life chances" (ibid.). Fowler refers here to that side of our nature that may be so over-bearing, demanding, and vindictive that it can hurt, diminish, or destroy others. In most of our closer, one-to-one relationships of an interdependent nature, we may discover that sometimes we do act in selfish or self-imposing ways that can usurp others' rights to be, grow, and have their own space.

Gandhi's self-righteous behavior in the "chamber pot cleaning" incidence, and his usurpation of his sons' rights to formal schooling, show this overbearing side of Gandhi. The eldest son Harilal's open rebellion and ruined life, and the second son Manilal's silent suffering, both reveal Gandhi's destructive side. "The Father of the Nation" could not be a father to his own sons.

The "Conscious" and the "Shadow Self"

The "shadow self" refers to that side of our nature that is hidden from our conscious self—and which could be destructive to the self or to others. The shadow self is our own "veiled face," which is not fully exposed to even our own eyes; it remains unrecognized in the form of ambiguities, weaknesses, and vulnerabilities, which if revealed, will make us feel ashamed of ourselves. For example, Gandhi, in insisting that his sons be as devoted to him as he was to his father (Kaba Gandhi), acted from the darker side of his nature or the "shadow self." Erikson (1969, 243) interpreted Gandhi's harsh treatment of his sons "in fact, as a facsimile of the very Demon King whom Prahlad[26] resisted!" Similarly, Gandhi's self-defensive confessions of his earlier domineering behaviors toward his wife in phrases like "I was a cruelly kind husband" or "a devoted but jealous husband" reveal the self that was even concealed to him.

Although Gandhi was less than perfect, more often than not he was aware of his imperfections; that awareness itself became his incentive for self-perfection. As he put it: "I am conscious of my own limitations. That consciousness is my only strength." (1958, 38) The more he was aware of his limitations, the more he struggled to overcome them; he largely succeeded in transforming his weaknesses into strengths. Three important steps in his journey toward self-perfection were: first, an awareness of his own limitations; second, an admission or public confession of them; and third, correction or retraction of a wrong step, thought, or action. The most powerful incentive in this journey was his relentless search for Truth and his incessant efforts to purge himself of all his inner impurities.

In summing up this chapter, in Gandhi's life, character, and faith is the most telling evidence of the fundamental characteristic of Stage 5 faith, namely the "coincidence of opposites," which proved to be largely complementary. Gandhi can be seen as a vulnerable, struggling, and striving mortal who, by his spiritual self-disciplines and drive for self-transformation, could still achieve extraordinary things. As Judith Brown observed:

> It is in Gandhi's struggles with himself and his society that some of his most powerful and lasting contributions to this century lie. ... In his strivings, his set-backs and even his self-contradictions, he faced crucial human questions which find resonances in almost any time and place. (1983, 392)

Gandhi never ceased to develop. As Margaret Chatterjee explained (1983, 132), "to develop is to move in a certain direction, to grow." Gandhi continued "to grow in the direction of his lifelong journey to Truth," and to move on to an even more radical stage of faith development.

11

From Death to Immortality

We now approach the grand finale of Gandhi's faith journey, the death of his ego self as well as his physical death by assassination—his ultimate self-sacrifice for nonviolence and the brotherhood of mankind. The world admires Gandhi as a martyr for peace, whose death was the very affirmation of his life and faith in the ultimate triumph of Truth. Of more interest than Gandhi's martyrdom, however, are the inroads and alleyways to his martyrdom—his inner struggles and the radical choices he had to make to be true to his larger-than-life vision of Truth.

While battling with the British for India's freedom, Gandhi battled with himself to get rid of all his impurities. In the midst of World War II, the Hindu–Muslim violence, and escalating Muslim demand for a separate state of Pakistan, Gandhi conducted his last most rigorous spiritual experiments in *brahmacharya*; he also fasted frequently—twice unto death, seeking his own radical remedies to cure the spiritually bankrupt outer world.

Now is Gandhi's transition from Stage 5 Conjunctive Faith to the final, more radical Stage 6 Universalizing Faith. This last stage of Gandhi's life is not only marked by his imperviousness to his personal comfort, health, and happiness but also by his solemn resolve to sacrifice his life at the altar of Truth, nonviolence, and peace. Previously, Gandhi has demonstrated radical traits and tendencies in his statements (at Benares), in his actions (accepting Untouchables in his Ahmedabad Ashram), and in his decisions (sudden withdrawal of the Non-cooperation Movement in 1921). From now on, however, these traits magnify into extreme forms and take on a martyr-like spirit of "do or die" for Truth and nonviolence in the larger interests of all.

To continue from the last chapter, because of his astounding success in leading the *salt satyagraha*, Gandhi's name spread across the world as a moral and political genius. As far as India was concerned, Gandhi had accomplished two major tasks by this *satyagraha*. First, he set the Indians free from their fear of the British. Second, he brought the British down from their high citadels of power to confer with Indians on equal terms about the future of India.

DHARASANA SALT RAID

Before Gandhi was imprisoned from the *salt satyagraha*, he had contemplated another salt raid in Dharasana (150 miles north of Bombay). In spite of his absence, his fellow *satyagrahis* carried out his plans under the leadership of a fiery female patriot and poet named Mrs. Sarojini Naidu.[1] Mrs. Naidu successfully led twenty-five hundred *satyagrahis*, dressed in the Gandhian-style, homespun, coarse cotton *dhotis* and triangular white caps, to raid the government-controlled salt works at Dharasana. In the spirit of her mentor, Mrs. Naidu held a huge prayer meeting before leading the march and exhorted them: "Gandhi's body is in jail, but his soul is with you. India's prestige is in your hands. You must not use any violence under any circumstances. You will be beaten but you must not resist; you must not even raise a hand to ward off blows" (Homer 1956, 248). True to her command, the *satyagrahis* demonstrated exemplary self-restraint and nonviolent courage under fire; Web Miller of the United Press provided a moving eyewitness account of the British brutality and Indian forbearance, which shamed the British and enhanced Indians' prestige around the world.

Jails were overflowing with more than one hundred thousand Indian nationalists, including the elderly Motilal Nehru, his son Jawaharlal Nehru, Sardar Patel, Mrs. Naidu, Khansaheb Abdul Gaffar Khan or the "Frontier Gandhi,"[2] and many other Congress leaders. The soul of India was astir, England was embarrassed, and the whole world was watching.

The crisis in India and the world uproar put extraordinary pressure on the newly elected Labor team of the British Prime Minister Ramsay MacDonald and the Viceroy of India Lord Irwin; both MacDonald and Irwin thought, "Gandhi in jail was as much a nuisance as Gandhi on the march or at the beach or in the ashram" (Fischer 1950, 276). Therefore, in keeping with MacDonald's conciliatory gesture, Irwin released Gandhi and other leaders from jail.

The Gandhi-Irwin Pact or the Delhi Pact

In appreciation, Gandhi wrote a letter to Irwin asking to meet with him not so much as "the Viceroy of India" but as one fair and decent human being meeting another. This was an innate quality of Gandhi—not to hold grudges but to remain open to mending a personal or political relationship with an adversary. The Indian Viceroy Irwin, resplendent in his royal regalia, and the "naked fakir of India" (as Churchill called Gandhi) formally met in the viceroy's new palace in New Delhi to discuss the future of India. The viceroy demanded from Gandhi a total withdrawal of civil disobedience, but he did not promise any Dominion status to India in the near future. Although Gandhi conceded at the moment, like a hard *Bania* bargainer, he asked two things in return: first, that Irwin release all *satyagrahis* from jail, and second, that the British acknowledge Indians' right to manufacture their own salt. Pending on the viceroy's agreement to these two stipulations, Gandhi was willing to send a Congress delegate to the Second Round Table Conference to be held in London in September 1931. The Delhi Pact, as it came to be called by the British, was signed on March 5, 1931, by Irwin and Gandhi.

Although not a big political victory, the pact nevertheless marked the first significant move on the British side to meet with Indians on equal terms and accept their right to negotiate the future of their country. Even though tacit, this was not only the beginning of the end of the British raj in India but also was Gandhi's moral victory over the enemy. At this time, Gandhi was riding on the highest wave of popularity and was unanimously elected by all at the next Congress convention in Karachi (now in Pakistan) as its sole delegate to the Second Round Table Conference in London.

With an entourage of close associates and chroniclers, Gandhi sailed to England on the S. S. *Rajputana* to attend the Second Round Table Conference in September 1931. Despite his popularity, Gandhi's claim of being "the sole representative of Congress" caused lots of resentment among the delegates of other minority groups including Muslims, Sikhs, Parsees, Anglo-Indians, and the Untouchables.

Though Gandhi entertained no high hopes regarding a positive political outcome of this conference, he still succeeded, with his disarming honesty and guileless humor, in this mission of goodwill toward the British. Not only did he win the hearts of the poor Lancashire mill workers, middle-class housewives, and children but also the minds of the Oxford and Eaton professors.[3] Politically, however, the conference was nothing but a "magnificent failure" for two reasons. First, the British were not yet ready to give up their control over India, and second, the Indians were divided among themselves, with each minority group pressing for a larger share in the future freedom pie. Gandhi's pleas for national unity were vehemently opposed by two minority groups in particular—the Muslim League represented by Aga Khan and the Untouchables, led by Ambedkar—who insisted on having their own separate electorates in the legislative assembly.[4] Gandhi saw these minority rivalries as an ill omen that foreboded nothing but a dark future for India as a house divided in itself.

WHY GANDHI RESISTED SEPARATE ELECTORATES

At the Round Table Conference, Gandhi said that he was against all kinds of "bar sinister," meaning distinctions based on caste, color, creed, culture, religion, and nationality. Though his was the only voice in that political wilderness, Gandhi severely protested MacDonald's "Communal Award" for the Untouchables' separate electorates; being an astute politician, he could sense that the British were up to their old trick again of "conquering by dividing" the people of India. As an ardent nationalist, Gandhi also foresaw the dangers inherent in the very diversity of India's multi-stranded cultures, religions, regions, and languages. In the interest of national unity, therefore, he wanted to prevent division of any kind, especially at that critical time when all Indians needed a unified front against the foreign British.

If political disharmony was perilous for Indians fighting for freedom, religious divisions were no less dangerous, even though Gandhi knew that such divisions (among the Hindus, Muslims, Sikhs, and others) had always existed since centuries past. However, he regarded the Untouchables as part and parcel of Hinduism; as long as he lived, he would not allow them to be separated from Hinduism. This was the other voice of Gandhi, the soul-keeper of India, who saw himself as a unifier and a peacemaker among all the warring minorities. To put it in Dennis Dalton's words, "Indian society saw Gandhi, and Gandhi regarded himself, as occupying the peculiar position of a figure above the discord around him, and uniquely capable of harmonizing it" (Zelliot 1992, 153).

Gandhi's moral stand on the Untouchables' separate electorate issue shocked both the orthodox Hindus and the Untouchables. The former had thought of Gandhi as an all-time champion of Untouchables' interests, whereas the latter could not conceive that Gandhi, who had worked all along for them, would now oppose their right to have separate voting just like other minorities. Both groups failed, however, to understand Gandhi's principled logic that "it would divide the Hindu community into two armed groups and provoke needless opposition" (Gandhi *Collected Works*, 48: 331).

GANDHI MEETS ROMAIN ROLLAND IN SWITZERLAND

On his voyage home to India, Gandhi's meeting with Romain Rolland in Switzerland must be marked for its high spiritual significance.[5] In his biography of Gandhi, Rolland described him as "too much of a saint," a religious man who was "too trusting of human nature." He argued that Gandhi never suspected evil in man, nor did he acknowledge man's destructive potential. Like Tagore, and occasionally like Andrews, Rolland criticized Gandhi's "civil disobedience techniques of bonfires, boycott, and others"; he considered such methods as rather dangerous as they could arouse a mob's inherent destructive tendencies. Gandhi, however, had infinite faith in basic human goodness, and believed that "even the hardest heart melts before the heat of nonviolence. And there is no limit to the capacity of nonviolence to generate heat" (Radhakrishnan 1944, 41). The French writer and Gandhi also differed in their views regarding what should have supremacy in life— Beauty or Truth (i.e., aesthetics or ethics)? To Rolland, as also to Keats and Tagore, "Beauty was Truth"; to Gandhi, however, "Truth was Beauty." Regardless of their ideological differences, Rolland deeply revered Gandhi, and it was in that historic meeting of two great men of the twentieth century that Miss Madeleine Slade—an English friend of Rolland and an admirer of Gandhi—was also present. Ever since Miss Slade met Gandhi, she became his disciple-cum-daughter, renamed by Gandhi as "Mirabehn."

Upon his return home, Gandhi was shocked to see India under an emergency power ordinance imposed by the new viceroy, Lord Willingdon. Deploring such dictatorial measures of the government, Gandhi tried to meet with the new viceroy, but Willingdon refused to see or correspond with Gandhi. Gandhi intimated to the viceroy that because of his iron-handed policies, he had no other option than to launch another civil disobedience campaign. The viceroy considered it a threat and imprisoned Gandhi along with Fourteen thousand other *swarajists* (freedom seekers). Gandhi was back again in the Yeravda jail with his close associates in February 1932.

As earlier, Gandhi could not be happier in jail. Besides reading classics such as Upton Sinclair's *The West Parade*, Goethe's *Faust*, and Kingsley's *Westward Ho*, Gandhi used his time to write a small but spiritually seminal book, *From Yeravda Mandir* (1932).[6] The booklet contained the quintessence of Gandhi's philosophy regarding the nature of God or Truth, and its inviolable connection with nonviolence or *ahimsa*, which meant to him "universal love." Gandhi also gave his own explication of other spiritual disciplines, such as *asteya* (non-stealing), *aparigraha* (non-possession), and *brahmacharya* or complete abstinence—which he had been observing since taking the vow of celibacy in 1906.

GANDHI'S FAST UNTO DEATH OR THE "EPIC FAST"

Gandhi felt so strongly about retaining the Untouchables within the fold of Hinduism that he declared, "If I was the only person to resist this thing, I would resist it with my life." (Collected Works, Vol. 48, 298) Accordingly, he went on a fast unto death on September 20, 1932, which came to be known as the "epic fast." [7] Gandhi clarified, however, "My fast is not meant to coerce the British, but to sting the Hindu conscience"; he added, "I would far rather that Hinduism died than that untouchability lived." Gandhi (Collected Works, Vol. 51, 62) This radical statement reveals that Gandhi had a twofold purpose in undertaking his fast unto death: one was practical and the other, moral. In the first, Gandhi the pragmatist nationalist wanted to prevent the country's division into several splinter minority groups; therefore, he urged all minority groups to forget their petty differences, and to unite and drive the British out of India. In the second purpose, Gandhi the moralist endeavored to awaken the Hindu conscience and purge Hinduism of untouchability, which he denounced as "the greatest blot on Hinduism," because it was "against the fundamental principles of humanity." (Harijan, February 11, 1933, 4) Gandhi insisted, "I have never regarded untouchability as an integral part of Hinduism." (Harijan, February 20, 1937, 9) Gandhi tried his hardest, through preaching and through personal example, to remove the blot of untouchability from the otherwise flawless fabric of Hinduism. His moral reasoning was that if the Untouchables were treated humanly, fairly, and respectfully by the caste Hindus, they would not want to separate from Hinduism. In order to stop the alienation of Untouchables from Hinduism, if he must fast even unto death, he would be more than willing and happy to do so.

The question still remains: Was it necessary for Gandhi to go to such an extreme as undertaking a "fast unto death" for this issue? Or as Fischer asked: "Was the Mahatma's torment unnecessary?" (1950, 318). In the answer to this question lies the key to understanding Gandhi, who he was, and what he meant to his people. It is important to remember here that

Gandhi saw himself primarily as a man of faith—a deeply religious man at heart, to whom religion meant being and living in the presence of God. By fasting unto death for expiating "the sin of untouchability" from Hinduism, Gandhi showed where lay his priorities. As the Untouchable cause assumed a God-value, his own life was reduced to a zero-value.

Ambedkar was neither convinced nor impressed; he considered Gandhi's decision to fast unto death a big "political stunt." He saw nothing heroic or "epic" about it. On the contrary, he saw Gandhi's fast as "an almost Machiavellian move, a veritable piece of blackmail" (Deliege 1999, 183), which made Ambedkar look like "a villain responsible for Gandhi's life."

All across India people prayed and fasted on September 20, 1932, the day Gandhi commenced his fast unto death. Every heart feared, "what if Gandhi died!" Every heart prayed that he would not. As Louis Fischer put it; "The possibility of losing Gandhi in the fast … the very thought sent a shiver through the spine of the nation. If nothing were done to save him, every Hindu would be Mahatmaji's murderer" (1950, 312).

The Gandhi-Ambedkar impasse was becoming critical; Gandhi's life was ebbing away. Even though suffering from nausea, excruciating aches and pains, weight loss, and high blood pressure, Gandhi remained peaceful and joyful. Time was ticking away; tension was mounting. India was praying for Mahatma's life.

THE POONA PACT OR YERAVDA PACT

All eyes were riveted on Ambedkar—would he or would he not relent? Ambedkar said that he was willing to help save the Mahatma's life but not without his "political compensation." He demanded 197 reserved seats to be guaranteed for the Depressed Classes in the provincial legislatures, instead of the 71 seats that MacDonald had recommended. In a series of negotiations between Gandhi, Ambedkar, and other Hindu leaders, Tej Bahadur Sapru brought up a new idea for holding the primaries. According to this plan, Hindus and Untouchables would nominate a portion of the reserved Untouchable seats jointly, and the remaining seats would be nominated only by the Untouchables for the Untouchables. Gandhi saw the wisdom in accepting the lesser of the two evils, namely, the "reservation of seats" for the Untouchables rather than their "segregation from the Hindu community." Although earlier Gandhi had rejected Ambedkar's proposal of the reserved seats for the Untouchables, fearing it would create in them a consciousness of being separate from Hinduism, he now not only agreed but also granted

Ambedkar even more than what he had originally demanded.[8] Why did he now change his mind? Upon reflection, Gandhi thought it wiser to allow the Untouchables more reserved seats to be elected by them rather than by the upper-caste Hindus, so that they would not be under any obligation to the Hindus; at the same time, the Untouchables would still cast their votes not as a separate minority like the Muslims, Sikhs, and others, but as a privileged group of Hinduism.

After Gandhi, Ambedkar, and the viceroy signed the Poona Pact, also called the "Yeravda Pact," Gandhi broke his fast on September 26 with a sip of orange juice. Although "the Poona Pact in itself accomplished little more than might have emerged from an earlier compromise," says Zelliot (1992, 168), "the dramatic circumstances in which it was forged gave a great deal of publicity to Gandhi's concern for the Untouchable and to Ambedkar's leadership."

Yet both great leaders could not see eye to eye on the problem of untouchability or its solution. "As political figures," observed Mendelsohn and Vicziany (1998, 111), "Gandhi and Ambedkar were highly asymmetrical."

GANDHI AND AMBEDKAR ON UNTOUCHABLES AND UNTOUCHABILITY

The fundamental disagreement between Gandhi and Ambedkar "centered around the place of Untouchables in the Indian politics," says A. K. Vakil (1991, 4). Political placement of the Untouchables, however, was Ambedkar's priority; it was not Gandhi's. Ambedkar firmly believed that until the Untouchables demanded and secured their rightful place in Indian politics, they would be totally left at the mercy of the caste Hindus. There was no power without politics, believed Ambedkar, and without the electorate power, Untouchables would remain the *pariahs* or the outcasts of society. All other rights—social, economic, educational, and religious—are contingent upon the mother of all rights, namely the legal and political rights. Therefore, Ambedkar was fighting tooth and nail with Gandhi for the Untouchables' right not only to vote for themselves but to have a fairly large number of guaranteed seats in the legislative assembly, in the state administration, and in local governments. Ambedkar insisted that the number-one need of the Untouchables was to have their legal and political rights guaranteed in the constitution of India. Political rights alone could improve the Untouchables' socioeconomic status and open up opportunities for higher education, higher positions, and better-paid jobs. Similarly, legal statutes alone could compel the caste Hindus to throw open the doors of their temples to Untouchables for worship, and make it punishable to those who violate the law. "According to Ambedkar," observed S. M. Michael (1999, 34), "it is wrong to say that the problem of the Untouchables is a social problem. ... the problem of the Untouchables is fundamentally a political problem."

Gandhi had no disagreement with Ambedkar about the place of the Untouchables in Indian politics; it was just not his first priority. His number-one priority was to ensure the human and social rights of the Untouchables, because unless they were treated equally and humanely by the Hindu society, political rights alone would do little to eliminate the cancer of untouchability from Hinduism. Gandhi's approach to the removal of untouchability was through an inner transformation of the heart, the attitude, and the behavior of the die-hard Hindu toward Untouchables. By peaceful persuasion and by his own personal example, Gandhi strove to awaken the Hindu conscience or even to "sting" it, if it was necessary. Mahatma Gandhi often exhorted his fellow Hindus to treat Untouchables as their equals, with love, dignity, and respect, and urged them to appreciate the Untouchables' contributions and the value of their work. He explained to the caste Hindus that because Untouchables do their dirty work, pick up their filth, and clean up their streets, they do not become "polluted." Nor should the Untouchables be considered inferior to the upper-caste Hindus in any way.

Gandhi believed that because Untouchables are the poorest of the poor, and the lowliest of the lowly, they are nearest and dearest to God. He therefore called them by the name of *Harijans* (*Hari*: God; *jana*: people) or "the people of God." From here on, I will use Gandhi's title "Harijans" when referring to this group. However, it is important to note that Ambedkar and the later generations of Untouchables rejected this title because to them it sounded paternalistic; they would rather be called the "Dalits" (depressed or downtrodden) or otherwise be known as the "scheduled classes."

The major disagreement between Gandhi and Ambedkar arose over their diagonally opposite perception of the Hindu *varnashrama dharma*, which Ambedkar saw as a hierarchical, hereditary, and discriminatory caste system, but Gandhi did not. Although Gandhi denounced untouchability in the strongest terms, like "a curse," "excrescence," "poison," "snake," "a blot," "a vice," and a "sin," he maintained his belief in the *varna vyavastha* (organization by occupations). He honored it as a divinely ordained grouping of society into four major occupations: the *Brahmins* (priests or educators), *Kshatriyas* (warriors or protectors), *Vaishyas* (businessmen or traders), and the *Shudras* (servers or cleaners). To Gandhi, *varna* did not mean caste (*jati*), which he considered to be a later interpolation, and the system did not endorse any caste-based discriminations. As Gandhi explained in *Young India* (November 17, 1927), "the law of *varna* is for the preservation of harmony and the growth of the soul." To him, our forefathers thoughtfully devised the whole system for the smooth functioning and maintenance of our society. The members of each group followed their ancestral occupation; no one's occupation was to be higher or lower than the other's and none, therefore, was superior or inferior. Each person knew his place and role in society, as he followed his prescribed occupational *dharma* (here, duties). Thus, stability, security, and harmony prevailed in this kind of *varna vyavastha*.

Ambedkar did not interpret *varna* the way Gandhi did; he vehemently rejected it as an outdated, discriminatory, and undemocratic Hindu institution. He maintained that it was the Brahmins' conspiracy to preserve maximum power in their hands, and to exploit all the lowly castes, of which Harijans were the lowliest. Ambedkar saw caste system as the root of all evils and condemned it in severest words: "Kill Brahmanism and it will also kill caste; you will succeed in saving Hinduism if you kill Brahmanism" (Mowli 1990, 74).

Besides their political and ideological differences, the two leaders' personal backgrounds were also vastly different. Ambedkar was a Harijan by birth; Gandhi was not. Gandhi did not suffer from the humiliations, deprivations, and social ostracism, but Ambedkar did. Unlike Gandhi, Ambedkar was still haunted by the painful memories of his childhood and youth. Ambedkar remembered how his colleagues at work hurled files at him from their desk; he recalled how the upper-caste children at school would not sit by him, and knowing that he was a Harijan, people would avoid his very shadow! Though he suffered silently, the pain lingered; the rage remained. He blamed the whole Hindu caste system, Hindu scriptures, and the Hindu priests for authorizing untouchability and perpetuating it.

Turning bitter, and even acrimonious, Ambedkar sought revenge and demanded justice. His monumental hatred toward Hinduism was expressed in three ways: first, he vented his fury through writing a caustic book, *What Congress and Gandhi Have Done to the Untouchables* (1946, 124–125), in which he called Hinduism "a mere camouflage" and accused Congress of playing "a strange game of political acrobatics!" He charged both Congress and Gandhi of betraying the trust of the Untouchables "in order to preserve political power" in their hands. He also resented that while Gandhi fasted unto death to defeat the Harijans' separate electorates, never once did he fast against the caste Hindus. Second, in the Nagput meeting

(1927), he publicly set fire to a copy of *Manusmriti*, the sacred Hindu Law book that he believed endorsed the idea of "pollution," and justified the ill-treatment of *panchamas* (*Shudras*) as the *pariahs* (Untouchables). Ambedkar's third and ultimate act of defiance was his conversion to Buddhism in 1956, which led to an en mass conversion of thousands of his Mahar caste Untouchables.

Thus, unfortunate as it is, although Gandhi and Ambedkar were working diligently for the same cause, their views, aims, and perception of their roles in resolving the problem did not match. Gandhi saw his role as a national leader, as a unifier and peacemaker between several warring minorities; he could never conceive that Harijans would want to sever their roots from Hinduism. As long as he lived and as long as he could help it, he could not and would not allow it to happen. As a reformer, Gandhi saw himself as someone who cherished his tradition but was not a die-hard traditionalist. As mentioned earlier, Gandhi was a critical traditionalist who would rather treat the disease than give up on the patient. Though Gandhi acknowledged "untouchability" as the "greatest blot on Hinduism" and tried to purge Hinduism of its "greatest sin," his approach to untouchability and his methods for its removal were not as radical or drastic as those of Ambedkar.

Keeping in mind, however, the larger picture as well as the long-term impact of the distinct contributions of Gandhi and Ambedkar, I would agree with Zelliot, that "the paths of Gandhi and Ambedkar, while they often diverged, ultimately converged, forcing on the Indian conscience the problem of untouchability as an issue of national concern," and that "there are no equivalents of either Gandhi or Ambedkar in India today" (1992, 173–174).

Furthermore, the way in which Gandhi approached the issue—through undertaking fast unto death—touched a spiritual chord in every human heart. Considering the cultural climate of India, and the Indian reverence for holy men and yogis who fasted unto death for God-realization, we can imagine the deep spiritual impact of Gandhi's fast on the hearts and souls of his people. Fischer has said that "No mystic himself, Gandhi affected others mystically" (1950, 318). I think only the second half of Fischer's statement is true, not the first half. In my judgment, "Gandhi affected others mystically" because he, too, *was* "a mystic," though not a stereotypical one. He was not a cave-dwelling yogi who renounced the world to seek God through deep meditation or *samadhi*; Gandhi stayed in the world and worked in it but selflessly. As Gandhi wrote in *Young India* (April 3, 1924), "To attain my end it is not necessary for me to seek shelter of a cave. I carry one about me, if I would but know it." Gandhi was a *karmayogi* to whom work was worship, prayers the yearning of his heart, fasting a feast for the soul, and his Inner Voice the Voice of God. His life was his message; there was no other.

GANDHI FASTS AGAIN FOR TWENTY-ONE DAYS IN 1933

While still in jail, on May 8, 1933, Gandhi went on another fast for twenty-one days for the dual purpose of self-purification and as penance for the moral lapse of some of his ashram residents, who had broken their vows of celibacy. The idea to undertake this fast as atonement for their moral failure came to him "in a flash," just as the idea of *hartal* had come to him earlier in a dream. Gandhi followed the dictates of his Inner Voice.

Gandhi called fasts his "inner eyes" with which he could see, feel, reflect, and function better. Like deep communion with God in profound silence or meditation, or like prayers from deep within the heart, these were the fasts that soothed his soul and calmed his nerves. As we have seen, Gandhi fasted frequently and for a variety of reasons. Some of his fasts were dietetic rituals for health and palate control, whereas others were revolutionary (like fasts unto death) in their content and in their "do or die" intent. However, only spontaneous fasts like this one in 1933 proved to be spiritually uplifting. Like his mother, Gandhi rejoiced in fasting for the sake of fasting; although a learned behavior, it eventually became as effortless as breathing itself. Moreover, like deep breathing, prolonged fasting reinvigorated Gandhi's body, refreshed his mind, and rejuvenated his spirit. He felt renewed all over. After twenty-one days, Gandhi broke his fast with orange juice in the presence of Harijans and people of different religions, chanting *shlokas* or prayer verses in Sanskrit and reading from scriptures.

GANDHI'S POLITICAL *SANNYASA* (RETIREMENT) AND CONSTRUCTIVE PROGRAMS

Even before his release from jail in 1933, Gandhi had social reform on his mind. In February 1933, while still in jail, he had started a new service organization called the "*Harijan Sevak Sangh*" or a service organization for the Untouchables. In the same year, he launched a new weekly paper, *Harijan*, that replaced *Young India*, which he had started in 1919. After his release from the Yeravda jail later in the year 1933, Gandhi wanted to devote himself totally to his multifarious constructive programs. Because Gandhi continuously traveled, mostly through the villages of Madhya Pradesh

(Central Provinces), it was not feasible for him to stay in permanently or to maintain his Sabarmati Ashram in Ahmedabad.[9] He therefore disbanded it and established another ashram at Wardha (in Central Provinces), which was later renamed *Sevagram* or Service Village.

From 1933 through 1938 Gandhi's political involvement remained only peripheral; he now plunged wholeheartedly into propagating his constructive programs, which aimed not only at educating the villagers but also making them self-sufficient. Among all the constructive programs, however, "service to Harijans" was Gandhi's prime priority. As he described it in his weekly *Harijan* (March 4, 1933), "It was a spiritual act of soul acting upon soul," which can be done only by those "who have courage of their conviction, faith in themselves, faith in their cause and faith in a living God." In 1934, at age sixty-five, Gandhi traveled again by third-class train passage from village to village through the central and northern provinces of India to root out both the prejudice and practice of untouchability. Gandhi considered it his sacred mission to replace hatred with love, and narrow-mindedness with a vision of the world united. As Stanley Wolpert (2001, 173) quoted Gandhi, "Harijan service would remain from now on the breath of life for me, more precious than the daily bread."

THE EARLIEST SIGNS OF THE GANDHI-CONGRESS RIFT

Gandhi's all-consuming passion for "Harijan emancipation and rural uplift work" created the first ideological rift between him and the largely orthodox Hindu Congress. Prominent Congress leaders like Nehru, Patel, Bose, and others resented Gandhi giving constructive programs a priority over national independence; to them it was as absurd as putting the cart before horse. Not only did most Congressmen fail to understand or approve of Gandhi's enthusiasm for social reforms, their concept of *swaraj* also drastically differed from that of Gandhi's. To the Congress, *swaraj* meant political independence from foreign rule; everything else was subservient to this one expedient goal. To Gandhi, however, *swaraj* meant total transformation of self and society from within and without. Gandhi's vision of *swaraj* was that of a self-sufficient village community that was not other-dependent, but interdependent. In his words: "Interdependence is and ought to be as much the ideal of man as self-sufficiency; man is a social being" (Prabhu and Rao 1946, 11). To Gandhi *swaraj* had to be comprehensive to include moral, social, political, economic, and internal freedom and it had to begin at the local village level. Localism and nationalism were not irreconcilable to Gandhi.

As George Woodcock (1971) observed, "localism was the very ground and guarantor of nationalism, and the latter, of universalism." Gandhi's national *satyagraha* itself had developed out of various local *satyagrahas*.

TRANSITION FROM STAGE 5 TO STAGE 6 UNIVERSALIZING FAITH

Earlier we touched on some of the telltale signs of transition from Stage 5 to Stage 6. The way in which Gandhi now adhered to truth at any cost is one of the biggest indicators of his moving away from the previous paradoxical Stage 5 and transitioning toward Stage 6.

The particular quality of becoming "an activist incarnation of the imperatives of love and justice" distinguishes Stage 6 from Stage 5 persons, the latter having only "partial apprehensions" of the same. For example, Gandhi's previous outspoken comments at Benares, and his disregard for social or religious conventions in accepting Harijans in his ashram, were only episodic, partial expressions of his moral and political absolutism. In Stage 6 we see the same "partial apprehensions" developing into more stabilized, uncompromising, full-fledged manifestations that may seem inconsistent to others but which are perfectly consistent with Gandhi's character and vision of Truth.

The first cataclysmic event to mark the onset of Stage 6 was Gandhi's serious confrontation with Ambedkar in 1931–1932 regarding Harijans' separate electorate rights. Gandhi took his most uncompromising stand so far against the "separation of Harijans from the Hindu fold." Both Hindus and Harijans considered Gandhi's opposition to be rather paradoxical or inconsistent; however, to Gandhi, nothing could be more consistent to his comprehension of truth. His radical moral stand on the Harijan issue exemplifies the Stage 6 characteristic that Fowler calls, "redemptive subversiveness and relevant irrelevance" (ibid.).

We just mentioned that according to Fowler, the "transition to Stage 6" is achieved through "a moral and ascetic actualization of the universalizing apprehensions." The words *moral* and *ascetic* are best exemplified by Gandhi's "epic fast" in 1932 for removing the "evil of untouchability" from Hinduism. Gandhi was an extremely moral person with deeply ingrained ascetic tendencies absorbed early in his childhood through his saintly mother. Fasting unto death was his ultimate moral weapon to sacrifice his very life for truth and "to sting the conscience of orthodox Hindus." We also saw that as Gandhi grew in his understanding and faith, he also used fasting in various ways to fight social, religious, and political injustices as well as for self-purification (the 1933 fast) and collective penance. His "epic fast" and another fast unto death toward the end of his life are the most powerful "moral and ascetic actualization of the universalizing apprehensions."

The representatives of Stage 6 are actively involved humans beings, who are willing to sacrifice themselves on the altar of truth, love, and justice. Not only are they visionaries but also the "doers" and "shakers" of the world. What they say and do can be so nonconformist that they may offend or shock others; they are the ones, however, who change the status quo, transform individuals, society, and the world at large.

For example, Gandhi's active involvement in his "Constructive Programs" illustrates the Stage 6 quality to "create zones of liberation from all kinds of shackles"—social, economic, educational, and others. Mere political freedom was meaningless to him without the liberation of the individual and the society from within. As Gandhi put it, "I do not divide different activities—political, social, religious, economical—into water-tight compartments. I look upon them as one indivisible whole each running into the rest and affected by the rest." (Iyer, 1986, Vol1, 408)

Similarly, Gandhi's concept of *swaraj* demonstrates the broadness of his humanistic vision beyond the parochial, geographical, political, or national boundaries. To Gandhi, *swaraj* was not restricted to gaining only political independence, as most congressmen interpreted it. Gandhi said, "My patriotism includes the good of mankind in general. Therefore my service of India includes the service of humanity." [10] His insistence on the right means for the right end lifted the Indian movement from a political plane to a spiritual plane and made it a "moral equivalent of war" or a *dharma-yuddha*. Gandhi explained that his vision of *Ramaraj* (*Rama*: God; *raj*: kingdom) was based on *Dharma*:

> Dharma is religion in the highest sense of the term. It includes Hinduism, Islam, Christianity, etc., but is superior to them all. ... we cannot achieve ... political and economic freedom without truth and non-violence. (1947, 11)

Gandhi's nationalism and religion were, therefore, all-inclusive. In this he exhibited one of the outstanding qualities of Stage 6 persons, that "their community is universal in extent," and that "particularities are cherished because they are vessels of the universal, and thereby valuable apart from any utilitarian considerations" (Fowler 1981, 201).

These were some of the qualities that demonstrated Gandhi's transition from Stage 5 to Stage 6. Toward the end of this chapter, further exposition of Stage 6 characteristics and an interpretation of Gandhi's faith and self-development from this point on in relation to Stage 6 criteria will be discussed.

AGING BODY AND AGELESS SPIRIT

At age sixty-nine, Gandhi's body was aging but his spirit was young. His blood pressure escalated again, and he contracted malaria, which was rampant in the village of Seagoan, Wardha, in central India. Assassins also pursued the old Mahatma during 1934–1936. Once, while walking through the tribal jungle villages in Bihar and Orissa (northeast) where he was preaching against untouchability, Gandhi was attacked by some orthodox Hindus, but he narrowly escaped. Once again in 1934, another Hindu extremist from Poone (Maharashtra), who was furious about Gandhi advocating Hindu–Muslim unity, threw a bomb at a car, thinking that Gandhi was riding in it (Gandhi occasionally traveled by car when his assistants insisted). Thus the assassins proposed, but God disposed, and the Mahatma miraculously survived.

In addition, some personal miseries plagued Gandhi at this time. His "prodigal son Harilal" had reappeared suddenly after a long exile. According to Stanley Wolpert (2001), Harilal had fallen in love with one of Gandhi's ashram disciples, and they asked for Gandhi's permission to marry. Gandhi had to turn them down for various reasons. Having avowed himself to *brahmacharya* along with other ashram residents, Gandhi could not allow his own son to break the celibacy vow as long as they remained in his ashram. Harilal also had no steady income, nor any sense of family responsibility (Gandhi and Kasturbai were still taking care of his children from his previous marriage). Gandhi also knew that the woman Harilal wanted to marry had a long history of mental illness; therefore, his answer was a definite "no."

Two more incidents further frayed Gandhi's nerves. In the first, he recalled having a sexual dream in 1936 at the age of sixty-seven. For someone like Gandhi, who had so arduously tried (since age thirty-six) to subdue and sublimate his sexual instinct, this proved to be a terrible blow and an extremely painful experience. As Gandhi said, "I ultimately conquered the feeling, but it was the blackest moment of my life" (Fischer 1950, 337). Gandhi, being a votary of truth, would not forgive himself if he kept any skeletons in his closet. He laid bare all his weaknesses and inner struggles so that others might learn from them and know that "even their Mahatma was only an erring mortal." In another incident, Gandhi found out that

Kasturbai (now on "Kasturba" for seniority and respect) and his disciple-cum-secretary Mahadevbhai Desai had gone secretly to worship at the famous Hindu temple of Jaggannath Puri, which was closed to Harijans.[11] Feeling betrayed by his nearest and dearest ones, Gandhi had a nervous and physical breakdown. His doctors now compelled him to rest for a few months at a friend's home on Juhu Beach in Bombay.

Amazingly, despite his setbacks and "bouts of depression," Gandhi bounced back to health and retained what he called his "incorrigible optimism" only because of his faith, which he said, "is not like a delicate flower which would wither under the slightest stormy weather. Faith is like the Himalaya mountains which cannot possibly change."[12]

Toward the end of the 1930s, the Gandhi-Congress relationship began to further deteriorate. The Congress membership had considerably changed with the coming of young, militant leaders like Subhash Chandra Bose who rebelled against Gandhi's nonviolent ways. Though Gandhi was disappointed in the present Congress leadership, he was still regularly consulted by the Congress, for which Nehru lightheartedly called Gandhi "the permanent super-President of Congress." Whenever he was summoned, Gandhi, like an old, wise grandsire, helped them tackle critical national crises and resolved their interpersonal power struggles.

WORLD WAR II AND THE PARTING OF WAYS

With the advent of World War II in 1939, the already existing rift between Gandhi and Congress became a gulf too wide to bridge. First, the Congress leaders could not share Gandhi's passion for nonviolence at any cost and under all circumstances. To the Congress, nonviolence was a matter of policy, not a principle; they supported it as long as it was expedient or politically correct to use. For example, in the 1921 national movement of Non-cooperation and in the 1930 *salt satyagraha*, nonviolence seemed to work like magic over the masses under Gandhi's leadership. Now, however, with an impending international crisis like World War II, they thought that unconditional nonviolence was not the need of the hour. Obviously, for Gandhi, nonviolence was a "creed," the "biggest article of his faith." Gandhi was against India having an army or using force to stop any violence whether internal or international; Congress was ready to support Britain in war if specified conditions were met. Although Gandhi had recruited Indians for the British army during the World War I (1918), he saw no inconsistency between his war advocacy then and his principled objection to India's participation in war now. He explained that in 1918, he still considered himself to be a loyal subject of Britain just like other Indians, so despite his endorsement of nonviolence he felt it his moral duty to help the British in their critical hour. Now, however, his views on nonviolence had evolved to become more uncompromising, for he could clearly see the Truth—the larger picture, which Gandhi presented to an English journalist (*Harijan*, September 29, 1946) in these words: "Unless now the world adopts nonviolence, it will spell certain suicide for mankind."

The impasse between Congress and Gandhi become insurmountable in June 1940. Congress regretfully told Gandhi that it could not fully agree with his insistence on nonviolence. As, Nehru wrote in his autobiography, "Gandhi went one way and the Congress went another." (in Fischer, 1950, 352)

Congress capitalized on the war crisis. Turning it to India's advantage, it now demanded *Purna Swaraj* (Complete Independence) from Britain in return for India's assistance in fighting the war. In the British parliament, Prime Minister Churchill and the new Viceroy Linlithgow disapproved of India's demand. Taking full advantage of the rising discontent of the Muslim minority, Britain devised a scheme to "divide and rule" over India. The viceroy rejected the Congress proposal for complete independence on two grounds. First, His Majesty could not allow Congress to rule over India without Muslim consent; second, Britain could not completely divest herself of her long investment in India (for more than 150 years), nor evade her responsibilities to see that India was capable of self-rule. Churchill put it even more bluntly, as Fischer quoted him, "I have not become the King's First Prime Minister in order to preside at the liquidation of the British Empire" (1950, 354).

The crestfallen Congress now came back to Gandhi toward the end of 1940. Realizing that Linlithgow was no Irwin, Gandhi adopted a different strategy this time of launching several individual *satyagrahas* instead of one mass-scale *satyagraha*; he handpicked proven *satyagrahis*, such as Vinoba Bhave,[13] Nehru, Sardar Patel, and Maulana Abul Kalam Azad, who, one after the other, released their nonviolent, antiwar "missiles." The British once again threw Gandhi, other key leaders, and more than 20,000 Indians into jail without a warrant, trial, or explanation of any kind.

Toward the close of 1941, World War II was escalating, consuming nation after nation. Germany attacked Russia. Japan bombarded Pearl Harbor, also taking China, Thailand, British Malaya, and Rangoon (the capital of Burma), thus arriving at the gates of India. While India was facing a war crisis outside, she was simultaneously facing an internal crisis of escalating animosities between the Hindus and the Muslims. India was writhing in pain and seething with anger. Indians were tired of remaining in jail with no end in sight. The whole country was restless.

Britain was now under pressure from all sides to offer India at least a tentative plan for a new self-government. The Labor wing in the British wartime coalition government had many friends who were sympathetic to the Indian demand for freedom. The American President Roosevelt urged Churchill to open negotiations with India; Chiang Kai shek of China also favored Indian independence and visited India.

The Cripps Mission Fails

Because of overpowering pressure from inside Britain and out, Churchill now reluctantly sent Sir Stafford Cripps to New Delhi on March 22, 1942, with a proposal of "His Majesty's Draft Declaration." [14] Gandhi was specially invited by Cripps to study the draft before it was formally presented to the Congress. After perusing it carefully, Gandhi shook his head in disapproval, suggesting that Cripps should go home. Cripps still waited to hear what Congress had to say. Articles A, B, C, and D in the proposed draft dealt with the postwar period and promised a "full-fledged Dominion" status to India with a right to vote herself out of the Commonwealth, if she desired. After the war, a legislative assembly consisting entirely of Indians would form a new constitution of India, about which Gandhi and Congress could not be happier.

However, the Cripps mission broke down on two major points. First, there was a stipulating clause that one-third of the constituent assembly would be appointed by the princes of India, provincial governments, and other minority groups, who could secede any time from the new Indian self-government at their own will. Gandhi foresaw the danger in accepting a proposal with a built-in provision for dividing India into "many little Indias" (a princely India, Muslim India, Sikh India). If any prince, province, or minority decided to withdraw from the federal Indian government, it could; any minor party could curry the British favor to retain its self-autonomy or the latter could play one against the other to regain control over India.

And second, according to article E in the draft, Britain would still retain its wartime powers and control over India's defense. As Gandhi was against any war or violence, he rejected article E in its entirety, whereas the Congress (Nehru, Azad, Rajgopalachari) pushed for gaining more power over India's wartime defense and military activities. It is important to bear in mind that even though Gandhi, being a votary of nonviolence, disliked article E related to war, he did not interfere with the Congress' demand for more military powers—the issue over which it rejected the Cripps proposal. Disenchanted India stood on the brink of a revolution.

THE 1942 QUIT INDIA MOVEMENT

The year was 1942. World War II was drawing dangerously close to India. Japanese invasion was expected any moment, and the British seemed unable to stop it. An atmosphere of doom and gloom prevailed. People were in a panic. Their panic turned into fury, and the fury needed an outlet. They needed Gandhi more than ever before.

Gandhi sensed the inflammatory mood of the nation. He forewarned the viceroy in a letter about what was coming—a nationwide civil disobedience or bloodless revolution that demanded the British to leave India to Indians, and to leave NOW. This was the ultimatum that later materialized as the 1942 Quit India Movement.[15]

In his letter to the viceroy, Gandhi clarified that he was not contemplating an overthrow of the British government. He was only alerting him about his people's irrepressible urge for self-assertion, their desperate cry for *swaraj*, for freedom. Gandhi also assured His Highness that as long as he remained in charge, it would be "a nonviolent revolution, and not a seizure of power." Gandhi further explained to the viceroy that *swaraj* to him was "a program of transformation of relationships ending in a peaceful transfer of power."[16] The viceroy did not reply; instead, he locked Gandhi up in the Aga Khan Palace in Poone.[17] Nothing could have infuriated people more.

The floodgates of fury opened. Wild with rage, people went on a killing spree. Gruesome riots spread all across India, thousands were arrested, and jails were overfilled.[18] In a series of letters that issued back and forth between Gandhi and the viceroy, each placed the blame on the other for this mass-scale violence. Gandhi held the government to be entirely responsible for the bloody revolt for two reasons. First, the viceroy had refused to see or even talk to him, nor had he replied to a letter in which Gandhi had disclosed his peace plan. Second, the government's even bigger blunder was to react in panic and imprison Gandhi prematurely. The news of this imprisonment had provoked people who were already on the brink of despair and desperation. The British, on the contrary, held Gandhi responsible for masterminding a mass-scale revolution that was potentially dangerous. The viceroy either failed to gauge the extent of people's anger and despair, or he simply refused to concede to Gandhi, whose letter he saw only as a threat or a political ploy to pressure the British to grant India her freedom. Gandhi maintained throughout that although he had given his people the *Guru-mantra*, or the slogan of "do or die," it never meant "kill or be killed." According to D. G. Tendulkar (1951, 6: 216), when Gandhi said "do or die," he meant "do your duty by carrying out instructions and die in the attempt, if necessary." Nonviolence was always a prerequisite for Gandhi. Gandhi also denied that his plan contained any threat, open or veiled. On the contrary, the Congress had laid all the cards on the table; instead of appreciating it, the government had drawn unwarranted inferences, reacted heavy-handedly, and provoked the people into violence.

Gandhi had intended the Quit India Movement to be a nonviolent revolution, but the masses, misled by extremist group leaders, had misinterpreted his message. Pragmatist as he was, Gandhi had expected some violence to creep into the movement; however, he also had full confidence that if he had been present on the scene, he could have controlled or reversed it. Francis Hutchins argues, however, that "Gandhi disdained violence as a blunt weapon, but he did not shun it; he endorsed violent resistance without advocating it" (1973, 138). On the contrary, an unbiased historical appraisal of Gandhi since his arrival on the Indian political scene shows that from the beginning of the Nonviolent Non-cooperation Movement in 1920–1921 through the 1942 Quit India Movement and thereafter, Gandhi never condoned violence, nor did he instigate it. What Hutchins fails to register is the "time factor"; he seems to overlook that the period between the early to mid-forties was perhaps the most volatile one in Indian history. The country was teetering on anarchy; people were angry, frustrated, and desperate.

Bear in mind also that the 1942 Quit India Movement could not remain entirely Gandhian in form or spirit. Subversive anti-British activities and powerful underground movements had been active (both in England and India) since the beginning of the twentieth century; if we recall, as early as 1911 Gandhi had written a fictitious dialogue confronting some of the revolutionary leaders (Vir Savarkar, Shyamji Krishnavarma, and others) in his book *Hind Swaraj*. In 1942, many other patriotic groups advocating force (Hindu Mahasabha, Rashtriya Sevak Sangh or R.S.S., Forward Bloc, Socialists, students of Carl Marx) and other Leftists were gaining in popularity. With Gandhi being removed from the scene, these extremist group leaders took over and changed the style and the direction of the movement. Others to join the extremists were some of the city lords (*shehar subas*) and provincial leaders, who turned the initially nonviolent movement into a violent rebellion. Arsons, bombings, lootings, overthrowing of trains, uprooting of telephone and telegraph lines, murders of the *sahibs*, and rapes of the *mem-sahibs* (wives of the British) became the order of the day. Gyanendra Pandey observed (1988, 12), "in 1942, the leadership was Gandhi's but the spirit was of Bhagat Singh" (a patriot-rebel or *shahid* who was hanged by the British).

GANDHI AGAIN FASTS FOR TWENTY-ONE DAYS

In 1943, Gandhi wielded from jail his ultimate moral weapon. He went on a fast for twenty-one days to "combat injustice and falsehood" of the British government, and to "spread truth and nonviolence among mankind in place of violence and falsehood in all walks of life" (Tendulkar 1951, 6:195). Strictly following the law of *satyagraha*, he wanted to crucify the flesh by fasting.[19] Once again, Gandhi fasted not for personal gain or for political power. His was an act of self-penance, a symbolic protest against political injustice. It was a spiritual gesture that had the most calming effect on him and on his people. Although very near death, the seventy-four-year-old Mahatma survived the ordeal. Exactly on the twenty-second day, on March 3, 1943, he broke his fast with six ounces of diluted orange juice, and with prayers from the *Gita* and the *Qu'ran*. Gandhi's friends and followers also sang one of his favorite Gujarati hymns of *Vaishnava Janato* (by the fourteenth-century saint-poet Narsimha Mehta). As India rejoiced, the British breathed a sigh of relief.

PERSONAL LOSS AND GRIEF

Gandhi's confinement in the Aga Khan Palace prison was marked by deep personal sorrow on account of the deaths of his two nearest and dearest ones, who had been in the same jail with him. On August 15, 1942, Mahadevbhai Desai, his devoted disciple-cum-chronicler, died of sudden heart failure at age fifty. Gandhi grieved and missed him acutely. As Kasturba put it, "Bapu has lost his right hand and his left hand! Both his hands Bapu has lost!" (Payne 1969, 496). Little did she know who was next to follow.

In 1943, Kasturba's health began to deteriorate in the Aga Khan jail. Gandhi nursed her tenderly day and night, and when she felt better he resumed giving her lessons in reading, writing, and geography. More sacrificing than Gandhi in domestic life, Kasturba retained her quiet strength, her loving, self-asserting yet self-suffering ways, her traditional beliefs, and even some of her habits.[20] Although illiterate, she had her own mind and a distinct individuality. She was not only a doting mother or "*Ba*" to her own children, but to all the children of the *ashrams*. To put it in Hindu terminology, Kasturba was not only a traditional, devoted and virtuous wife but also a true *sahadharmacharini* or a spiritual partner of Gandhi.

Kasturba breathed her last breath, with her head in Gandhi's lap, on February 22, 1944. Grieving deeply, Gandhi said: "I cannot imagine life without *Ba*; her passing has left a vacuum which never will be filled" (Fischer 1950, 394). Soon thereafter, Gandhi's own health collapsed; he suffered from malaria, anemia, and high blood pressure. Not willing to take the blame of Gandhi's death in jail, the government released him on May 6, 1944. After a brief respite, Gandhi was ready to wrestle with his former Congress colleague turned enemy—Mohammad Ali Jinnah.[21]

GANDHI AND JINNAH

Both Jinnah and Gandhi hailed from the Kathiawar peninsula (in Gandhi's native Gujarat) and spoke the Gujarati language; both were also barristers educated in London—Gandhi studied at the Inner Temple, and Jinnah at Lincoln's Inn. But that is where the similarities ended, as they were poles apart with respect to religion, dress, manners, personality, and politics. In 1915 when Gandhi returned home from South Africa, Jinnah was present at his reception in Bombay. It was "hate at first sight" at least on the part of Jinnah, as he perhaps saw everything in Gandhi that he was not. "Austere and arrogant, upper-crust, well-dressed in European style, Jinnah did not suggest a demagogue. Yet possibly he was helped by being so wildly unlike Gandhi," described Geoffrey Ashe (1968, 339). Westernized Jinnah was a non-religious Muslim with a sharp intellect, fierce political ambition, and remarkable oratorical skills. Gandhi was a deeply religious man of simple living, high thinking, humble at heart and manners, and broad in his human sympathies. Jinnah detested Gandhi's rural style, his saintly politics and most of all, his immense popularity. Gandhi knew this very well, but as we have seen throughout, he believed in turning an enemy into a friend.

JINNAH DEMANDS PAKISTAN

Ever since he attended the First and Second Round Table Conferences in London in 1931 and 1932, respectively, Jinnah began to push for Muslim rights as a minority. Once a prominent leader of the Congress party (for thirty-five years), Jinnah claimed to have Gandhi and Nehru working under him in the 1920 Home-rule Movement. Jinnah was for Hindu–Muslim unity until 1920, when he claimed Gandhi came into the picture and began to convert the once-elite Congress into a mass-based, Hindu-dominated organization. Jinnah resented what he saw as an increasing Hindu predominance in Congress especially after 1930, with the rising popularity of Gandhi, Nehru, Patel, and Bose. After 1935, Jinnah parted from the alleged Hindu Congress, joining the Muslim League and its campaign for Pakistan— a separate, new nation of the Muslims for the Muslims. Soon thereafter, Jinnah assumed the role of *Quaid-e-Azam* or "The Great Honorable Leader."

Gandhi and Jinnah met—early in 1939, twice again in 1944 and thereafter—to decide the fate of India. Interestingly, through all their sessions, Gandhi addressed Jinnah informally as "Brother Jinnah," or *Quaid-e-Azam,* whereas Jinnah continued to address Gandhi only formally as "Mr. Gandhi." Gandhi, who since the 1940s had been focusing on India's independence struggle, urged Jinnah to work together in first procuring India's independence from the British, and later settle the Hindu–Muslim differences after the British departure from India. Jinnah vehemently opposed, insisting on creating a new separate nation of Pakistan before the British left. He also wanted Gandhi to admit that he came to see him (Jinnah) not on personal grounds but as a Hindu leader representing the Hindu Congress. Likewise, Jinnah insisted that Gandhi accept him as a Muslim leader speaking for the entire Muslim population of India.

Gandhi could not agree with Jinnah, nor approve of his separatist mentality. To Gandhi, Hindus and Muslims were sons of the same soil of India; they were brothers who must therefore strive to keep India free and united. Gandhi was totally against the "vivisection of India" (Iyer, Vol III, 273–274) and would give his life to stop it. Jinnah was adamant on the division of India into two separate religion-based states—Hindu India and Muslim Pakistan. The Gandhi-Jinnah talks broke down when Jinnah refused to budge an inch; he wanted the partition now, not later. On September 9, 1944, Gandhi made one last effort by writing to Churchill and Jinnah, says Wolpert (2001, 210), imploring both "to forestall the vivisection of Mother India," but his plea fell on deaf ears.

THE 1945 SIMLA CONFERENCE FAILS

The year 1945 saw the end of Churchill's power in England and the beginning of the Labor party administration of Prime Minister Clement Attlee,

Lord Wavell, the new viceroy of India, and Sir Pethick-Lawrence, the secretary of state of India. On June 25, 1945, Viceroy Wavell held his first conference in Simla (the British summer capital) in which he proposed the formation of a new executive council consisting entirely of Indians, who would be in charge of finances, foreign affairs, safety, and so on. The viceroy was still to retain his right to veto the decisions of the Congress council; he promised, however, not to exercise his right unreasonably, and even if he did, all Indians could withdraw from the council and thus nullify the viceroy's veto. The plan provided for equal proportions of Muslims and Hindus in the viceroy's council. Even though Congress was at first reluctant to accept this equalization, it finally did. Only Jinnah did not; he insisted that he be the sole spokesman of the Muslim League and that only he designate the Muslims in the viceroy's council. Thus, the Simla Conference failed on account of this stalemate regarding who should select the Muslim members of the executive council—Congress or the Muslim League.

THE 1946 CABINET MISSION ALSO FAILS

In May 1946, another Cabinet Mission met in New Delhi to iron out the differences between Congress and Jinnah and to decide the future of India. Gandhi was specially summoned from where he was living at this time—in a *Bhangi* colony or Harijans' quarters, which he had renamed as *Valmiki Mandir*.[22] This conference also broke down because of a disagreement between Congress and the Muslim League regarding the composition of a provisional government[23] proposed by the new viceroy (and the last one), Lord Mountbatten. In order to avoid another deadlock, and to avert the painful "partition of India," Gandhi reportedly offered Jinnah the first choice of forming a provisional government and selecting his own personnel. Nehru, Patel, Azad, and other Congressmen considered this as far too generous an offer on Gandhi's part to placate Jinnah. The latter, however, declined it until his demand was met, namely, to carve out of India a separate Muslim nation of Pakistan. Thus the deadlock remained.

THE DIRECT ACTION DAY

Regardless of Jinnah's cooperation, the new provisional government (with Nehru as prime minister) and a Constituent Assembly were formed. In retaliation, Jinnah and the Muslim League declared August 16, 1946, as

Direct Action Day or "A Day of Mourning." The Muslims of India treated it as a "Day of License to Kill the Hindus." Holding black flags and shouting slogans of "*Hindustan Murdabad*" (Death to Hindu India), and "*Pakistan Zindabad*" (Long Live the Pure Muslim Nation), Muslim hooligans went on looting, butchering Hindus, raping their women, and converting Hindu males by forcibly circumcising them. The most gruesome violence wrecked the city of Calcutta (known as the "Great Calcutta killings"), the Noakhali district in East Bengal, and Bihar.

"Do or Die for Peace"

Deeply anguished by the raging violence and darkness all around him, Gandhi prayed and fasted; he was determined to "do or die" for Hindu–Muslim harmony. Peace was now the only passion and mission of the remaining years of his life. Gandhi knew the Congress was not with him; India was not with him. Not too long ago he had desired to live up to 125 years to make true "the India of his dreams" where there was no high class or low class of people, no untouchability, and no room for hatred based on religion or race. The India of his dreams was a nation free and united, where love ruled and peace prevailed. But that India of his dreams was dying today. Partition was around the corner. Gandhi wanted to live no more.

India Free at Last But Not without Partition

On August 15, 1947, India became a free nation at last under the last viceroyalty of Lord Louis Mountbatten, but not without the vivisection that Gandhi had dreaded. At the stroke of midnight, two nations were carved out of the same geographical-historical land that had been home to both Hindus and Muslims for centuries untold. One nation was India or *Bharat*; the other nation was *Pakistan*—the pure land of Muslims.

Intoxicated with joy, Indians were celebrating their independence all across the country, but the "Father of the Country" was mourning the death of a united India (see Preface). To him, the partition was a spiritual tragedy and therefore the freedom of India, a hollow victory.

Though his heart was broken, Gandhi was still sustained by his faith in the ultimate triumph of Truth and nonviolence. Like his childhood mythological heroes—King Harishchandra, and the boy Bhakta Prahlad—Gandhi wanted to sacrifice his very life for Truth. Until God called him away, he would live to spread the gospel of peace and nonviolence among the warring Hindus and Muslims in the aftermath of the partition. In the darkest hour of his life, Gandhi remembered a poem by his revered friend, Gurudev Tagore.

> Walk alone
> If they answer not to thy call, walk alone;
> If they turn away and desert you when
> crossing the wilderness,
> O thou of evil luck,
> trample the thorns under thy tread,
> and along the blood-lined track travel
> alone.
> (Quoted in Pyarelal, 1966, Vol 1, Book Two, 139)

Determined to walk alone, Gandhi prayed God "to lead him from darkness to Light."

THE ULTIMATE PILGRIMAGE FOR PEACE

The seventy-seven-year-old Mahatma went on his ultimate pilgrimage for peace through the riot-ridden Calcutta, Noakhali, and Bihar to wipe tears from every eye, to spread the gospel of love and forgiveness, and to quench the fires of revenge and hatred that still consumed the Hindu and Muslim refugees, the innocent victims of partition. Gandhi walked barefoot through the hardest-hit villages and cities, which looked like ghost towns deserted by the living and surrounded by skeletons. Calcutta was "a city of the dead" where men had gone mad committing acts so savage they shamed a savage. Muslims massacred Hindus, and the Hindus took revenge. Gandhi was inconsolable; he felt helpless. This was the dark night of his soul, when he cried out in agony: "I invoke the aid of all-embracing Power to take me away from this 'vale of tears' rather than make me a helpless witness of the butchery by man become savage. Yet I cry, 'Not my will but Thine alone shall prevail." (Harijan, October 12, 1947)

SIGNIFICANCE OF *BRAHMACHARYA* EXPERIMENTS

Gandhi faced an unprecedented crisis of faith. Being a true *bhakta* or man of prayers, he turned to God for guidance, solace, and strength. Gandhi was also a seeker after Truth, who subjected everything he experienced in the outer and inner world to a severe self-scrutiny. Whenever pressures or problems mounted outside, he turned the searchlight inward; he became introspective, not to blame himself but to find the strength within—to purify himself, or as he said, "to be a fit instrument of God." (Gandhi used this expression in (1932) reference to fasting to purify the body and make it 'a fit instrument of God.')

In order to be "a fit instrument of God," Gandhi considered it absolutely necessary to test his purity by conducting severe experiments in *brahmacharya*. In keeping with his Hindu and Jain traditions, Gandhi strongly believed that the practice of *brahmacharya* was power-enhancing; not only did a *brahmachari* (practitioner) acquire extraordinary powers to command the environment but also he could affect the outcome of events.

It is worthwhile at this point to give a stage-by-stage account of Gandhi's gradual advancement in *brahmacharya*. As discussed earlier, since taking his vow of *brahmacharya* in 1906, Gandhi had been strictly observing abstinence. At that time, Gandhi's purpose was twofold. First, he wanted to curb what he considered to be his excessive sexual appetite, and second, to restrict the size of his family so that he could free himself for public service.

Now, however, in these last, most crucial years (1946–1947) of Gandhi's life, *brahmacharya* occupied supreme importance. He put himself through his most severe tests so far in *brahmacharya*, probably because he felt that desperate times called for desperate measures. This time his experiments in *brahmacharya* were not only for self-purification, nor were they solely for enhancing his inner spiritual strength in order to control outer conditions, although the influence cannot be denied.

I refer here to Gandhi's unconventional practice at this time of sleeping naked with a young woman, who was none other than his grandniece, Manubehn Gandhi, whom he and Kasturba had adopted as their daughter. Gandhi had consulted Manubehn beforehand, and with her consent, he slept in the same bed with her while keeping the doors open all the time. Nirmalkumar Bose, Gandhi's Bengali interpreter and a psychologist, criticized Gandhi for this in his book *My Days with Gandhi* (1974). Bose objected to Gandhi's "sex-control experiment" not because he suspected or found anything improper between them, but for the psychological effect it may have on the young woman. Manubehn, however, in her book *Bapu— My Mother* (1949), casually mentioned that ever since she came to live with Ba and Bapu, she had shared her "Bapu's bed." She also reported no "ill effect" on her then or thereafter.

The idea to undertake these most unusual tests in *brahmacharya* came to him, said Gandhi, "not as an *experiment* but as a matter of sacred duty and so became a part of his penance or *yajna*" (Pyarelal 1966, 216). That is why, after undertaking his *brahmacharya yajna* (sacred duty), Gandhi reportedly experienced ineffable calmness and peace everlasting. He felt inwardly shielded to bear all the pain inflicted from the outside. He developed a new detachment similar to that of the "man of equipoise" described as "*sthitaprajnya*" in the *Bhagavad Gita*. Gandhi passed his penultimate crisis of faith.

Thus, when death danced all around him, he "went in search of the divine in maddened men," said Fischer (1950, 445). Tirelessly, the Mahatma walked through the rivers of blood, crossing rickety bridges, visiting refugee camps, comforting grieving mothers, fathers, and orphans. He beseeched Hindus and Muslims to give up their arms, their hate, and their thirst for revenge. When Gandhi could not stop the mass lust for blood and revenge by his personal appearance or word, he decided to once again wield his ultimate weapon.

GANDHI FASTS UNTO DEATH FOR PEACE

Gandhi declared his fast unto death on September 1, 1947, to ensure permanent peace in Calcutta. While he was groping in the dark, Gandhi saw the light; it was the light of his inner voice, the voice of God. He was determined to put his life on the line for stopping the carnage. Gandhi refused to break his fast until peace and sanity returned to Calcutta, and until both the Muslims and Hindus were safe. On the fourth day of his fast, like a miracle, the maddened mankind returned to sanity, and peace prevailed. "Fasting unto death" was Gandhi's most potent weapon in the armory of nonviolence; it spoke louder than words. Gandhi awakened their nobler self and peace prevailed. Sanity returned. Brotherhood lived. When the riots in Calcutta and Noakhali abetted, Gandhi left for Bihar, where the families of butchered Hindus had gone on a revenge spree. He was deeply pained to see that the Hindus' heinous acts of revenge even exceeded the Muslim atrocities to Hindus. Gandhi's peace efforts were not appreciated by the Hindus, nor were they eager to listen to his message: "We ought to overcome violence with love. ... Are we going to match barbarism with even more barbarous acts?" Rather than do so, he argued, "why not to use a new weapon that India has placed before the world?" (Wolpert 2001, 231). Regardless of their hostility, Gandhi retained his "incorrigible optimism" rooted in faith that even the most hardened hearts are capable of transforming themselves by the power of pure *ahimsa*.

While Gandhi was still busy with his peace mission in East Bengal, Nehru urged him to immediately return to New Delhi, where riots were raging, spreading to Amritsar, Punjab, and Bombay. Hindus, Muslims, and Sikhs were violently reacting there to the partition of Punjab on account of the partition of India.

Gandhi's peace mission was not yet over. What he saw in Delhi and in the Punjab was religious violence at its worst. Bodies were piled upon bodies; the stench of the dead polluted the air, contaminating the joy of freedom. Fear was in every human heart; no one felt safe. Despite a strict curfew, rioters roamed the streets of Delhi with nothing but murder on their minds. But Gandhi had nothing but peace on his mind. Although under enormous mental stress and emaciated by fasting, exhaustion, and high blood pressure, Gandhi dismissed all thoughts of personal comfort, rest, health, or safety. Like a wick lamp burning at its brightest before running out of oil, he used the last drop of his energy touring the riot-ridden areas and attempting to stop the violence. As in Calcutta and Bihar, Gandhi went out in Delhi visiting refugee camps, comforting and speaking to thousands of homeless and heartbroken Hindus, Muslims, and Sikhs pouring in and out of Delhi from east Punjab (India) and west Punjab (Pakistan).

Gandhi wanted to stay again in the *Bhangi* (Harijans') colony, but this time, upon the insistence of colleagues concerned about his safety, Gandhi stayed at the house of his industrialist friend Ghanshyamlal Birla in New Delhi. Every evening he held prayer meetings to teach the gospel of peace, love, and forgiveness and to urge Hindus not to mistreat Muslims residing in India. He told them it was more valiant to be killed for peace than to kill for revenge. Twice at the prayer meetings he escaped attempts on his life by infuriated militant Hindus. During those last critical months in New Delhi, Gandhi's life was hanging on a thread; death was hovering around.

"The One-Man-Boundary Force" in Punjab

Just as Nehru had urgently called Gandhi away from Bihar to appease the violent crowds in New Delhi, now Lord Mountbatten was urging him to rush to Punjab to stop the killings. The last British viceroy of India did not want to leave behind a burning inferno. He knew that the British governor of Punjab had failed to curb the widespread rioting, and the British army had also proved impotent. The only army that could now help consisted of one old man, Mahatma Gandhi. The Indian in loincloth had once again converted a foe into a friend, who said, "In the Punjab we have 55,000 soldiers and large-scale rioting on our hands. In Bengal our forces consist of one man, and there is no rioting. As a serving officer, as well as an administrator, may I be allowed to pay my tribute to the one-man boundary force!" (Tendulkar 1963, 8: 111).

GANDHI'S LAST FAST FOR INDIA'S PURIFICATION AND PENANCE

Gandhi's last fast on January 13, 1948—only two weeks prior to his death, was a symbol of collective prayer for peace and penance. The whole nation, barring a few militant Hindus, fasted with Gandhi and prayed for his life. On the seventh day of his fast, the Central Peace Committee signed a Peace Pledge with joint signatures of Hindus and Muslims; only now did Gandhi agree to break his fast. During the last fateful weeks, Gandhi was joyfully busy treating people with his "nature-cure" remedies, while contemplating an amicable settlement of the Kashmir issue between India and Pakistan.

PREMONITION OF DEATH

But these last few weeks of Gandhi's life were also filled with intuitive allusions to his imminent death. Not only did he have a strong premonition of death but also of the kind of death, and the manner in which he would like to embrace death. At a prayer meeting in Calcutta on October 15, 1946, he said, "It is not death that matters, but how you meet your death; to die at the hands of one's brother is a privilege, provided you die bravely." (Payne, 1969, 573 and 579) After having escaped a bomb explosion on January 20, 1948, Gandhi confided his thoughts to one of his close associates, that though he was under God's protection, he also believed that God might very well have ordered his death and that his death would crown his life. In two more private conversations with Manubehn (ibid.), Gandhi said: "As I said yesterday at the prayer-meeting, I wish I might face the assassin's bullets while ... repeating the name of *Rama* with a smile on my face." He also told her by which criteria should she and posterity judge him:

> If I die of an illness, you must declare me to be a false or a hypocritical Mahatma, ... and if an explosion takes place, as it did last week, or if

someone shot at me and I received his bullet in my bare chest without a
sigh and with *Rama*'s name on my lips, only then should you say that I
was a true Mahatma.

THE LAST WORDS—"*HE RAMA*"

On January 30, 1948, Gandhi was assassinated at the Birla House prayer
grounds in New Delhi. Natthuram Godse, an orthodox Hindu, while pretending to bow down to Gandhi, fired shots at him. The Mahatma died as
he had wished, with "*He Rama*" on his lips and love in his heart for the
enemy. "My life is my message," said Gandhi. His death was a crowning
affirmation of his life-message of Truth, nonviolence, and peace.

GANDHI AND STAGE 6 UNIVERSALIZING FAITH

Throughout the chapter we witnessed Gandhi's enlarging global vision to
include all human beings as brothers (or sisters) united by love if not
blood, and by the way they were all connected to their divine roots. He
believed that because all humans originated from a common divine source,
they all partook of the nature of God—that that they all possessed within
them certain powers for good, nonviolence, unselfish love, and forgiveness.
The problem begins when people forget in their ignorance or under extreme
circumstances that they have these noble, God-given qualities in them. It
is the life mission of Stage 6 persons, therefore, "to remind them," and "to
rekindle" those inherent divine qualities of love, compassion, and forgiveness. Gandhi did just that whenever he found the Hindus and Muslims
fighting and killing one another. The most inspiring proof, however, of his
"universalizing faith" were his last heroic efforts of risking his life for nonviolence, peace, and brotherhood in Noakhali, Calcutta, Bihar, Delhi, and
Punjab. Even the enemy—the British Viceroy Lord Mountbatten had to
pay a glowing tribute to Gandhi, that what his entire army of 50,000
trained soldiers could not accomplish in the Punjab, Gandhi—the "one-
man boundary force" (Tendulkar 1963, Vol. 8, 111)—did single-handedly.
Gandhi thus "incarnated and actualized" the Stage 6 "spirit of an inclusive
and fulfilled human community." (Fowler, 1981, 200)

   Gandhi believed in transforming the level of human relationship
before trying to resolve an actual conflict. To him conflict was only the tip of
the iceberg; the root of any conflict lay deeper in a defective relationship or

in negative communication that fed on mutual distrust, long-run hostility, fear, and hatred. Believing that "love contains more energy and endurance than anger" (Gregg 1959, 50), Gandhi allowed both warring parties of the Hindus and Muslims to grow together in an environment of renewed mutual trust, love, and goodwill. Among other examples, in all his *satyagrahas* as well as in his encounters with Ambedkar, Smuts, Irwin, orthodox Hindus, and the British (Lord Mountbatten), he largely succeeded in converting the heart of the enemy by genuine overtures of love. In the language of Stage 6, Gandhi achieved "an epistemological decentration from self" through the "gradual qualitative expansion in perspective taking" (1984, 68). He could succeed at this "double conversion"—of the party who is wronged, and the party alleged of wrongdoing. The Indians and the British thus remained friends even after Indian independence, and Gandhi was largely responsible.

Gandhi embraced a wide variety of persons of dissimilar backgrounds, tempers, temperaments, and ideologies and also helped transform the lives of many individuals Eastern or Western, Hindu or Muslim, Christian or non-Christian. Transforming others through his own self-transformation was one of the unique features of Gandhi's spirituality. In Stage 6 terms, Gandhi engaged himself "in spending and being spent for the transformation of present reality in the direction of transcendent actuality" (ibid.).

To put it in less formal language, in this stage of his spiritual development, Gandhi was largely successful at reducing his ego to a zero or becoming less and less self-centered and more and more God-centered. Each one of his self-austerities—vow-taking, observing truth, nonviolence, non-possession, and *brahmacharya*—was meant for subduing his lower self (passions, sex, palate, other senses and desires) and moving toward the higher "Self-realization." For Gandhi it was seeing God in everyone and in God, the whole universe. As we discussed before, Gandhi's last, most radical, tests in *brahmacharya* toward the end of his life show the extreme tendencies typical of Stage 6 people (in the Indian context) to strip off their bodily identity in order to realize their "trans-body identity." In *Bhagavad Gita* terminology, this Stage 6 "self-relinquishment" means to acquire complete detachment from all pairs of opposites and paradoxes, and to be utterly selfless (or without an individual ego) in order to be fully grounded in God. Through his severe self-austerities and spiritual self-control exercises, Gandhi was able to submerge his ego-self into God.

The way most Stage 6 people embrace death sums up the tragic yet redeeming radical nature of Universalizing Faith. As Fowler puts it, "many persons in this stage die at the hands of those whom they try to change"

(1981, 201). Stage 6 persons like Gandhi are more venerated than under-stood. Despised during their lifetime (by some), they are widely worshipped after their death. More often than not, these messengers of peace become victims of the very violence they strive to stop. Death actually proves to be their most eloquent affirmation of life. These rare exemplars of Stage 6 transform the world as much by their manner of living as by their dying.

Most Stage 6 persons meet tragic deaths by assassination and Gandhi was no exception. A certain shadow of death had been lurking in the dark to claim his body and take his life, which we especially saw during the last two decades of his life when a martyr-like spirit of "do or die" permeated his actions. The supreme test of his faith was to come, however, just before and after the partition of India in 1947, which sent him onto his ultimate peace pilgrimage through the riot-ridden East and West Bengal, Bihar, and New Delhi. With nothing but peace on his mind and God in his heart, as the seventy-eight-year-old Gandhi walked without fear and without com-pany among the most bloodthirsty and revenge-hungry mobs of Muslims and Hindus in Calcutta and Noakhali, he proved that "truth can be stranger than fiction." No ordinary act of human courage, this was an extraor-dinary triumph of the human spirit inspired by "the providence of God and the exigencies of history," as Fowler put it (ibid., 202). In no other way can we explain Gandhi—this rare phenomenon of a man who was so fully human and yet so deeply immersed in the spirit divine. Gandhi had con-quered the fear of death long back, but here he chose "death as his coveted companion" to traverse from "darkness to Light, from death to Immortality, from untruth to Truth." Although alone, confused, and helpless, this cru-sader of Truth fought single-handedly against all untruth because he felt that God was walking with him. It was because of this "Himalayan faith" that he could retain what he called his "irrepressible optimism" and trust in the Godliness of all humans—their basic goodness and kindness that would ultimately triumph over everything evil, everything unholy. He saw the Light at last as he survived the dark night of the soul. As Rev. John Haynes Holmes wrote to Gandhi in a letter in January 11, 1948:

> Single-handed you saved the situation and brought victory out of what seemed for the moment to be defeat. I count these last months to be the crown and climax of your unparalleled character. You were never so great as in these last dark hours. (1953, 91)

Gandhi died but his faith lived. Hope survived. Peace prevailed. Gandhi knew he was only an ordinary mortal with many flaws. He never claimed to be a saint although he had a passion for purity and perfection, for truth and nonviolence, by which he transformed himself and others whose lives he touched. As Geoffrey Ashe put it:

> Gandhi had the rarer and truer sainthood which ritual canonization purports to recognize. He was raised, by communion with whatever it is that religions call God, on to a level where human nature is changed and ordinary human understanding falls short. ... He became, ... a supreme and quintessential revolutionary, an apostle of endless transfiguration. (1968, 388–389)

12

Conclusion: From Darkness to Light

The multifaceted Mahatma Gandhi played many a role in his life. The "Father of India's Independence" was also the beloved father (*Bapu*) to all his ashram residents, close colleagues, and followers around the world. Gandhi, the charismatic leader and wielder of *satyagraha*, was not only an astute politician but also a bold social reformer, religious visionary, and a servant of humanity. These myriad images of Gandhi, however, only highlight his outer achievements and tell half the story. The other half of the story of Gandhi, the inner man, the serious spiritual seeker, has not been explored in its entirety until now. Gandhi himself started out telling his story in his *Autobiography: The Story of My Experiments with Truth*, but could not finish because of his intense political involvement during the last two decades of his life.

This book has attempted to finish that unfinished story of Mohandas Gandhi's faith pilgrimage by providing a comprehensive study of an ordinary man's extraordinary efforts to first find and build a strong self-identity, and then relinquish it in order to find his higher Self or Truth. The book has undertaken the task of exploring Gandhi's interior journey to Truth in light of Fowler's Theory of Stages of Faith, which allows us to focus on the internal structural developmental process of Gandhi's gradually evolving identity and spirituality.

Gandhi claimed to be neither a Mahatma nor a prophet, but only a votary of Truth. As we discussed in the book, the title *Mahatma*, which implied sainthood, actually pained him because he knew he was far from being a perfect man, much less a saint. The only claim Gandhi ever made was that he was a "humble seeker after Truth," a "weak aspirant ever failing, yet ever trying." (Harijan, September 14, 1934, 244) Gandhi's "ordinariness," however, had two self-redeeming aspects. First, he was painfully aware of his human imperfections—his angers, passions, and other weaknesses of the flesh—which kept him humble. Second, because he was self-aware or conscious of his limitations, he continued to struggle with himself to become a "fitter instrument of God." In Gandhi's words, "This consciousness is my only strength. Whatever I might have been able to do in my life has proceeded out of the realization of my limitations" (1958, 38).

This very humanness of Gandhi that the book has endeavored to show made him not only a beloved leader but also a believable man of faith who was approachable by all. Because Gandhi was as weak and vulnerable as any other mortal, people in general were interested in his ongoing battles with himself, and their results. This was one of the secrets of Gandhi's universal appeal—that people found him to be like them, yet above them; he inspired them by his example that even an ordinary person can climb the Mount Everest of Truth if he has a deep faith in God, in himself, and others. Gandhi considered his failures as much a blessing from God as his successes. He said, "A perfect man would have been their (people's) despair. When they found that one with their failings was marching towards *ahimsa*, they too had confidence in their own capacity" (ibid., 51).

Two major points of this book cannot be overstressed. First, that Gandhi was, above all, a man of deep and abiding faith in God or Truth. Second, his journey to Truth was neither as smooth nor rapid as taking one giant leap to the mountaintop. Gandhi's faith pilgrimage was a long process, protracted and painful every step of the way. However, as Gandhi said, "it is by a process of trial and error, self-search and austere discipline, that a human being moves step by painful step along the road to fulfillment" (ibid., xiii).

Gandhi's approach to faith was not pedantic, doctrinaire, or sectarian. To him, faith was not confined to structured religion, ritual worship, sectarian beliefs, dogmas, or caste rules; it was, rather, a deep yearning of the human soul to connect and unite with its Maker. Gandhi said, "Faith is not a thing to grasp; it is a state to grow to. And growth comes only from within" (Desai 1932). Notice how Gandhi ties in his concept of faith with the *inwardness* of the human spirit pining for God, and with the idea of *growth*. Gandhi was a deeply religious man, but as he wrote to Samuel E. Stokes, "religion consists not in outward ceremonial but an ever-growing inward response to the highest impulses that man is capable of" (Iyer 1986, 1: 460). To him, religion was not for display but for a real communion with God in the private chambers of one's heart and soul.

Gandhi's underlying motive in every one of his activities—whether political, social, or religious—was to serve God as Truth through nonviolence, which he defined as "the largest love" for all. Although Gandhi was not a metaphysician, the whole structure of his *satyagrahas* stood on three metaphysical pillars: truth (both absolute and relative), active nonviolence, and voluntary suffering. Gandhi thus translated metaphysics into ethics, and ethics into the very ground of politics.

Although this book is not about analyzing Gandhi's religious philosophy or his moral and political thoughts, we still need to understand his basic philosophy of God/Truth, which constituted his faith. As we showed earlier, Gandhi, as a *Vaishnava* Hindu child, was introduced early to the worship of a personal God or *Ishvara* (as *Rama* and *Krishna*). However, after his exposure to other world religions, the young Gandhi learned that God could also be known by many other names and forms. Further on, after his deep inquiry into religion through his correspondence with Raychandbhai and his reflection on books by Tolstoy, Ruskin, and others, the adult Gandhi learned that "the soul of religions is one, but it is encased in a multitude of forms" (*Young India*, September 25, 1924). Yet it was not until he began to live a life of simplicity, austerity, and selfless service, that Gandhi understood God as Truth only—Truth which is one, yet many-sided:

> To me God is truth and love; God is ethics and morality; God is fearlessness. God is the source of Light and Life and yet He is above and beyond all these. God is conscience. He is even the atheism of the atheist. ... He is the searcher of hearts. He transcends speech and reason. ... He is personal God to those who need His personal presence. He is the purest essence. He simply Is to those who have faith. ... He is in us and yet above and beyond us. (Iyer 1986, 1: 572)

Two points are necessary to explain Gandhi's above approach to God. First, though he continued to worship God as "personal" in the heart of his heart, he logically accepted the truth of the *Advaita* (non-dualistic) *Vedanta* tradition that God is really "impersonal"; God is *Sat-Chit-Ananda*—That which alone is, pure intelligence, pure bliss. God is pure undefiled consciousness, which, though unseen, indefinable, and formless, pervades the whole universe, and is the very essence of life. As Glyn Richards put it (1983, 2), "Gandhi's expressed preference for the impersonal and the formless does not prevent him from recognizing that God is personal to those who need to feel his presence and embodied to those who desire to experience his touch." Gandhi was very fond of the first verse of the *Isha*

Upanishad, which contained the gist of the Vedanta philosophy: Everything which is visible and invisible, manifest as well as un-manifest in this universe, is filled by *Isha* or God, and everything belongs to God alone; therefore, enjoy what is given by God but only after renouncing the idea of possessing it.

Second, Gandhi's concept of "God as Truth" kept evolving—starting with the simplistic faith of child Mohandas in the holy name of *Rama*, and ending in his deeply personal experience of God as a living presence more real than tangible reality. K. L. S. Rao's observation (1978, 73) that "the concept of God itself keeps evolving with the advance of the emotional, intellectual and spiritual life of man," verifies the truth of Gandhi's own experience and his structural developmental process of spiritual growth as shown in this book.

Gandhi's philosophy of Truth is based on his three core beliefs, which are all logically interconnected. The first one is that if this whole universe is pervaded by the spirit of God or Truth, then there is an essential unity of existence. Gandhi believed that all life is of one piece, which includes not only human life but also the sub-human world (animals), the vegetation world (plants, trees, herbs, and all), as well as the whole ecological world (air, water, fire, earth, sky, and other planets).

Gandhi's second core belief is that if all life is essentially one, then "one must be able to love the meanest of creation as oneself." This is *ahimsa*—which is not a passive virtue of non-injury, but an active principle of positive love; it is more like the Christian *agape*—an unconditional, all-embracing, and all-forgiving love rising from the depths of the human spirit. *Ahimsa*, as Gandhi used it, is also similar to the Buddhist concept of *karuna*—a deep compassion for or identification with everything that lives. The creativity of Gandhi, however, is that he retrieved this passive virtue of *ahimsa* from the scriptures, and made it a practicable means to an end of truth. As Joan Bondurant said (1965, 112), "The especial contribution of Gandhi was to make the concept of ahimsa meaningful in the social and political spheres." To which I would add that Gandhi used *ahimsa* as a powerful weapon not only to combat social and political injustice but also to resolve human conflict in every walk of life, and to resist untruth anywhere in the world.

Third, Gandhi argued that because all human beings have their origins in the same transcendental source, they are all "sparks of God"; they therefore possess an innate ability to love, trust, and respond to others' love and trust. He believed that love begets love and trust generates trust. This particular quality of putting trust in the other's ability to be trustworthy formed the core of Gandhi's own relationships as well as his philosophy of *satyagraha*. To him, every person possessed an infinite reservoir of love, goodness, and forgiveness that only needs to be tapped. Gandhi himself demonstrated this ability to love and trust—first in his adolescent encounter with his father (Chapter 5), then with General Smuts in South Africa (Chapter 9), and later with the British in India (Chapters 10 and 11). It was not that Gandhi was never betrayed, but that even after being so, he refused to abandon his faith in the other's capacity to change for better. It was not because Gandhi was naïve, or that he was "a prisoner of hope," as Judith Brown implied in her book (1989). He was, on the contrary, a practical idealist who would rather win over his enemies by trusting them than not trusting at all; even when he sometimes lost, he said he at least had the satisfaction of not losing his soul.

Gandhi wanted to be remembered not for his achievements but for his ceaseless strivings for purity and perfection, for his continuous battles with himself to overcome his weaknesses in order to come closer to God. He felt that what he could accomplish was difficult, but not impossible. In his own words, "I have not the shadow of a doubt that any man or woman can achieve what I have, if he or she would make the same effort and cultivate the same hope and faith" (1958, 46). The important words in this sentence are *effort*, *hope*, and *faith*.

For Gandhi, faith required continuous effort and constant self-vigilance. This explains why his self-austerities like *brahmacharya*, non-possession, and others were crucially important to him as a spiritual seeker. We also need to keep in mind Gandhi's Indian heritage, which gives supreme importance to the *sadhana* (spiritual disciplines) of self-purification and self-control (*yama-niyama*) for Self-realization. As we saw earlier in the book, the child Gandhi learned from his "saintly mother" Putliba the art and science of fasting, vow-keeping, self-restraint, and self-purification. It was Putliba who taught him the rigors and pleasures of keeping his body and mind under the control of his spirit. Her living example of cheerful self-austerities and selfless giving helped her Moniya to later become "Mahatma Gandhi: The Son of His Mother."[1]

Though his mother's positive examples of faith gave Gandhi a good head start, his faith needed to be tried and tested against the later challenges of his life; it needed to be developed into a deeper and fuller faith. This is where Fowler's Theory of Stages of Faith is most helpful as a heuristic guide to show us the continuous process of Gandhi's self-development and the implicit structures of his ever-growing faith in God or Truth.

ADVANTAGES OF USING FOWLER'S THEORY OF STAGES OF FAITH

At this point I would like to point out three outstanding features of Fowler's theory that proved to be particularly helpful in understanding the complexities of Gandhi's character and the developmental dynamics of his faith.

At the very outset, what is striking about Fowler's theory is the broad and comprehensive conception of "faith" as a deeper and inclusive dimension of human living; it is freed from the narrow confines of religion or beliefs, dogma or doctrines. Despite its Judeo-Christian roots, the term *faith* is described as "the most fundamental, generic and universal feature of human quest for meaning in relation to transcendence" (Fowler 1981, 14). This open-ended approach to transcendence and inclusivity makes the theory capable of cross-cultural and cross-religious application, especially suitable to study a man of "universalizing faith" like Gandhi. Specifically encouraging are the parallels between Fowler's concept of faith and Gandhi's approach to truth. (see Introduction, 12–13)

Another feature that helped trace the continuity of Gandhi's moral and spiritual development is that of the "invariant sequential" pattern in the stages of faith theory. Though not all figures of faith go through this gradual developmental process, Gandhi certainly went through the continuously changing and evolving dynamic patterns of knowing (both intuitive and intellectual), valuing, and construing meaning of his experiences. One particularly noteworthy example is Gandhi's unusual courage and nonviolent resistance to the apartheid at Maritzburg railway station in South Africa (Chapter 7), which was not sudden or dramatic but rather was a deliberate response, which, as we have shown, was the culmination of his long-simmering resentment of all authority figures in the past. It was because of the "invariant sequence" feature of the theory that we could see the inevitable link of this event with his earlier similar experiences; we could also connect the links and see through the inner workings of Gandhi's mind; we could empathize with his agonizing dilemma.

That brings us to still another strong feature of the faith theory, namely, its provision for transitions from one stage of faith to another. Stage transitions serve as preludes to a person's underlying structures of the ongoing transformational process; they allow us to see the earliest signs of his or her changing thought patterns and emotional turbulence and prepare us for the kind of new development that is likely to follow. For example, Gandhi's increasing dissatisfaction with his prosperous lifestyle as a successful Indian attorney in South Africa (Chapter 8), alerted us to the first telltale signs of his upcoming transformation in faith. The ever-changing undercurrents of Gandhi's mind and his increasing disillusionment with a material life indicated the first stirrings of his soul; these prepared for his next decision to take the *brahmacharya* vow in order to seriously embark upon a totally spiritual life of selfless service. Though this was a landmark transition, we know now that Gandhi's life consisted of not one, but many a little and big transition or turning point.

In this book I have given as much importance to Gandhi's roots and his earlier, pre-Mahatma stages of faith as to the later, post-Mahatma stages, in order to show an inevitable link between the beginning, the middle, and the end. The whole tree of faith—its leaves, branches, flowers, and fruits— depend on the roots for their nourishment and growth. "Gandhi made very frequent use of the tree metaphor," says Margaret Chatterjee (1983, 131), "for the tree is perhaps the most powerful natural symbol of grounding and outreach, a symbol too of the connection between outreach and blossoming."

This is not to suggest that whatever Gandhi accomplished in later stages was entirely owing to his early solid foundation in faith. Even though it was strong and positive, early experience cannot in itself be enough. The early structures of one's intuitive-imaginative faith need to develop into conceptual and intellectual knowledge. Since faith is a comprehensive stance of life, it consists not only of emotions but also convictions, not only symbols and images but also the logical structures of reason and reflection. Faith, therefore, cannot be a blind acceptance of one's given tradition; it must become an informed choice. As Fowler says, "Faith must combine passionality as well as rationality," or "the logic of rational certainty" and "the logic of heartfelt conviction."

Just as the windmills of God grind slowly, so also the logical struc- tures of reasoning develop gradually with a person's ability to think and reflect; though the process is neither easy nor speedy, it is necessary for one's development in identity and faith. For example, Gandhi's London stay (Stage 3 Synthetic-Conventional Faith in transition to Stage 4 Individuative Reflective Faith), which seemed to be so unproductive, was highly productive considering both his inner and outer learning process. It was not a period of Gandhi's "moratorium," as Erikson suggested; rather, it was, as Judith Brown observed, "a time of his social, moral and intellec- tual ferment" (Chapter 6). It is true that Gandhi was then young and naïve, awkward and immature. It is also true that he was continuously

experimenting with his diets, clothes, and Anglicization; however, this is
precisely how one discovers one's identity—by trial and error, by conscious
as well as unconscious experimentation with self and truth. The journey of
self-development, which is intertwined with that of faith, is hardly smooth
or straight; it is rather a twisting and winding journey with many a detour
and distraction. There are obstacles from outside and roadblocks from
inside. I strongly contend that every experience of the adolescent Gandhi
in London, no matter how embarrassing or erroneous, was necessary for
the development of his inner self-confidence and for his intellectual
growth. The critics who see no hint of the future Mahatma in this period,
forget that growth in personhood has never been an overnight phenomenon; it cannot be without pain or without trial and error, and requires continuous self-search by experimentation with truth. The meaning of truth
at this point for Gandhi was about his "becoming in identity." Without
acquiring first a solid sense of "self," one cannot begin to search for one's
larger or truer Self. It was London that made South Africa happen, and it
was South Africa that gave us a glimpse of the Mahatma-to-be in India.

     During his whole South African experience, we saw Gandhi building
up his strong sense of self-identity, or in faith terminology, his "executive
ego." Interestingly, however, everything that the ambitious young barrister
had dreamed of becoming, he achieved in South Africa, plus something
unexpected. From the faith developmental perspective, he also "found his
God in a God-forsaken country." Gandhi's gradual self-transformation
began from this period onward; it was sealed by his *brahmacharya* vow and
his determination to live a totally selfless life in service of the needy and the
downtrodden. Only after having acquired a sense of the "self" (ego identity), was Gandhi ready to relinquish it for finding his "truer Self" in India.

     Gandhi's Indian saga saw the consistent development and culmination
of his diminishing self-interest and increasingly selfless human service. As
he became more involved in the Indian independence movement and in
the "constructive programs" and social reforms, his inner spiritual life grew
even stronger, deeper, and more austere. For example, in the midst of his
ongoing battles with the British, Gandhi engaged in battles with himself—
to conquer his passions and to purify himself by fasting and other austerities. As the war and violence escalated outside, he intensified his
brahmacharya experiments not only for self-purification but also as a token
of collective penance and peace for all mankind.

     At the same time, Gandhi experienced deep anguish during this phase
in both his private life and public career. The gradually worsening father-
son relationship with his eldest son, Harilal, remained a reminder that the

one who was *Bapu* to all, miserably failed to be a father to his first son. This was only one of the many sad paradoxes of Gandhi's personality and life, which represented the classic characteristics of Stage 5, "the coincidence of opposites" (Chapter 10): the shadowy and the destructive sides of Gandhi, as well as the brighter and constructive sides. What is surprising, however, is not that Gandhi was as imperfect and dichotomous as any other human being, but that he could still manage to keep his passions and paradoxes in control; he even succeeded in integrating and sublimating most of them in the larger interests of all.

A final observation: Gandhi's true greatness lay more in his inner conquests than in his outer political victories. A humble seeker after Truth, Gandhi was a man of deep faith, prayers, and austerities; he practiced what he preached and followed the dictates of his Inner Voice. Though an erring and imperfect human, Gandhi continuously struggled—through prayers and introspection—to be a purer and fitter instrument of God. Starting out as "Everyman," Gandhi grew, says Bhabani Bhattacharya in *The Good Boatman: A Portrait of Gandhi* (Gandhi 1995, 458), "to an extraordinary towering height" through a process that "involved him in the most sustained and most agonizing struggle for self-transformation that no man in the world has ever experienced." It was through this painful process of transforming himself that Gandhi could transform others; through seeking his own true self-identity, he saw the light of Truth shining within every human soul. Gandhi searched for the Infinite in the finite; he yearned to see God, not in temples, mosques, or churches, but in the hearts of the poorest of the poor peasants, in the slums of Harijans, and in the faces of all the oppressed of the world.

Gandhi said his life was his only message, his legacy, the power of the human soul. He lived as he believed that the "the divine is reflected within every individual as his inalienable core of Truth" (Iyer 1986, 1: 9). He had infinite faith in the power of Truth and nonviolence to remove all darkness of human ignorance, apathy, and violence. As he said, "My faith in truth and nonviolence is ever growing ... as ... I too am growing every moment. I see new implications about them. I see them in a new light every day."[2] Gandhi perceived faith not as an end in itself, but as a journey from untruth to Truth, darkness to Light, and ultimately, from death to Immortality.

Notes

PREFACE

1. Dr. Fowler, Charles Howard Candler Professor of Theology and Human Development at Emory University, has a doctorate from Harvard University and has taught at Harvard Divinity School and Boston College. As director of the Center for Research in Faith and Moral Development, Fowler is well-known for his pioneering research in the field and for his book *Stages of Faith*, which was followed by many more (see bibliography). Since 1994, he is also the director of the Center for Ethics and the Public Policy and the Professions at Emory.

2. A leading figure in the field of psychoanalysis and human development, Erikson has been awarded the Pulitzer prize and the National Book Award for his major psychobiographies, *Young Man Luther: A Study in Psychoanalysis and History* (1958), and *Gandhi's Truth: On the Origins of Militant Nonviolence* (1969).

INTRODUCTION

1. Jawaharlal Nehru was Gandhi's political heir, confidant, and the first prime minister of India after its Independence from the British in 1947.

2. Gandhi, at a later stage, preferred to say, "Truth is God" to "God is Truth." As Margaret Chatterjee explains in *Gandhi's Religious Thought* (1983, 58), "the word Truth is not substituted for God, but serves to elucidate what 'God' means for Gandhi."

3. The *Journal of the American Academy of Religion* (JAAR) 68, no. 4 (2000) offers a wide variety of perspectives on the "insider versus outsider" issue by current scholars in the field, who raise the most fundamental question: Who is entitled to speak with authenticity and authority for Hinduism or any religion? Should it be an academic scholar who approaches the subject from outside the tradition, or should it be someone who is born into, raised in, and practicing that tradition? Although scholars do not reach consensus, they all acknowledge the "complex relationship" between an academic scholar of any religion and its actual practitioner. Representative voices of the discussant scholars include Sara Caldwell, S. N. Balagangadhara, Arvind Sharma, Vivek Dhareshwar, John Hawley, Vasudha Narayanan, and Laurie Patton.

CHAPTER 2. GANDHI'S ROOTS

1. A great medieval Vaishnava saint-poet from Junagadh in Kathiawar, whose hymn—"*Vaishnava jana to tene re kahiye je peed parayi jane re,*" meaning, "Know him to be a true Vaishnava, whose heart melts at the suffering of others"—was very dear to Gandhi's heart.

2. Swami Yogeshananda of the Vedanta Center of Atlanta provided the translation.

3. Kathiawar or Saurashtra is now a sub-province of the western state of Gujarat, but then it was a princely province of hundreds of small kingdoms in British colonial India.

4. Sudamapuri means the city of Sudama, who was a childhood friend and devotee of Lord Krishna; it was one of the pilgrimage places in Kathiawar, the others being Prabhas Patan, Dwarika (the golden capital city established by Krishna), Tulsishyam, and others. The information is drawn from *Mahatma Gandhi*, Volume 1: *The Early Phase* (Pyarelal 1965).

5. According to *The Early Phase* (Pyarelal 1965, 190), Sheth Nanji Kalidas, a merchant-prince of Porbandar, built this costly memorial as a token of his devotion to Gandhiji. Pyarelal describes it as "an impressive edifice crowned with a graceful spired pinnacle. The main entrance opens upon a spacious marble-paved courtyard. Surrounding it on all sides is a running verandah with marble floor and twenty-six pillars, bearing suitable inscriptions from Gandhiji's writings. The monument houses a modest collection of Gandhiji's works and relics and a miniature living museum of his various constructive activities."

6. Gandhi's childhood name "Moniya" was a nickname derived from "Mohan," which was one of the many names of Lord Krishna.

7. In most Indian languages (including Gandhi's language of Gujarati), there are specific words besides "mama" and "papa," such as *nana* (mother's father), *nanima* (mother's mother), *mashi* (mother's sister), *mama* (mother's brother), and *kaka* (father's brother). In Gujarat, the titles can be more specific, e.g., *motakaka* (father's older brother) and *motiben* (older sister).

8. The title of the book refers to "an ivory statuette of the god Vishnu," which Girindrasekhar Bose—the founder of the Indian Psychoanalytical Society of Calcutta—had sent to Sigmund Freud on his seventy-fifth birthday; since then, Freud had given it a place of honor on his desk. The book [edited by T. G. Vaidyanathan and Jeffrey J. Kripal, with a foreword by Sudhir Kakar (Delhi: Oxford University Press, 1999)] is a comprehensive collection of essays on psychoanalysis and Hinduism by prominent writers in the field. Scholars whose insights proved to be particularly helpful to this chapter are Christiane Hartnack (pp. 81–106) and A. K. Ramanujan (pp. 109–136).

9. Manubehn Gandhi (Gandhi's grandniece) wrote the book *Bapu—My Mother* (1949).

10. The three *basic gunas* or properties of mind are: *the sattva guna*, which denotes the light of knowledge and wisdom, purity, brightness, selflessness, nobility of heart, and all Godly attributes; the *rajas guna*, which is associated with kinetic energy, restlessness of mind, drive, and attachment to all the worldly desires; and the *tamas guna*, which stands for darkness, ignorance, ignoble passions, inertia, indolence, and an indifference to everything good and positive in life.

CHAPTER 3. THE SEED AND THE SOIL

1. The original Sanskrit prayer reads like this: "*Twameva Mata cha Pita twameva, Twameva bandhu shcha sakha twameva; Twameva vidya, dravinam twameva, Twameva sarvam mama Deva Devam.*"

2. Prabhudas Gandhi first wrote *Jivan Prabhat* in Gujarati; it was later translated into English as *My Childhood with Gandhiji* (1957).

3. There are four major castes or *Jatis* in the Hindu religious and social hierarchy— *Brahmins* (the priestly, educated class), *Kshatriyas* (the warrior class), *Vaishyas* (the commercial class), and *Shudras* (the serving class). In Gandhi's time, caste rules and restrictions were strictly applied, and family and society looked down upon marrying outside one's own caste.

4. The value of a son-bearing woman escalates on the social scale for several reasons. (1) A son is expected to not only carry on his father's legacy, family name, and profession but also can perform religious funeral rights for his deceased father in a ceremony called *shraddh.* (2) Daughters later have to be given away as a bride in a ceremony called *kanyadan.* (3) In most of India, an exorbitant dowry must be given by the bride's family to her husband's family.

5. The word *Jain* is derived from the Sanskrit word *Jin,* the individual who has conquered his or her passions such as anger, pride, lust, and greed. The followers of Jin are called "Jains" and their religion is called "Jainism."

6. The *Mahabharata* says, "*ahimsa paramo dharmaha*" (nonviolence is the biggest religious precept).

CHAPTER 5. A CRISIS OF IDENTITY AND FAITH

1. Uka belonged to the lowest caste of the *Shudras,* the Untouchables, who perform menial tasks, such as cleaning filth, butchering animals, or burning corpses, and were therefore considered polluted and impure. For more on the fourfold Hindu caste system, see chapter 3, note 3.

2. A convention still prevails in highly conservative societies in which young married couples must observe *amanya* (respectful distance and modesty) in the presence of elders; they should not meet or talk, much less show any affection in front of them.

3. Fistula is an abnormal opening leading from an internal organ, such as the bladder and the rectum, to the body surface. It can be caused by an abscess. If the general health is good, it can be corrected by surgery.

4. Recently, a plethora of books have been published on homosexuality and same-sex love in India. A few noteworthy authors, included in the bibliography, are: Arvind Kala, Jeremy Seabrook, Ruth Vanita, Saleem Kidwai, and Giti Thadani, but it is beyond the parameters of this book to cover their varying viewpoints.

5. In the Hindu philosophy, there are four major *ashramas* or stages of life. Each has its own time period and stage-appropriate duties and obligations. These are called the *ashrama-dharmas.* The first is the *brahmacharyashrama*—related to the life of a *vidyarthi* or

a student who is not married and who observes celibacy (from the age six or seven through young adulthood). The second is the *grihasthashrama*—or the stage of the householder—one who is married and lives with his family (young adulthood stage). The third refers to the *vanaprasthashrama*, that is, the mid to late adulthood stage in which one should usually retire from all the worldly desires and entanglements and devote time in self-search and quiet contemplation. The fourth and the last one is the *sannyasashrama*—the forest-dweller's stage in which one seeks nothing but God and *moksha*—that is, self-liberation or nirvana.

CHAPTER 6. A LAW STUDENT IN LONDON

1. Gandhi presented a paper, "The Foods of India," before the London vegetarians and because they liked it, he presented it again at Portsmouth. He also wrote articles published in the *Vegetarian*, such as "Indian Vegetarians," "Some Indian Festivals," "The Foods of India," and others.

2. Arjuna, the bravest warrior representing the Pandavas' army against the Kauravas on the Kurukshetra battlefield, feels sudden loss of energy and desire to fight. He consults Lord Krishna and describes his psychological condition in verse 29 (First Discourse) of the Bhagavad Gita: "My limbs fail and my mouth is parched, my body quivers, and my hair stands on end."

3. James Hunt's *Gandhi and the Non-Conformists* (1986) provides a thorough description of the radical assortment of this group.

CHAPTER 7. A BARRISTER IN SOUTH AFRICA, PHASE I

1. The first son Harilal was born in 1888, and the second son Manilal was born in 1892.

2. We discussed in the previous chapter "two faces of shame"—one in the form of modesty (Sanskrit *lajja*) which serves as a shield, and the other face of shame makes one follow others blindly out of what Gandhi called, "a false sense of shame."

3. All dark-skinned people, including native Africans, Asians, and indentured Indian laborers were called "coolies."

4. The veteran Parsee leader, Dadabhai Naoroji, was revered as the "Grand old man" of Indian nationalism.

5. Gandhi mentions *Commentary*, by Dr. Parker of the City Temple, Pearson's *Many Infallible Proofs*, and Butler's *Analogy*.

6. Gandhi's questions and Rajchandra's answers are based on information given by Pyarelal (1965, 1: 327–331).

7. English translation. *Mahatma Gandhi and Shrimad Rajchandra* from the original in Gujarati (*Samvat*, 2005 according to the Gujarati Indian calendar).

8. Another Developmental Theorist, Sharon Parks (1986), has proposed a distinct stage of "the young adult faith," which should fall in between the Adolescent Stage 3 and

the Adulthood Stage 4 in Fowler's theory. Fowler has recognized the features that Sharon Parks marks as distinctive of the young adult faith, such as ambivalence, vulnerability, and fragile self-dependence. However, he includes them as part of the process of "transition" from Stage 3 to Stage 4.

9. In the Hindu epic of *Mahabharata*, Ravana is the evil king of Lanka (modern Shri Lanka) who abducted Sita, the wife of King and Lord Rama of Ayodhya in North India. Rama, one of the incarnations of Vishnu, represented Dharma or righteousness—the good and noble forces.

CHAPTER 8. A LEADER IN SOUTH AFRICA, PHASE II

1. A footnote in Gandhi's autobiography (1948, 231) introduces *Maya* as "the famous word in Hindu philosophy which is nearly untranslatable, but has been frequently translated in English as delusion or illusion."

2. In her book *Gandhi and the South African Experience* (46–47), Maureen Swan observed that "The Legislative Assembly's specific antagonism towards Indian commercial interests was nowhere more evident than in the proposal of the government to introduce a Bill providing that no person of Asiatic race, birth or descent, should be allowed to take out a license for the purpose of trading as a shopkeeper."

3. Three most noteworthy Jewish friends who played a key role in Gandhi's life and in his South African *satyagraha* were Henry S. L. Polak, Lewis W. Ritch, and Hermann Kallenbach. Polak, an Englishman and journalist (the third editor of *Indian Opinion*), was not only Gandhi's close friend and follower, but also his critic and advisor; he was the one to give Gandhi a copy of Ruskin's book *Unto This Last* in 1904. Ritch, co-worker and theosophist, served as a link between Tolstoy and Gandhi by facilitating correspondence between the two. Perhaps emotionally closest to Gandhi was Kallenbach, a wealthy Jewish German architect; until he died in 1945, he remained a loyal, lifelong friend and follower of Gandhi. Kallenbach earned his place in Gandhi's heart and in history by donating acres of land for the establishment of the Tolstoy Farm. Gandhi's other Jewish friends included Albert West, Herbert Kitchin, Miss Dick, and Miss Schlesin; the latter was also an ardent follower and an excellent stenotypist. This information is based on Margaret Chatterjee's comprehensive book *Gandhi* and this *Jewish Friends*, especially chapter 3, pp. 39–71.

4. Pyarelal mentions (1980, 182) that Gandhi's three younger sons were also "disgruntled with their lot" just like their eldest brother, Harilal. They also confided in Pyarelal that "their father had been less than fair to them and had used them as guinea-pigs in his educational and other experiments in life." "However," says Pyarelal, "in course of time they completely shed that feeling and learnt to appreciate the worth of what they had received in place of the tinsel they had missed."

5. Just like the English, the Dutch (or the Boers) came to South Africa more than four hundred years ago in search of green pastures for their expansion. The British and the Boers vied with one another for the possession of the African colonies and fought many a war. See Gandhi's book *Satyagraha in South Africa* (1928, 8–20) for a history of South Africa and his glowing account of the Boers.

6. While in Calcutta, Gandhi visited prominent reformers of the Brahmo Samaj, such as Keshav Chandra Sen and Maharshi Devendranath Tagore (The Nobel poet laureate Rabindranath Tagore's father). With great enthusiasm Gandhi also went to Belur Math on the banks of the holy river Ganges; he was disappointed, however, that he could not meet Swami Vivekananda, who was seriously ill at the time.

7. Geoffrey Ashe (1968, 87) observed that "People called him *Mahabhangi*, the Great Scavenger, long before they called him Mahatma, the Great Soul."

8. Before Gandhi's arrival on the Indian political scene in 1915, the Congress party was divided into two groups: the Moderates and the Extremists. The former believed in a slow but steady constitutional approach to gain independence from the British, whereas the latter did not eschew subversive means or methods for the same. Gokhale represented the Moderates, and Tilak, the Radicals.

9. In a letter to his older brother in India, Gandhi explained that from now on his concept of "a family" had widened and therefore, his brother may not expect any more monetary help. Offended and disapproving of Gandhi's ideas, his brother discontinued writing to Gandhi for many years. Only much later did he understand Gandhi's spiritual intents and his inclusive ideals enough to reconcile with him.

10. Emperor Ashoka (fifth century B.C.) also underwent a change of heart after witnessing the carnage of the Kalinga War, which he had waged himself. He transformed himself thereafter, adopting nonviolence through Buddhism.

11. In terms of the *Gita*, Raychandbhai was a *jitendriya* or one who had mastered all his senses, passions, and desires. He was a true *sthitaprajnya* or a person whose mind was equipoised between all pairs of opposites, such as pleasure and pain, love and hate, praise and blame.

Chapter 9. A Satyagrahi in South Africa, Phase III

1. According to Gandhi, in *Satyagraha in South Africa* (90), the arguments advanced by General Smuts and others were: "South Africa is a representative of Western civilization while India is the centre of Oriental culture. ... The West is opposed to simplicity while Orientals consider that virtue to be of primary importance. ... The Indians are disliked in South Africa for their simplicity, patience, perseverance, frugality and otherworldliness. Westerners are enterprising, impatient, engrossed in multiplying their material wants. ... How can these opposite views be reconciled?" The South African White supremacist government's anti-Indian attitude echoes Rudyard Kipling's similar sentiment in: "The East is East and the West is West, and the twain shall never meet."

2. Thoreau's statement was: If one thousand, if one hundred, if ten men whom I could name—if ten honest men only—aye, if only one honest man, in this state of Massachusetts, ceasing to hold slaves, were actually to withdraw from this co-partnership, and be locked up in the country jail therefore, it would be the abolition of slavery in America" (1966, 232).

3. In his letter (9/10/1935) addressed to Mr. P. Kodanda Rao of the Servants of Indian Society, Gandhi wrote: "The statement that I had derived my idea of Civil Disobedience from the writings of Thoreau is wrong. The resistance to authority in South Africa was well advanced before I got the essay of Thoreau on Civil Disobedience" (Fischer 1950, 87).

4. Gandhi wrote in *Young India*: "I believe in *Advaita*. I believe in the essential unity of man" (December 4, 1924, 398). In the metaphysical tradition of *Advaita* (non-dualistic) Vedanta, Gandhi also believed that a single cosmic spirit or *Brahman* pervades the universe, and that one Truth underlies the many. The cosmic spirit, which pervades the universe as Truth or Sat, also dwells in every human heart. Therefore, in the Hindu, *Advaita* tradition, God is both transcendental and immanent, impersonal and personal."

5. According to Gandhi (1928, 18), "after the treaty of Vereeniging (following the Boer War), the Boers were immediately entitled to a gradual but complete internal autonomy." The new self-autonomous Transvaal government under Prime Minister Botha and General Smuts was called the "Responsible Government."

6. Gandhi graduated from the Inner Temple in London, and Smuts from the Middle Temple.

7. Secret bomb attacks, bomb explosions, murders of the British, train derailment, underground conspiracies, and acts of terrorism were at their peak in India at this time. The partition of Bengal in 1905 added to this explosive environment.

8. While living in Ahmedabad, Harilal had fallen in love with Gulab, the young daughter of his hosting family, and at the age of seventeen he had fathered his first child. His parents knew nothing about this until the penniless Harilal retuned to South Africa with his young family.

9. Gopal Krishna Gokhale, a Chitpavan Brahmin from Maharashtra, emerged in the early 1920s as an eminent leader of the Moderates in the Indian Congress. A member of the Imperial Legislative Council and a well-respected, veteran Congressman, Gokhale founded the Servants of India Society in 1905.

10. According to the Indian Relief Bill, the three-pound poll tax was removed, Indian marriages regained their legal status, and the educated Indians were granted entry in South Africa. They also decided to stop all importation of indentured laborers from India by 1920.

CHAPTER 10. INDIA WELCOMES HOME HER MAHATMA

1. Erik Erikson (1969, 235) explains "ambivalence" as "an act, which is seemingly guided by one conscious emotion," but which is, "at the same time, unconsciously co-determined by the opposite emotion: an act of love by hate, an act of kindness by vindictiveness."

2. Jinnah was a Muslim Gujarati barrister and Gandhi's future political adversary, whose career we will cover in the next chapter.

3. The third-class railway compartments in India at that time were so tightly packed that people barely had room to breathe.

4. Tagore was a versatile man of myriad talents. A Nobel prizewinning poet laureate (of *Gitanjali* and other poems), a playwright, storywriter, and novelist, Tagore was also a painter, composer, and a musician, famous for his folk-style Bengali *Rabindra sangeet*. An ardent nationalist, Tagore played a prominent role in India's cultural regeneration.

5. In "Saint Gandhi" (Jergensmeyer 1987), it mentions that Tagore knew about Gandhi being a "saintly man" from the letters of their mutual friend, Missionary C. F. Andrews. Andrews was Tagore's disciple at Shantiniketan and had met Gandhi in South Africa in early 1914. Andrews and his friend Willy Pearson were struck by Gandhi's "sanctity"; they compared Gandhi with St. Francis of Assisi (189–190).

6. This location had a sacred significance and many advantages. First, for several ages, there has existed a special cultural-spiritual chemistry between an ashram and a river in India. Second, by having his headquarters in Ahmedabad, Gujarat, Gandhi secured a solid base in his own home region. Third, Ahmedabad was well-known as a booming, textile-industrial city of Gujarat, known as the "Manchester of India." Fourth, the city had always been a home of the finest handloom industry in India, which played a crucial role in Gandhi's future "constructive programs" related to spinning and weaving.

7. Remaining on only the groundnut (or peanut butter) and lemons during his recruiting campaign, he had ruined his constitution. He refused all Western medical aid, fruit juices, and even milk, because of the cruel way in which "the cow and the buffalo were subjected to the process of *phooka* (forcibly squeezing out the last drop of milk)." Only when he was "near death's door," he yielded, reluctantly, to Kasturbai's suggestion of taking "goat's milk".

8. Erik Erikson's psychobiography (1969) focuses on "The Event"—of the 1918 mill workers versus mill owners' *satyagraha* in Ahmedabad, under Gandhi's leadership, which contributed to his own search for identity as well as to the historical struggle for the Indian independence.

9. In his autobiography (1948, 520–521), Gandhi explained to the workers the conditions of a successful strike:
   1. Never to resort to violence.
   2. Never to molest the blacklegs.
   3. Never to depend upon alms, and
   4. To remain firm, no matter how long the strike continued, and to earn bread, during the strike, by any other honest labour.

10. In Patanjali's *Yoga Sutra*, the *yamas* are described as spiritual "restraints," which include veracity and abstinence from injury (*ahimsa*), theft, sex, and avariciousness. And the *niyamas* refer to spiritual observances such as cleanliness, contentment, purificatory action, study, and the making of the Lord the motive of all action. From *A Source Book in Indian Philosophy* (Radhakrishnan and Moore 1957, 467 and 468).

11. Lokmanya Bal Gangadhar Tilak, an orthodox Brahmin from Maharashtra, was a highly popular Extremist leader, Sanskrit scholar, orator, and patriot; he joined Mrs. Annie Besant in her Home-rule movement in 1914. Tilak's slogan: "*Swaraj* is my birth-right," became a household word or *guru-mantra* in the pre-independence era.

12. To fill the gap left by the suppression of the *Bombay Chronicle*, Gandhi launched the weekly *Young India* in October 1919. Before that, in September 1919, Gandhi had also

started publishing in Gujarati a monthly newspaper titled *Navajivan,* which later became a weekly.

13. Four hundred innocent, unarmed Indian men, women, and children, who had silently gathered to oppose the martial law in this bagh (a garden used for public mass meetings), were deliberately trapped inside (with all the exits closed), and then shot at sight by General Dyer upon Sir Michael O' Dwyer's order.

14. From "Gandhi's Religion and Politics" in *Essays and Reflections on Gandhi's Life and Work* (Radhakrishnan 1944).

15. From his speech on *Swadeshi* at Missionary Conference, Madras, in Gandhi's book *India of My Dreams* (1947, 41).

16. Gandhi admired "the enterprising spirit, courage, and common sense" of this horse-riding Gujarati widow of the Nagar community, who went from village to village in search of the original *charkha* or spinning wheel. In 1917 she found it at last in the small town of Vijapur in the then Baroda State, and persuaded the original spinners to resume their spinning. This information is based on Gandhi's *Autobiography* (1948, 601–602).

17. By the Hindu lunar calendar, Gandhi was born on *barash* (the 12th day) of the eleventh month called Bhadrapada. Because people knew Gandhi's great love for rentia (Gujarati word for the spinning wheel), they called his birthday "*rentia barash.*" By the English calendar, Gandhi's birthday continues to be celebrated on October 2nd.

18. A young, brilliant, fiery patriot from Bengal, "Netaji" Subhash was highly popular among the young radicals. The future President of Indian Congress (1938–1839), Bose even secretly trained and recruited his own army ("Azad fauj") to overthrow the British Empire from India; he disapproved of Gandhi's slow-moving, nonviolent approach to freedom.

19. As proof of his "loyalty to the British" Gandhi cited his repeated wartime services both in South Africa and India, up until the most recent governmental acts of atrocities, such as the Rowlatt Act, the Jallianwala Bagh massacre, the "crawling order," Khilafat injustices, and so on. He still "fought for cooperation" he said, working for the "Montagu-Chelmsford reforms" to succeed.

20. This time he read all 6,000 pages of the *Mahabharata* and studied the *Ramayana,* the *Q'uran,* the *Bhagavata,* the *Upanishads,* and many valuable works on Christianity, Buddhism, Sikhism, Zoroastrianism, and the lives of great saints.

21. Manilal had secretly lent Harilal several hundred rupees from the ashram funds to help the latter establish his new business in Calcutta. As soon as Gandhi found out that Manilal was responsible for this huge "misappropriation of the public money," he banished him from the ashram, overriding all family members' pleas for mercy. Manilal was sent to Madras to work on a newspaper and then back to South Africa to edit *Indian Opinion.*

22. Gandhi wished all his sons practiced *brahmacharya,* lived in perpetual poverty, and dedicated themselves to God through prayers, self-restraint, and human service. At one point or another in their lives, all the sons had joined their father in his various *satyagrahas,* gone to jail, and carried on his newspaper work as well. Gandhi's youngest son, Devadas (who married Rajgopalachari's daughter, Laxmi), became the managing editor of the *Hindustan Times* in Delhi.

23. In one of his letters from the jail, Gandhi wrote to Manilal (age 26, in 1919): "I think you should not marry. In *Brahmacharya* lies your good." In the same letter, however, he also wrote: " I am not your jailor but your friend. ... I will give you some good advice and you may consider it, and then do what you think best" (Desai 1968, 19).

24. Sardar (Commander or Sergeant) Vallabhbhai Patel was also a brilliant, London-educated barrister with a thriving practice in Ahmedabad and excellent leadership qualities. Later, he became known as "the Iron Man of India," as he could accomplish the most difficult task of persuading the "princes of more than 250 states" to give up their separate kingdoms, and join in the one, united and free India in 1950. Sardar Patel and Nehru were Gandhi's two closest colleagues.

25. From Sita Kapadia's article, "A Tribute to Mahatma Gandhi: His Views on Women and Social Change." According to Prof. Kapadia, women like Sarojini Naidu and Kasturbai led some of the *satyagrahas*, whereas many other women disciples of Gandhi—including Olive Schreiner, Sonya Schlesin, Millie Polak, Rajkumari Amrit Kaur, Maniben Patel (Vallabhbhai Patel's sister), Mrudula Sarabhai, and others—participated in one or more of Gandhi's *satyagrahas*.

26. In this mythological story, Prahlad, the devotee of God and son of a powerful Demon King named Hiranyakashyapu, was put through all kinds of tortures by his father, who wanted his son to believe that he (the king) was more powerful than his God. Prahlad, however, went through every test and torture but would never be shaken from his faith in God as the most powerful force of all. The outraged father now challenged the son to embrace a burning, hot pillar to prove that God resided even in a pillar and had the power to save him. This time, God not only saved his young devotee, but bursting out from the pillar, God appeared in the form of *Narasimha* ("half man and half lion") and killed the Demon-King.

CHAPTER 11. FROM DEATH TO IMMORTALITY

1. Ever since she met Gandhi in London, Mrs. Naidu became his ardent follower and friend, who lovingly referred to Gandhi as "Mickey Mouse." Mrs. Naidu was an inspiring leader, orator, and an accomplished poet, whom Tagore referred to as "the Nightingale of India."

2. Abdul Gaffar Khan was chief Muslim leader of the war-like *Pathans* from the wild northwest frontier (Afghanistan). After the Rowlatt crisis, Khansaheb became one of the most faithful disciples of Gandhi; he earned the title of "Frontier Gandhi" for successfully converting his ferocious frontiermen into a nonviolent religious army, called the *Khudai Khidmatgars* or the "Red Shirts."

3. At the conference, Gandhi met professors Gilbert Murray and Edward Thompson. After an in-depth interview with Gandhi, Thompson wrote: "The conviction came to me that not since Socrates has the world seen his equal for absolute self-control and composure" (Radhakrishnan 1944, 307). Gandhi also had a tête-à-tête with Charlie Chaplin, George Bernard Shaw ("Mahatma Minor"), the Archbishop of Canterbury, Madame Montessori, and Harold Laski. Churchill and the Pope, however, refused to see him.

4. Bhimrao Ramji Ambedkar, born into an Untouchable Mahar caste in Maharashtra (West India), was gifted with a superior intellect testified by his extraordinary educational credentials: B.A. (Elphinstone College, Bombay University), M.A. and Ph.D. (Columbia University, New York), M.Sc., D.Sc., and Barrister-at-law (Grey's Inn, London, England). A statesman, reformer, and crusader of Untouchables' legal and political rights, Dr. Ambedkar became the first law minister in 1947, and the chief architect of the constitution of free India. He was posthumously honored by the government of India (1990) with the most prestigious award of "Bharat Ratna" (the "Diamond of India").

5. Romain Rolland, the great twentieth-century French writer and novelist (*Jean Christophe*), singer, musician, and artist, was greatly influenced by Tolstoy and Gandhi. Although he did not meet Gandhi until 1931, he had known of him through their common friends—Tagore and C. F. Andrews. Rolland had written biographies of Gandhi, Beethoven, Goethe, and the Hindu mystic, Shri Ramakrishna (Fischer 1950, 291).

6. "Mandir" is a temple; it signifies what prison meant to Gandhi, a holy place to invoke and worship God.

7. The term *epic fast* was coined by Pyarelal, who wrote a book by the same title *The Epic Fast* (1932).

8. Instead of a panel of two Harijan candidates suggested by Ambedkar, Gandhi offered him five. In the final agreement, both Gandhi and Ambedkar agreed to 147 reserved seats for the Depressed Classes. The correlated issue of abolishing "separate primaries" was kept for a later date to be decided in the future.

9. He offered the ashram to the Servants of Untouchables Society, and it was known thereafter as the *Harijan Ashram*.

10. From his article, "To My American Friends," in *Young India* (Gandhi 17-9-1925, 31).

11. Like the legendary Hanuman to Lord Rama, Mahadevbhai was the most devoted follower, companion, and confidant of Gandhi.

12. From Gandhi's Speech at Public Meeting, Alleppey (January 18, 1934) in the Collected Works of Mahatma Gandhi (1951, 57: 17).

13. Vinoba Bhave was a scholarly and ascetic disciple of Gandhi who continued the *Bhoodan* or land-donation activity as part of the larger, *Sarvodaya* project, long after Gandhi's death by assassination.

14. A left-wing Laborite Member of Parliament, and a brilliant lawyer, Sir Stafford Cripps had abandoned his lucrative practice and toured India to know what leaders such as Gandhi, Nehru, Tagore, Jinnah, Ambedkar, Muslim leader Maulana Abul Kalam Azad, Southern leader Rajgopalachari, and others had on their minds; and what kind of constitutional changes they wanted.

15. According to K. K. Chaudhari (1996, vii), "Quit India" was actually an expression Gandhi used in his conversation with Horace Alexander, his Quaker friend. Gandhi referred to "an orderly British withdrawal," suggesting to "leave India to Indians"; this was later translated into a passionate cry "Quit India."

16. From *My Week with Gandhi* (Fischer 1942), in which he had given an account of his daily conversations with Gandhi for a week in June 1943. He published it separately and also as a part of the biography, *The Life of Mahatma Gandhi* (1950, 363–380).

17. This time Kasturbai and Gandhi's disciple-cum-secretary, Mahadevbhai Desai, were also with him in the same jail.

18. The centers where the movement was most intense were Bombay and Ahmedabad in the west, Punjab and Bihar in the north, and Bengal and Orissa in the east.

19. In the Indian tradition, an ascetic practiced *tapas* (penances) to ask for specific boons or rare powers. Self-austerities were supposed to have a power-enhancing effect, which their practitioner could use for himself or for controlling the environment.

20. Kasturbai loved sweets and coffee; Gandhi did not approve, but he accepted lovingly.

21. Early in his career, Jinnah was an active congressman, who risked his popularity among his Muslim League friends by saying he was "first and foremost an Indian, and then only a Muslim." However, Jinnah parted ways with Gandhi and the Congress when he felt that the Muslim minority interests were being swallowed up by a large Hindu majority.

22. Before the great poet *Valmiki* wrote his Hindu epic of *Ramayana,* he was a robber, and therefore assumed to have been born in a lowly caste—possibly, of the Untouchables.

23. The new interim government was to have five Hindu representatives from Congress, five members of the Muslim League, one Sikh, one Anglo-Indian, and one Muslim member selected by Congress. The last was not acceptable to Jinnah and the Muslim League.

CHAPTER 12. CONCLUSION: FROM DARKNESS TO LIGHT

1. The title of Sebastian De Grazia's article in the *Political Quarterly* (19, no. 4: 336–348).

2. From *Harijan* (May 1, 1937, 92–93).

Bibliography

Ambedkar, B. R. 1946. *What Congress and Gandhi Have Done to the Untouchables*. Bombay: Thacker.

Appadurai, Arjun. 1978. "Understanding Gandhi." In *Childhood and Selfhood*. Ed. Peter Homans. London and Lewisburg: Bucknell Univ. Press.

Ashe, Geoffrey. 1968. *Gandhi: A Biography*. New York: Cooper Square Press.

Basil, Williams. 1948. *Botha, Smuts and South Africa*. New York: Macmillan.

Bondurant, Joan V. 1965. *Conquest of Violence: The Gandhian Philosophy of Conflict*. Berkeley and Los Angeles: Univ. of California Press.

Boreman, Williams. 1986. *Gandhi and Nonviolence*. Albany: State Univ. of New York Press.

Bose, Nirmal Kumar. 1948. *Selections from Gandhi*. Ahmedabad: Navajivan.

———. 1974. *My Days with Gandhi*. Calcutta: Nishana.

Brailsford, H. N. 1949. "The Middle Years." In *Mahatma Gandhi*. Brailsford H. N., H. S. L. Polak, and Lord Pethick-Lawrence. London: Odhams Press.

Brown, Judith. 1989. *Gandhi: Prisoner of Hope*. New Haven, Conn.: Yale Univ. Press.

Burch, George Bosworth. 1964. "Seven Valued Logic in Jain Philosophy." In *Intercultural Philosophical Quarterly: An Intercultural Forum*. Vol. 4.

Chatterjee, Margaret. 1983. *Gandhi's Religious Thought*. Foreword by John Hick. Indiana: Univ. of Notre Dame Press.

———. 1992. *Gandhi and His Jewish Friends*. London: Macmillan Academic and Professional.

Chaudhari, K. K. 1996. *Quit India Revolution: The Ethos of Its Central Direction*. Mumbai: Popular Prakashan.

Complete Works of Swami Vivekananda. Vol. 3. 1979. Calcutta: Advaita Ashram.

Deliege, Robert. 1999. *The Untouchables of India*. Trans. from French by Nora Scott. English edition Berg Publishers.

Desai, Mahadev Haribhai. 1932. *The Diary of Mahadev Desai*. Vol. 1. Trans. from Gujarati and ed. Valji Govindji Desai. Ahmedabad: Navajivan.

———. 1968. *Day-to-Day with Gandhi*. 3 volumes. Ahmedabad: Navajivan.

Dhawan, Gopi N. 1951. Rev. Ed. *The Political Philosophy of Mahatma Gandhi*. Bombay: Popular Book Depot.

Diwakar, R. R. 1948. *Satyagraha: The Power of Truth*. Hinsala, Illinois: Henry Regnary.

———. 1949. *Glimpses of Gandhiji*. Foreword by Sardar Vallabhbhai Patel. Bombay: Hind Kitabs.

———. 1963. *Gandhiji's Life, Thought and Philosophy*. Bombay: Bharatiya Vidya Bhavan.

Doke, Rev. Joseph. 1909. *M. K. Gandhi: An Indian Patriot in South Africa*. London: Indian Chronicle Press.

Downing, Frederick L. 1986. *To See the Promised Land: The Faith Pilgrimage of Martin Luther King, Jr.* Foreword by James Fowler. Macon, Georgia: Mercer Univ. Press.

Erikson, Erik. 1958. *Young Man Luther: A Study in Psychoanalysis and History*. New York: W. W. Norton.

———. 1968. *Identity, Youth and Crisis*. New York: W. W. Norton.

———. 1969. *Gandhi's Truth: On the Origins of Militant Nonviolence*. New York: W. W. Norton.

———. 1975. "Identity Crisis in Autobiographic Perspective." In *Life History and the Historical Movement*. New York: W. W. Norton.

———. 1975. "In Search of Gandhi." In *Life History and the Historical Movement*. New York: W. W. Norton.

Fischer, Louis. 1942. *My Week with Gandhi*. New York: Duell, Sloan and Pearce.

———. 1950. *The Life of Mahatma Gandhi*. New York: Harper & Brothers Publishers.

Fowler, James W. 1981. *Stages of Faith: The Psychology of Human Development and the Quest for Meaning*. San Francisco: Harper & Row.

———. 1984. *Becoming Adult, Becoming Christian: Adult Development and Christian Faith*. San Francisco: Harper & Row.

———. 1987. *Faith Development and Pastoral Care*. Ed. Don S. Browning. Philadelphia: Fortress Press.

Fowler, James W., and Sam Keen. 1978, 1985 *Life Maps: Conversations on the Journey of Faith*. Ed. Jerome W. Berryman. Waco, Texas: Word Books Publisher.

Fowler, James W., and Robin W. Lovin, with Katherine Ann Herzog and others. 1980. *Trajectories in Faith*. Nashville: Abingdon.

Gandhi, Arun, and Sunanda Gandhi with Carol Lynn Yellin. (Foreword by Lord Richard Attonborough) 2000. *The Untold Story of Kasturba, Wife of Mahatma Gandhi*. Mumbai: JAICO.

Gandhi, Manubehn. 1949. *Bapu—My Mother*. Trans. from Gujarati by Chitra Desai. Ahmedabad: Navajivan.

———. 1962. *Last Glimpses of Bapu*. Trans. from Gujarati by Motilal Jain. Foreword by S. Radhakrishnan. Delhi: Shiva Lal Agarwala.

Gandhi, Mohandas Karamchand. 1893–1894. "A Guide to London." In *Collected Works of Mahatma Gandhi*. New Delhi: Publications Division, Government of India.

———. 1894. *An Appeal to Every Briton in South Africa*. Durban: Natal Indian Congress.

———. 1894. *The Indian Franchise: An Appeal*. Durban: Natal Indian Congress.

———. 1896. *The Grievances of the British Indians in South Africa: An Appeal to the Indian Public*. Madras: Price Current Press.

———. 1928. *Satyagraha in South Africa*. Trans. from Gujarati by Valji Govindji Desai. Stanford, California: Academic Reprints.

———. 1930. *A Guide to Health*. Trans. from the Hindi by A. Rama Iyer. 2nd Rev. Ed. Madras: S. Ganesan.

———. 1932. *From Yeravda Mandir*. Trans. from Gujarati by Valji Govindji Desai. Ahmedabad: Navajivan.

———. 1938. *Hind Swaraj or Indian Home Rule*. Ahmedabad: Navajivan.

———. 1941. *Constructive Programme: Its Meaning and Place*. Ahmedabad: Navajivan.

———. 1944. *Gandhi-Jinnah Talks*. Preface by C. Rajgopalachari. New Delhi: Hindustan Times.

———. 1945. *Gita—the Mother*. Ed. Jag Parvesh Chander. Lahore: Indian Printing Works.

———. 1946. *The Gospel of Self-less Action or The Gita According to Gandhi*. Trans. by Mahadev Desai. Ahmedabad: Navajivan.

———. 1947. *India of My Dreams*. Compiled by R. K. Prabhu. Foreword by Rajendra Prasad. Bombay: Hind Kitab Limited.

———. 1948. *Autobiography: The Story of My Experiments with Truth*. Trans. from Gujarati by Mahadev Desai. Washington, D.C.: Public Affairs Press.

———. 1948. *Delhi Diary*. Ahmedabad: Navajivan.

———. 1948. *Key to Health*. Trans. by Sushila Nayar. Ahmedabad: Navajivan.

———. 1948. *Nonviolence in Peace and War*. 4 volumes. Ahmedabad: Navajivan.

———. 1948. *Self-restraint and Self-indulgence*. Ahmedabad: Navajivan.

———. 1949. *Bapu's Letters to Mira*. (1924–48). Ahmedabad: Navajivan.

———. 1950. *Hindu Dharma*. Ahmedabad: Navajivan.

———. 1954. *Nature Cure*. Ahmedabad: Navajivan.

———. 1954. *The Removal of Untouchability*. Ahmedabad: Navajivan.

———. 1954. *Sarvodaya*. Ahmedabad: Navajivan.

———. 1955. *Ashram Observances in Action*. Ahmedabad: Navajivan.

———. 1955. *Gokhale: My Political Guru*. Ahmedabad: Navajivan.

———. 1955. *Truth is God*. Ahmedabad: Navajivan.

———. 1958. *All Men Are Brothers: Life and Thought of Mahatma Gandhi as Told in His Words*. Unesco: Columbia Univ. Press.

———. 1961. *In Search of the Supreme*. 3 volumes. Compiled and Ed. V. B. Kher. Ahmedabad: Navajivan.

————. 1958–2002. *The Collected Works of Mahatma Gandhi.* 100 volumes.

————. The Collected Works of Mahatma Gandhi, 2000. Vol 26. New Delhi: Publications Division, Government of India.

————, ed. *Indian Opinion.* Natal, South Africa (1903–1914).

————, ed. *Young India.* Ahmedabad, India (1919–1932).

————, ed. *Navajivan.* Ahmedabad, India (1919–1931).

————, ed. *Harijan.* Ahmedabad, India (1933–1948).

Gandhi, Prabhudas. 1957. *Jivan Prabhat.* Trans. *My Childhood with Gandhiji.* Ahmedabad: Navajivan.

Gandhi, Rajmohan. 1995. *The Good Boatman: A Portrait of Gandhi.* New Delhi: Penguin Books India.

Grazia, De Sebastian. 1948. "Mahatma Gandhi: The Son of His Mother." *Political Quarterly* 19 no. 4 (Oct–Dec 1948).

Green, Martin. 1993. *Gandhi: Voice of a New Age Revolution.* New York: Continuum.

Gregg, Richard. 1959. *The Power of Nonviolence.* Nyack, N.Y.: Fellow Publications.

Hawley, John, ed. 1987. *Saints and Virtues.* Berkeley and Los Angeles: Univ. of California Press.

Hay, Stephens. 1969. "Between Two Worlds: Gandhi's First Impressions of British Culture." *Modern Asian Studies* 3, no. 4.

————. 1970. "Jain Influences of Gandhi's Early Thought." In *Gandhi, India and the World.* Ed. Sibnarayan Ray. Philadelphia: Temple Univ. Press.

Holmes, John Haynes. 1953. *My Gandhi.* New York: Harper & Brothers Publishers.

Homans, Peter, ed. 1978. *Childhood and Selfhood: Essays on Tradition, Religion and Modernity in the Psychology of Erik Erikson.* London and Lewisburg: Bucknell Univ. Press.

Homer, A. Jack, ed. 1956. *The Gandhi Reader: A Source Book of His Life and Writings.* Bloomington: Indiana Univ. Press.

Hoyland, John S. 1944. "Gandhi's Satyagraha and the Way of the Cross." In *Mahatma Gandhi.* Ed. S. Radhakrishnan. Allahabad: Kitabistan.

Hunt, James, D. 1978. *Gandhi in London.* New Delhi: Promilla.

————. 1986. *Gandhi and the Non-Conformists: Encounters in South Africa.* New Delhi: Promilla.

Hutchins, Francis. 1973. *India's Revolution: Gandhi and the Quit India Movement.* Princeton, N.J.: Princeton Univ. Press.

Huttenback, R. A. 1971. *Gandhi in South Africa.* Ithaca, N.Y.: Cornell Univ. Press.

Iyer, P. Krishnamurty. 1970. *The Divine Message of Lord Prannath.* Jamnagar, Saurashtra. N.P.

Iyer, Raghavan, ed. 1986. *The Moral and Political Writings of Mahatma Gandhi.* 3 volumes. Oxford: Clarendon Press.

————. 1987. The Moral and Political Writings of Mahatma Gandhi, Volume III, Oxford: Clarendon Press.

Jergensmeyer, Mark. 1984. *Fighting with Gandhi*. San Francisco: Harper & Row.

———. 1987. "Saint Gandhi." In *Saints and Virtues*. Ed. John Stratton Hawley. Berkeley and Los Angeles: Univ. of California Press.

Jones, E. Stanley. 1983. *Gandhi: The Portrayal of a Friend*. Nashville: Abingdon Press.

Jordens, J. T. F. 1998. *Gandhi's Religion: A Homespun Shawl*. London: Macmillan Press. New York: St. Martin's Press.

Journal of the American Academy of Religion. 2000. Vol. 68, no. 4.

Kakar, Sudhir. 1979. *Identity and Adulthood*. Introduction by Erik Erikson. Delhi: Oxford Univ. Press.

———. 1981. *The Inner World: Psychoanalytic Study of Childhood and Society in India*. Delhi: Oxford Univ. Press.

———. 1989. *Intimate Relationships*. Delhi: Viking Press.

———. 1997. *Culture and Psyche: Selected Essays*. Delhi: Oxford Univ. Press.

Kala, Arvind. 1991. *Invisible Minority: The Unknown World of the Indian Homosexual*. New Delhi: Dynamic Books.

Kapadia, Sita. 1995. "A Tribute to Mahatma Gandhi: His Views on Women and Social Change." Essay presented on October 2, 1995, at the hundred and twenty-sixth anniversary of Mahatma Gandhi's birth.

Kopf, David. 1969. *British Orientalism and the Bengal Renaissance*. Berkeley and Los Angeles: Univ. of California Press.

Kripalani, J. B. 1970. *Gandhi: His Life and Thought*. Delhi: Publications Division, Ministry of Information and Broadcasting, Government of India.

Krishnaswamy, Revathi. 1998. *Effeminism: The Economy of Colonial Desire*. Ann Arbor: University of Michigan Press.

Kunz, Paul Grimley. 1982. "Gandhi's Truth." *International Publications Quarterly* 22, no. 3. Issue no. 87.

Mahatma Gandhi and Shrimad Rajchandra. Original Gujarati. Samvat 2005. Unjha, Gujarat: Bhogilal Nagindas.

Maitland, Edward, with Anna Kingsford. 1890. *The Perfect Way*. London: Field and Turner.

Mendelsohn, Oliver, and Marika Vicziany. 1998. *The Untouchables: Subordination, Poverty, and the State in Modern India*. Cambridge: Cambridge University Press.

Metcalf, Thomas R. 1990. *The Aftermath of Revolt: India, 1857–1870*. New Delhi: Manohar Publications.

Michael, S. M., ed. 1999. *Untouchable: Dalits in Modern India*. Boulder: Lynne Rienner Publishers.

Morton, Eleanor Pseud. 1953. *Women in Gandhi's Life*. New York: Dodd, Mead.

———. 1954. *Women Behind Mahatma Gandhi*. London and New York: Max Reinhardt. Bombay: Jaico Publishing House.

Mowli, V. Chandra. 1990. *B. R. Ambedkar: Man and His Vision*. New Delhi: Sterling Publishers.

Nag, Kalidas. 1950. *Tolstoy and Gandhi*. Patna: Pustak Bhandar.

Nanda, B. R. 1965. *Mahatma Gandhi: A Biography*. Woodbury, N.Y: Barron's Educational Series.

———. 1985. *Gandhi and His Critics*. Delhi, New York: Oxford Univ. Press.

———. 1994. "Gandhi and Religion." In *Facets of Mahatma Gandhi*. Vol. 4. Ed. Subrata Mukherjee and Sushila Ramaswamy. Delhi: Deep and Deep Publications.

Nandy, Ashish. 1983. *Intimate Enemy: Loss and Recovery of Self under Colonialism*. Delhi: Oxford Univ. Press.

Natesan, G. A. 1922. *Speeches and Writings of M. K. Gandhi*. Introduction by C. F. Andrews. Madras: G. A. Natesan.

Nayar, Sushila. 1948. *Kasturba: Wife of Gandhi*. Introduction by M. K. Gandhi. Pennsylvania: Pendle Hill.

———. 1989. *Mahatma Gandhi: Satyagraha at Work*. Vol. 4. Ahmedabad: Navajivan.

Nehru, Jawaharlal. 1941. *Toward Freedom: An Autobiography*. New York: John Day.

———. 1948a. *Nehru on Gandhi*. New York: John Day.

———. 1948b. *A Selection Arranged in the Order of Events from the Writings and Speeches of Jawaharlal Nehru*. New York: John Day.

———. 1960. *The Discovery of India*. New York: John Day Co.

Pandey, Gyanendra, ed. 1988. *The Indian Nation in 1942*. Calcutta and New Delhi: K. P. Bagchi.

Parekh, Bhikhu. 1989a. *Colonialism, Tradition and Reform*. London: Sage Publications.

———. 1989b. *Gandhi's Political Philosophy: Critical Examination*. London: Macmillan.

Parks, Sharon. 1986. *The Critical Years: The Young Adult Search for a Faith to Live By*. Cambridge: Harper & Row.

Patel, Dinubhai Muljibhai. 1988. *Bhavna Bodh* Trans. from Gujarati by Shrimad Rajchandra. Agas: Shrimad Rajchandra Ashram.

Patil, V. T. 1984. *Gandhi, Nehru and the Quit India Movement: A Study in the Dynamics of a Mass Movement*. Delhi: B. R. Publishing.

Payne, Robert. 1969. *The Life and Death of Mahatma Gandhi*. New York: E. P. Dutton.

Polak, Henry S. L., H. N. Brailsford, and Lord Pethick-Lawrence. 1949. *Mahatma Gandhi*. London: Odhams Press.

Polak, Millie G. 1931. *My Gandhi: The Man*. London: George Allen & Unwin.

Prabhu Ramchandra Krishna, ed. 1944. *Sati Kasturba: A Life Sketch with Tributes in Memorium*. Foreword by M. R. Masani. Bombay: Hind Kitabs.

Prabhu, R. K., and U. R. Rao, eds. 1946. *The Mind of Mahatma Gandhi*. Foreword by S. Radhakrishnan.: Oxford Univ. Press.

Prasad, Nageshwar. 1985. *Hind Swaraj: A Fresh Look*. New Delhi: Gandhi Peace Foundation.

Prasad, Rajendraprasad. 1961. *At the Feet of Mahatma Gandhi*. New York: Asia Publishing House.

Pyarelal. 1932. *The Epic Fast*. Ahmedabad: Mohanlal Maganlal Bhatt.

———. 1965. *Mahatma Gandhi*. Volume 1: *The Early Phase*. Foreword by Jawaharlal Nehru. Preface by Sarvapalli Radhakrishnan. Ahmedabad: Navajivan.

———. 1965 *Mahatma Gandhi*. Volume 1: *The Last Phase*. Introduction by Rajendra Prasad. Ahmedabad: Navajivan.

———. 1965. *Mahatma Gandhi*. Volume 2: *The Last Phase*. Ahmedabad: Navajivan.

———. 1956 (first edition) 1966 (second edition). *Mahatma Gandhi*. Volume 1, Book 2: *The Last Phase*. Ahmedabad: Navajivan.

———. 1980. *Mahatma Gandhi*. Volume 2: *The Discovery of Satyagraha—On the Threshold*. Bombay: Sevak Prakashan.

———. 1986. *Mahatma Gandhi: The Birth of Satyagraha: From Petitioning to Passive Resistance*. Ed. James D. Hunt. Introduction by Sushila Nayar. Ahmedabad: Navajivan.

Radhakrishnan, Sarvapalli, ed. 1944. *Mahatma Gandhi: Essays and Reflections on His Life and Work*. Presented to him on his seventieth birthday, October 2, 1939. Allahabad: Kitabistan.

Radhakrishnan, Sarvapelli and Charles A. Moore, eds. 1957. *A Source Book in Indian Philosophy*. Princeton, N.J.: Princeton University Press.

Rao, Seshagiri, K. L. 1978. *Mahatma Gandhi and Comparative Religions*. Delhi: Motilal Banarasidas.

Rao, M. B., ed. 1969. *The Mahatma: A Marxist Symposium*. Bombay: People's Publishing House.

Ray, Baren. 1996. *Gandhi's Campaign Against Untouchability (1933–34): An Account from the Raj's Secret Official Reports*. New Delhi: Gandhi Peace Foundation.

Ray, Sibnarayan, ed. 1970. *Gandhi, India and the World. An International Symposium*. Philadelphia: Temple Univ. Press.

Richards, Glyn. 1983. *Philosophy of Gandhi: A Study of His Basic Ideas*. London and Dublin: Curzon Press.

Rolland, Romain. 1924. *Mahatma Gandhi Who Became One with the Universal Being*. New York: Garland Publishing.

Roy, Ramashray. 1985. "Moral Foundation of Hind Swaraj and Nonviolence." In *Hind Swaraj: A Fresh Look*. Ed. Nageshwar Prasad. New Delhi: Gandhi Peace Foundation.

Royle, Trevor. 1989. *The Last Days of the Raj*. London: Michael Joseph.

Rudolph, Susanne Hoeber, and Lloyd I. Rudolph. 1983. *Gandhi: The Traditional Roots of Charisma*. Chicago: Univ. of Chicago Press.

———. 1967. *The Modernity of Tradition*. Chicago: Univ. of Chicago Press.

Sarma, D. S. 1938. *The Gandhi Sutras*. Madras: Mountroad Press.

Schneider, Carl D. 1977. *Exposure, Shame and Privacy*. Boston: Beacon Press.

Seabrook, Jeremy. 1999. *Love in a Different Climate: Men Who Have Sex With Men in India*. London and New York: Verso.

Sheean, Vincent. 1955. *Mahatma Gandhi: A Great Life in Brief.* New York: Alfred A. Knopf.

Shrimad Bhagavad Gita. 1967. Text in Devnagari (Sanskrit). Trans. by Annie Besant. Adyar-Madras: Theosophical Publishing House.

Shukla, Chandrashankar. 1951. *Reminiscences of Gandhiji.* Bombay: Vora.

Slade, Madeleine (Mirabehn). 1960. *The Spirit's Pilgrimage.* New York: Coward-McCann.

Smuts, J. C. 1944. "Gandhi's Political Method." In *Mahatma Gandhi.* Ed. Sarvapalli Radhakrishnan. Allahabad: Kitabistan.

Swan, Maureen. 1985. *Gandhi and the South African Experience.* Johannesburg: Ravan.

Tendulkar, D. G. 1951. *Mahatma: Life of Mohandas Karamchand Gandhi.* 8 volumes. New Delhi: Publications Division, Ministry of Information and Broadcasting, Government of India.

Tendulkar, D. G. 1963. Mahatma: Life of Mohandas Karamchand Gandhi. Volume 8. New Delhi: Publications Division, Ministry of Information and Broadcasting.

Thadani, Giti. 1996. *Sakhiyani: Lesbian Desire in Ancient and Modern India.* New York: Cassell.

Thoreau, Henry David. 1966. *Walden and Civil Disobedience.* Ed. by Owen Thomas. New York: W. W. Norton.

Tolstoy, Leo. 1896. *The Gospel in Brief.* Trans. from Russian. New York: Thomas Y. Crowell.

———. 1899. *The Kingdom of God is Within You.* New York: Thomas Y. Crowell.

———. "Letter to a Hindoo." In *Collected Works of Mahatma Gandhi.* Vol. 9. New Delhi: Publications Division, Government of India.

Vaidyanathan, T. G., and Jeffrey J. Kripal. 1999. *Vishnu on Freud's Desk: A Reader in Psychoanalysis and Hinduism.* Delhi: Oxford Univ. Press.

Vakil, A. K. 1991. *Gandhi-Ambedkar Dispute.* New Delhi: Ashish Publishing House.

Vanita, Ruth, ed. 2002. *Queering India: Same Sex Love and Eroticism in Indian Culture and Society.* New York: Routledge.

Vanita, Ruth, and Saleem Kidwai. 2000. *Same Sex Love in India: Readings from Literature and History.* Houndmills, Basingstoke, Hampshire: Macmillan.

Varma, Vishwanath Prasad. 1959. *The Political Philosophy of Mahatma Gandhi and Sarvodaya.* Agra: Lakshmi Narain Agarwal Educational Publishers.

Vivekananda, Swami. 1920. *Raj Yoga or Conquering the Internal Nature.* 5th Ed. Calcutta: Visweswarananda.

Vivekananda, Swami. 1979. *The Complete Works of Swami Vivekananda.* Calcutta: Advaita Ashram.

Winsten Stephen. 1951. *Salt and His Circle.* London: Hutchinson.

Wolpert, Stanley. 2001. *Gandhi's Passion: The Life and Legacy of Mahatma Gandhi.* Oxford and New York: Oxford Univ. Press.

Woodcock, George. 1971. *Mohandas Gandhi.* New York: Viking Press.

Zelliot, Eleanor. 1992. *From Untouchable to Dalit: Essays on the Ambedkar Movement.* New Delhi: Manohar Publications.

Index

Abdulla, 120
Adajania, Parsee Sorabji Shapurji, 146
Adolescent Mohandas, 7, 15, 58, 70
Advaita Vedanta, 12, 186, 235. *See also*
  Vedanta
Advaita Ashram, 255, 262
Alfred High School, 57
Aga khan, 200; Aga Khan palace prison,
  216, 218
Agape, 140, 236
Ahimsa, 16, 44, 67, 71, 104; and
  satyagraha, 139; in Jainism and
  Hinduism, 140; *satya* and ahimsa 140;
  141, 152, 165, 167–168, 192, 202,
  226, 234; as an active principle, 236,
  245; in Patanjali, 250. *See also*
  nonviolence
Ahmedabad, xi, xiii, 74, 119, 149, 163,
  171–172, 188, 249–250, 252,
  254–258, 260–261
satyagraha in, 168, 250; Great Trial in,
  178
Ahmedabad ashram. *See* the Sabarmati
  ashram *under* Gandhi
Alexander, Mrs., 115
Ali brothers, 167, 180
Ali, H. O., 141
Allinson, Dr., 80
All India Spinners'Association, 181
All men are brothers, 154, 257
Alter ego, 70. *See also* the negative
  identity
Ambedkar, Bhimrao Ramji, 181, 200,
  203–207, 210, 229, 253 (bio), 255,
  260, 262; on Untouchables, 204

Ambedkar–Gandhi impasse, 203
Ampthill, Lord, 147
Anasakti-yoga, 103, 128. *See also* the
  Bhagavad Gita
Andrews, C. F., 119, 167, 176, 180, 250,
  253, 260
Anekantvada, 44. *See also* syadavada
Anglicization, 81, 89, 240. *See also*
  English experiments under Gandhi
Aparigraha, 44, 202. *See also* non-
  possession
Apartheid, 1, 13, 16, 98, 99, 101, 108,
  110, 238
Appadurai, Arjun, 69, 255
Arjuna, 65, 83, 246
Arnold, Edwin, 85
Arya samaj, 24
Asahakara, 177. *See also* the Non-
  cooperation Movement
Ashe, Geoffrey, 255
Ashoka, Emperor, 248
Ashram, 209; ashrama-dharma, 245
Asiatic Department, 124, 134
Asiatic Law Amendment Ordinance, 134
Asteya, 44, 202
Atheism, 71, 84, 87, 235
Atithi, 37
Atman, 12
Attlee, Clement, 220
Attonborough, Richard, 256
Augmented Indian, 89
Autobiography. *See under* Gandhi
Ayurveda, 119
Azad fauj, 251
Azad, Maulana Abul Kalam, 214, 253

263

relationship, 15; Colonial India,
19–20, 22–23, 26–27, 73, 244;
character, 13; culture, 13, 15, 258;
democratic principles, 159; etiquette,
47, 79; lifestyle, 20; orientalists, 22,
23, 85, 259; German, 23; parliament,
116, 180, 183, 214; salt monopoly,
17, 183; salt taxation, 183, 185; non-
conformists, 138; Viceroy, 116, 226,
228–229; British raj, 15, 147–148,
183, 199; British rule, 19, 21, 25, 27,
147–148, 167, 173, 183
British–Boer war, 120–121, 128, 131,
249
Brown sahibs, 20
Brown, Judith, 86, 90, 139, 190, 195,
237, 239
Buddha, 85; teachings of, 86; and
Mahavir, 103; 104, 129, 181, 187
Buddhism, 23, 44; Tibetan, 85; 140;
Ambedkar converts to Buddhism,
207; 248, 251

Cabinet mission, 221
Calcutta, 21, 108, 122–123, 162, 172,
222–223, 225–228, 230, 244, 248,
251, 255; the Great Calcutta killings,
222
Camp Karadi, 185
Carlyle, 86, 105, 143
Cartwright, Albert, 144
Caste, 42, 62, 76, 117, 154, 200, 205,
245; Ambedkar on caste, 206; caste-
based discriminations, 206; caste
barriers, 20, 24; caste elders (and
authorities), 75–76, 79, 88, 92, 94,
108, 109; folly of caste, 23; four major
castes, 245; lowly castes, 206, 254;
lowest caste (shudras), 245; caste
members, 76; Mahar caste
Untouchables, 207, 253; caste
ostracism, 75–76; social ostracism,
206; prohibitions, 76; rules and codes,
95, 123, 234, 245; upper caste
Hindus, 20, 117, 123, 188, 202–206;
sub-caste, 36; caste system, 190, 205,
206, 245. See also jati

Celibacy, 16, 37, 130, 136, 202, 208,
212, 246. See also brahmacharya
Celibration of India's independence, xii
Champaran Satyagraha. See under
satyagraha
Chandala, 51
Chaplin, Charlie, 252
Charkha, 176, 251. See also the spinning
wheel
Chastity, 107. See also celibacy, and,
brahmacharya
Chatterjee, Bankim Chandra, 20, 23
Chatterjee, Margaret, 49, 51, 104, 136,
164, 184, 186, 195, 239, 243, 247
Chauri Chaura violence, 177, 178, 182
Chinese, the,143
Christians missionaries, 80, 87,
101–102, 104, 112, 114, 116–117,
119, 143, 148, 151, 174, 180, 190,
193, 229, 236, 256; Trappist
missionaries, 106
Christianity, 42, 101–103 Gandhi's
views about Christianity. See under
Gandhi
Chum relationship, 7
Churchill, Winston, 142; his remark
about Gandhi, 185, 199; 214,
215; and Jinnah, 220; and the
Pope, 252
Civil Disobedience, the consequences,
167; nationwide civil disobedience,
171, 216; implications of, 173;
different from non-cooperation, 175;
179, 183, 184; 199; techniques, 201.
See also under Thoreau, his Essay on
Civil Disobedience
Clifford, Dr., 138
Coates, Mr., 101–102, 112
Coincidence of opposites, 185, 188, 191,
195, 241; coincidentia oppositorum, 10
Colonel Olcott, 85
Colonial-born Indian Christians in
South Africa, 100, 141
Communal Award. See under
MacDonald
Compassion, ix, 11, 12, 16, 37, 66, 86;
of Buddha, 104; for the Zulus, 129;

Swaminarayana sampradaya, 42
Swan, Maureen, 100, 114, 247
Swaraj, Gandhi's interpretation of, 45;
 meaning of, 147; true swaraj, 154;
 Gandhi's vision of, 164; 176; to the
 Congress, 209; 211; purna swaraj,
 214; 216; Tilak's slogan, 250;
 swarajists, 179, 201
Syadavada, 44. See also Anekantvada
Symbiotic existence, 5; infant-mother
 symbiosis, 30
Symbols, 5, 9, 52, 112; Gandhi's gift for,
 146; 166, 177, 184, 239
Synthetic–Conventional faith. See under
 Fowler, Stages of faith

Tagore, Maharshi Devendranath, 248
Tagore, Rabindranath, 161–162, 176,
 201; 223 (poem, "walk alone");
 Rabindra sangeet, 250; 250–253
Tagore and Gandhi, comparison, 162
Taj Mahal, 2
Tapas/tapasya/tapashcharya, 22, 130, 136;
 as voluntary suffering, 141; 170
Tendulkar, D. G., 2, 180, 217–218,
 227–228, 262
Thakore saheb, 34, 39, 47. See also Rana
 Thakorji, 39
Theosophy, 85; theosophists, 80,
 84–85, 87
Third-person perspective-taking, 9
Thompson, Edward, 252
Thoreau, Henry David, 23, 262; his
 essay on the "Civil Disobedience,"
 137, 248– 249; the reading of the
 essay by Gandhi, 146; Gandhi
 denies borrowing from Thoreau's
 essay, 249
Three cardinal principles of satyagraha,
 138–141
Three Moderns, 95; influence on
 Gandhi, 104
Three vows, 75, 78
Tilak, Bal Gangadhar, 24, 108, 167; and
 the radicals, 248; Lokmanya, 250;
 slogan, 250
Tinkathia system, 165

Tolstoy, Leo, 16, 95, 103–105, 107, 112,
 126, 143; letter to a Hindoo,
 148–149, 151, 154, 235, 260, 262;
 and Gandhi, 247, 253;
 correspondence with Gandhi, 148;
 impact on Gandhi, 103
The Kingdom of God is Within You, 16; its
 impact on Gandhi, 103–104; 262
Tolstoy farm, 148–149, 151, 154, 247.
 See also Tolstoy ashram under Gandhi's
 Ashrams
Touts, 93
Traditionalists,20; Gandhi as, 21
Traga, 26
Transcendence, 4, 5, 12, 238;
 Transcendent, 10–12, 140, 229;
 transcendental source, 236, 249
Transcendentalism, 85; transcendental
 movement, 23
Transformation, in faith, 239; of
 relationships, 216; of society, 136,
 205; total, 164, 209 ; world transfor-
 mation, 45; transformation of self.
 See also self-transformation
Transitions and transitional process.
 See under Fowler
Trappist missionaries, 106; monastery,
 106–107
Travankore, 180
True religion, 102–103
True self-identity, 3, 70, 82, 139, 241
Truth is God, 139, 186, 243, 257. See
 also God is Truth
Truthful King Harishchandra. See the
 Harishchandra story
Tulsi beads necklace, 102, 235
Tulsidas, poet, 43; Tulasi-Ramayana, 43
Tulsima. See under Gandhi
Two faces of shyness. See under shyness
Tyebji, Badruddin, 93
Tyranny of the they, 7, 8, 70, 82

Uka, the Untouchable, 58, 245
Ultimate Environment, 5, 7, 8, 9, 11,
 54, 77
Ultimate triumph of truth, 3, 139, 197,
 222